Irish Writers in their Time

Series Editor: Stan Smith

This innovative series meets the urgent need for comprehensive new accounts of Irish writing across the centuries which combine readability with critical authority and information with insight. Each volume addresses the whole range of a writer's work in the various genres, setting its vision of the world in biographical context and situating it within the cultural, intellectual, and political currents of the age, in Ireland and the wider world. This series will prove indispensable for students and specialists alike.

1. Patrick Kavanagh
(Editor: STAN SMITH)

2. Elizabeth Bowen
(Editor: EIBHEAR WALSHE)

3. John Banville
(JOHN KENNY)

FORTHCOMING

4. Sean O'Casey
(JAMES MORAN)

5. James Joyce
(Editor: SEAN LATHAM)

6. Jonathan Swift
(BREAN HAMMOND)

John Banville

JOHN KENNY

National University of Ireland, Galway

IRISH ACADEMIC PRESS

DUBLIN • PORTLAND, OR

First published in 2009 by Irish Academic Press

44 Northumberland Road,
Ballsbridge,
Dublin 4, Ireland

920 NE 58th Avenue, Suite 300
Portland, Oregon,
97213-3786, USA

www.iap.ie

British Library Cataloguing-in-Publication Data
An entry can be found on request

978 0 7165 2900 2 (cloth)
978 0 7165 2901 9 (paper)

Library of Congress Cataloging-in-Publication Data
An entry can be found on request

Printed by Biddles Ltd, King's Lynn, Norfolk

For my mother and father

Contents

Preface

Literary criticism is a gesture of love towards the very *idea* of literature, and it should therefore never set out merely to prove a self-serving point. Not too long ago, one version of this justification went that criticism is a *debt* of love to an author or text. The critic, from this point of view, is always up against it; he *owes* something. However, in the same way that no 'creative' book can be said to be strictly *necessary*, no 'critical' book is necessary, neither as a tribute to an author, however warranted, nor as a filling of some kind of hole in the grand scheme of things. Criticism is rather a chosen performance of free love, brought on – sometimes spontaneously, sometimes carefully – by aspects of beauty, diversion, wisdom, humour, yearning and confusion in the phenomenon of attention. It declares, to itself and others: look, isn't this worthy of scrutiny? Inscribed in that urging is the suspicion that such worthiness might not otherwise be readily acknowledged or understood. The performance, therefore, should be unjealously aimed at encouraging the attentions of others.

It is conventional in academic criticism to assertively, sometimes aggressively, set up one's own arguments and procedures against previous work in the domain one is hoping to also lay some claim to. This book wishes to avoid erecting the straw-men targets necessary to such criticism. When I want to express disagreement in what follows here with some tendencies in the existing body of criticism on John Banville, I try to offer my suggested correctives in a generalizing way rather than, as it were, distractingly naming names. I quietly pass over many areas of the Banville ground that are well trodden discursively. Rather than waste the reader's time in overly comfortable accord with others or in attempts at point-scoring, I aim as far as possible to offer my own vision or version of Banville with positive force and thereby hope to provide others in turn with something stout to take with them or to take against.

Some basic differences between previous books on Banville and what is afoot here should be quickly outlined nonetheless. With the exception of most of Chapter 3, because it is a companion to ideas outlined in Chapter 2, and some individual sections of other chapters, I do not engage in extended self-contained readings of individual Banville works. Most of what I have to say is based not just on close readings of Banville's primary publications but also on readings of two kinds of source material: the extensive list of essays, reviews and articles that he has turned out over the course of his career, and, to a lesser extent, the voluminous collection of his manuscripts held at Trinity College Dublin. In a second book emanating from my original doctoral thesis on Banville and which will follow the present one as a companion, I will include full bibliographies of material by and on Banville as well as various items and essays on his sources and his practices as a literary journalist. But I include in the present bibliography only the sources directly used in the text and those that are the major starting points for secondary reading.

While the extensive material available can provide for a rigorous empirical investigation into Banville, I do not have a sustained thesis to present here. Certain patterns of emphasis certainly begin to appear as I proceed – a preoccupation with concepts of silence, autonomy and religion, for instance – but rather than behave as though always conclusively proving something, my chapters, and even sections within individual chapters, attempt instead to be as often speculative as definitive, as often mixed as unified in approach. I have no hesitation in employing critical approaches that are not entirely bound by the empirical. Banville is a deeply philosophical writer – he has regularly mentioned that, along with poetry, he reads far more philosophy than fiction – and so discussions here will sometimes take us into the realms of conceptualism and speculative thinking.

Even a single Banville novel is far too rich and textured in design, far too layered in its intelligence, far too elusive and allusive in tandem for any one critical study to assume anything like comprehensiveness. Rather than be exhaustive in a circumscribed area of concentration and illustration, my overall discussion is intended to be suggestive in a number of respects. In illustrating, sometimes quickly, what I think important, I do not discuss all the work equally. The potential imbalance that this might otherwise cause is alleviated by the close correspondences between individual Banville works in terms of thematic exposition and development to the degree that, more than with most fiction writers, his œuvre can be said particularly to constitute an organic whole. What applies at one point in his work usually applies at some other stage along his way.

I try to incorporate most of Banville's own important statements on his art and world-view, some of which occur only once in the source material, but most of which assume their importance by very virtue of his frequently repeating them, sometimes verbatim. By way of his regularly expressed puzzlement about his creative procedures, Banville need not of course be believed on anything to do with the nature of his work, even when it might be clear that he is speaking sincerely. But we should at least give him plenty of space to present his own case.

What I principally want to provide here is a range of frameworks for thinking not just about Banville's œuvre but also about his aesthetic first principles and the artistic traditions which might best help us place and understand his styles and themes. I therefore occasionally allow his individual works to recede in favour of explorations of these frameworks, as in Chapter 4 in particular. Rather than always read what is on Banville's pages as such, I want to provide some readings of what is underneath or behind or beyond the stylistic and thematic happenings of those pages – not always to the extent of carrying through to single conclusions, but to various suggestions as to how at least some of the more hidden doors of Banville's house of fiction may be prised ajar, how its beautiful windows might best be kept shut so that we might properly admire their colour. All explorations are, however, at some point referred back directly or contextually to the works themselves.

Banville's works are more or less consecutively figured in this book, though many of the discussions also range forwards and backwards freely across the œuvre. Overview is as often the intent here as microscopic attention to single works since a considerable level of this attention has already been granted Banville by other book-length studies.

So this is not exactly an introduction to John Banville since that function has been served by some of the existing books; nor is it a focused monograph on particularized aspects of Banville because variations on that function have also been offered elsewhere. Plot summaries that might be used as a substitute for a first-hand reading of Banville's novels will not be found here; neither will there be found any assumption that the reader is already familiar with the entire œuvre. Instead, this book hopes to perform an in-between function. While it recaps on some of the important fundamentals in Banville criticism, it also quickly moves away at various points from these in the knowledge that they have already been minutely examined in dedicated articles and essays perhaps not readily available to the non-specialist reader.

I have tried to keep in sight those who are unfamiliar, or in the early stages of familiarity, with Banville, so that the general application of ideas and arguments can be understood even without first-hand or detailed knowledge of the works under discussion at any particular stage. But I also try to keep in sight those who are well acquainted with the Banville œuvre, not least the established specialists, so that they too might find new details and new aspects of emphasis embedded in the whole.

While there is no getting away, even when taking a brief reading dip, from the implicit and explicit intellectualism of Banville's fiction and the requirement of referring to other writers and various intellectual and literary traditions, I try in establishing his contexts here to keep references to, and quotes from, other writers to a minimum. Where I need to bring in categorical or theoretical terms I try to quickly define these, and when works of any kind are mentioned for comparative or illustrative purposes I include all relevant dates on first mention so that a practical sense of chronology can be maintained. Where authors of previous eras are mentioned, their life dates are similarly given on first mention; where none are given, it can be assumed that the relevant author is alive and well at the time of writing.

My hope in all this is that my provisional disassembling of Banville's work and aesthetics will be of decent assistance in both subsequent reassembly and further deconstruction. When readers take a Banville book in hand, I would have long and reasonably lit virtual avenues of larger and smaller ideas open up in front of them, along which the ghosts of certain literary and philosophical monuments and figures would be lined, their own books open, ready to lean in and help.

Acknowledgements

Work on this book was made easier and more enjoyable by a number of people.

Firstly, sincere thanks to John Banville for his courteous help and for his kindness in allowing me to quote from his work and papers.

Thanks to Dr. Riana O'Dwyer who supervised the doctoral work on which this book is based, and to Professor Kevin Barry for his congenial support.

A conversation with Professor Joseph McMinn at the early stages of research was of great benefit, and the readiness of his support in recent times is gratefully acknowledged.

I would like to thank colleagues at the English Department, NUI Galway and in the wider university community who were also my friends and who extended kindnesses. Particular thanks to Professor Adrian Frazier whose close reading of a draft of this book was invaluable and who was my mentor during the period when it was in the final stages of completion in my time as a researcher at the Moore Institute at National University of Ireland, Galway, 2004–06. Thanks to all researchers and staff based at the Institute during that time, especially to the director, Professor Nicholas Canny, and to Martha Shaughnessy.

Noel O'Neill was a vital help many years ago in getting research underway and I specially thank him for the *Nightspawn* first edition. Thanks also to Caitriona O'Connell of *The Arts Show* and Joan O'Sullivan and Nina Ward at the Press and Information Office, RTÉ; to Geraldine Mangan of Reed Books; to Emily Hill of the *Guardian* and Emma Costigan of the *Telegraph*; to Kate O'Connor and Paul Rainbow of Sheil Land Associates; to Siobháin O'Reilly of Lilliput Press; to Imre Laszlo of the Embassy of the Republic of Hungary, Dublin; to Thaddeus O'Sullivan for his helpful points of information; to Professor Gearóid Ó Tuathaigh for his lightening insights on Irish literature and society.

Many thanks to the librarians and all the staff at the James Hardiman Library, NUI Galway. I gratefully acknowledge permission from The Board of Trinity College Dublin to quote from John Banville's manuscripts and thank the librarians at the College for their help in accessing these.

Years of thanks to Charlie Byrne's Bookshop, Galway, especially Vinny and Charlie. Thanks also to Des Kenny of Kenny's Bookshop for throwing in the book; to the Brownen family for their hospitality when the original work was ongoing; to Laura Izarra for kindly lending me a copy of her book on Banville. Thanks to my fine neighbours in Dangan Heights in Galway.

I'll also take this opportunity to thank Caroline Walsh of The Irish Times who has been a delight to know and work with these past few years.

Thanks to my agent, Jonathan Williams, especially for his professionalism, alacrity, and sharp editorial eye, and to my editors Lisa Hyde and Stan Smith, not least for their sturdy patience.

I am fortunate to have a number of hard-thinking friends who also know the importance of sociability and hospitality and all the other good old things. Especial thanks to Frank Shovlin for his help, to James Shovlin, Enda Leaney, Mike Griffin, Keith and Siobhán Duggan, James Whyte, Paul Moran, Patrick Griffin, Seán MacAodha, Maura Kennedy, Patrick O'Sullivan, John Foley and Farah Hasanli, Gregg McClymont, Mike McCormack, Mark Stansbury, Jimmy Ryan, Sven Trakulhun, Martin Dyar.

Anne and Teddy O'Shea have been a constant source of encouragement and their kindness and goodwill is ever appreciated.

Beyond my parents, Nell and Paddy, to whom this book is dedicated, I hope all my family, including extended, will accept collective thanks for everything.

Hello to small Séamus, and my love to Karen, whose help is measureless and who was with it all from start to finish.

I gratefully acknowledge the Irish Research Council for the Humanities & Social Sciences, which, under the auspice of its Post-Doctoral Fellowship scheme, funded me on a full-time basis when this book was in development.

Chronology

1945

John Banville born in Wexford town on 8 December to Martin Banville, a garage worker, and Agnes Banville (née Doran), a housewife. He has an older sister, Vonnie, and an older brother, Vincent, who will also become a novelist. Educated in Wexford, first at St John of God primary school near his home in the Faythe area of the town, then at the Christian Brothers' primary school, and finally at the Brothers' secondary school, St Peter's College.

1957–58

By his own account, at the age of 12 he is writing regularly.

1963–68

After finishing secondary school, works in Dublin as a computer operator for the national airline, Aer Lingus. Finds the work boring but uses the perk of major discounts on international flights to visit cities around the world. Begins to submit work for consideration to magazines, and in 1966 *The Kilkenny Magazine* publishes 'The Party', his first short story. (This story remains uncollected.) The following year, begins to publish some of the stories that will comprise his first book when the same magazine publishes a second submission, 'A Death'. These first works are well received and in 1967 he wins the Allied Irish Banks Award and the Irish-America Foundation Literary Award.

1969

Begins working as copy-editor for *The Irish Press*, one of the leading newspapers in the country, where he will rise to the position of chief sub-editor. Has begun to write book reviews for the Irish political and cultural periodical Hibernia, for which he will be a prolific commentator on literature, particularly fiction, over the next decade.

1970
Between 1968 and early 1970 six further stories have been published, three in The Transatlantic Review ('Summer Voices', 'Sanctuary' and 'Nightwind'), two in The Irish Press ('Lovers' and 'Island'), and one in The Dublin Magazine ('Wild Wood'), and these and 'A Death' are now collected with two previously unpublished stories and a novella to make up his first book, Long Lankin.

1971
Nightspawn, his first novel, is published. Despite some good reviews and American publication also, it is not especially successful and it will not be reissued until 1993, by which time his intervening success will have raised considerable new interest.

1973
Second novel, Birchwood, is published. Wins the Irish Arts Council Macaulay Fellowship.

1976
Doctor Copernicus, the first of what will become a 'Science' Tetralogy (four novels), is published. Wins the Whitbread Prize and the James Tait Black Memorial Prize.

1981
Kepler is published. Wins the Guardian Prize for Fiction.

1982
The Newton Letter: An Interlude is published.

1983
His reputation as a novelist is growing. Leaves his job at The Irish Press to have more time for writing. Begins regularly reviewing books for The Sunday Tribune, and this will continue for four years.

1984

Second version of Long Lankin is published – the novella included in the first version of 1970 has been dropped, and 'Persona', which closed the original stories section, is replaced by 'De Rerum Natura', a story first published in The Transatlantic Review in 1975. A film version of The Newton Letter, entitled Reflections, adapted by Banville and directed by Kevin Billington, is broadcast in cooperation between Channel Four and RTÉ. Elected to Aosdána, an important new government-funded body of Irish artists.

1986

Mefisto, the final instalment of the Tetralogy, is published. Returns to the newspaper business as a sub-editor with The Irish Times. Begins regular reviewing with The Sunday Independent, and this will continue for two years.

1987

Begins regular review duties for The Irish Times. This will continue to the present day.

1988

Appointed Literary Editor of The Irish Times.

1989

The Book of Evidence is published. Short-listed for the Booker Prize and wins the prestigious and highly lucrative Guinness Peat Aviation Award. The award becomes somewhat controversial when one of the judges, Graham Greene, a writer whose work Banville had read from a young age, wants to give it to another contender instead and a compromise and new award have to be concocted.

1990

Begins to regularly appear as a reviewer-essayist with The New York Review of Books and this will continue to the present day.

1993

Ghosts is published. Profiled on ITV's South Bank Show.

1994

The Broken Jug, his first adaptation of the plays of Heinrich von Kleist, is premièred under the directorship of Ben Barnes at the Peacock Theatre, Dublin on 1 June, and is also published. *Seachange*, a film adapted from his uncollected story 'Rondo', which had been published in *The Transatlantic Review* in 1977, broadcast as part of a series of two-actor screenplays by RTÉ, directed by Thaddeus O'Sullivan.

1995

Athena is published.

1996

The Ark, an adaptation of the Noah's Ark story for children, is published in a lavishly produced limited edition (260 copies) illustrated by Conor Fallon. The project is designed to raise funds for The Ark centre, a new designated cultural space for children at Temple Bar, Dublin.

1997

The Untouchable is published. Wins the Lannan Literary Award.

1999

Adapts a novel he has long admired, Elizabeth Bowen's *The Last September*, for the screen, directed by Deborah Warner. Concludes a decade of work as Literary Editor of *The Irish Times*, but remains with the paper as a feature reviewer.

2000

Eclipse is published. *God's Gift*, his adaptation of Kleist's play *Amphitryon*, is directed by Veronica Coburn and premièred on 12 October at the O'Reilly Theatre, Dublin as part of the Dublin Theatre Festival, and is published. The first three books of the Tetralogy (*Doctor Copernicus*, *Kepler* and *The Newton Letter*) are published together as *The Revolutions Trilogy*.

2001

Resigns from Aosdána in December. This causes something of a stir, and related matters are subsequently discussed on the pages of *The Irish Times*. He points out in the process that he has not taken part in the proceedings of Aosdána nor has availed of its annuity for some years, and that he feels it would be wrong for a frequent absentee to continue to occupy a place that could be better filled perhaps by a younger or needier artist. *The Book of Evidence, Ghosts* and *Athena* are published together under the Trilogy title, *Frames*.

2002
Shroud is published. *Dublin 1742*, an unpublished play for 9 to 14-year-olds, about the last week of the original rehearsals for Handel's *Messiah*, is performed at The Ark in Dublin on 5 June.

2003
Prague Pictures: Portraits of a City, his single non-fiction work, is published as a contribution to Bloomsbury's 'The Writer and the City' series.

2005
The Sea, his thirteenth novel, is published and wins the Man Booker Prize for Fiction. His third Kleist adaptation, *Love in the Wars*, a version of *Penthesilia*, is published. *A World Too Wide*, a radio play about Shakespeare's 'sixth age of man', is broadcast by RTÉ.

2006
Christine Falls, his first novel under the pseudonym Benjamin Black, is published. *Todtnauberg*, a radio play about a 1967 meeting between the Holocaust survivor and poet Paul Celan and the Nazi philosopher Martin Heidegger, is broadcast by BBC4.

2007
The Silver Swan, his second Benjamin Black novel, is published.

2008
He is the subject of a major new documentary film, *Being John Banville*, directed by Charlie McCarthy and broadcast as part of RTÉ's 'Arts Lives' series. *Conversation in the Mountains*, the script of *Todtnauberg*, is published.

Periods

While one of the purposes of this book is to offer a holistic assessment of Banville's work and general aesthetics and thus to discover organic relationships between his writing and thinking from all stages of his career thus far, I also want to maintain a sense of his chronological development. As a compact of the chronology above, a fairly conventional periodization is useful in this regard. With a publishing history that spans five decades, Banville is now at the point where further criticism should recognize that his œuvre can be sectioned into identifiable periods. Over the past few years he himself has frequently admitted that he has completed his 'early', 'middle' and 'late' phases. These phases do apply, though there may be some doubt as to where the demarcations should be placed since the terminus of periods of aesthetic development can sometimes be anterior to related publication dates. Four periods can arguably be identified, and these will be employed throughout this book mindful of their provisionality and potential slippage, and especially of the ongoing necessity to review the context of the 'late' phase.

The Formational Period: mid-1960s to early 1970s
What would perhaps more conventionally be referred to as the early period is best subdivided so that a formational period can be identified. The formational period encompasses what can justifiably be termed Banville's apprentice work, up to and including his first two books. Along with some uncollected pieces, the major works of the formational period are *Long Lankin* (1970) and *Nightspawn* (1971).

The Early Period: early 1970s to mid-1980s
The early period proper sees the characteristic Banville style emerge and

develop into the four novels of the science Tetralogy, which begins to bring him significant critical recognition. The novels of the early period are *Birchwood* (1973) and the Tetralogy novels, *Doctor Copernicus* (1976), *Kepler* (1981), *The Newton Letter* (1982) and *Mefisto* (1986).

The Middle Period: late 1980s to late 1990s

After the Tetralogy, Banville entered a second period of writing interrelated novels, and his set of three concerning the world of art was followed by a fourth, related but stand-alone novel. The novels of the middle period are the Trilogy of *The Book of Evidence* (1989), *Ghosts* (1993), *Athena* (1995), and also *The Untouchable* (1997).

The Late Period: 2000 to the present

The present late period opens as Banville publishes a new novel at the very beginning of the new millennium, followed by another partially related literary novel, then a further apparently stand-alone novel, and adopts the pseudonym of Benjamin Black under which to publish a new popular brand of fiction. The late works thus far are *Eclipse* (2000), *Shroud* (2002), *The Sea* (2005), and the two crime thrillers, *Christine Falls* (2006) and *The Silver Swan* (2007).

Editions and Referencing

Because there are currently a number of different Irish, British and American editions and reprints of most of Banville's books in circulation, for the sake of uniformity all references are to the first British editions, except in the case of *Long Lankin*, of which there are two versions – the first edition of 1970 was significantly revised in 1984 and, unless indicated as '1st edn', all references are to this second version (see Works by John Banville in the Bibliography for all relevant publication details).

For ease of reading, I have not used any abbreviations. Conveniently, Banville's titles are predominantly brief, and I have shortened the longer ones only in the cases of referring to *Doctor Copernicus* as *Copernicus*; dropping, where suitable, the word 'The' from the beginning of all relevant titles; and dropping the subtitle *An Interlude* used for the first British edition of *The Newton Letter*.

As a planned group of novels, *Doctor Copernicus*, *Kepler*, *The Newton Letter* and *Mefisto* (1976–86) have generally been referred to in the relevant criticism as Banville's science 'tetralogy'. Equally, *The Book of Evidence*, *Ghosts* and *Athena* (1989–95) have come to be known as his art 'trilogy'. These grouped titles have variously appeared with and without quotation marks, with and without capitals. In the interests of clarity, these terms appear thus throughout this book: the Tetralogy; the Trilogy. At no point should Trilogy be taken to refer to the reissue of the first three books of the Tetralogy as *The Revolutions Trilogy* (2000); nor should Trilogy be taken to refer to the reissue of the Trilogy novels in the omnibus volume *Frames* (2001).

CHAPTER ONE

The Belief in Autonomy: Intellectual and Cultural Contexts for Banville's Work and Reception

THE WRITER IN THE STREET: POPULARIZING BANVILLE

The process of becoming a popular writer after a considerable period of repute as a literary elitist seems to have its hazards. Over the course of five decades, during which he has published seventeen books of fiction and a number of other works of non-fiction and adaptation, John Banville has experienced three moments of exposure that provide for a general overview of the career of this key figure of Irish and world literature, and also for usefully suggestive ways of approaching his work in the context of its wider critical reception.

Banville has often told an anecdote against himself to point to a favoured kind of critic for his books:

> I remember, after The Book of Evidence came out, going for the bus one day and this guy came cycling towards me on a bicycle. I thought: I'm going to be attacked, because he was really coming at me. At the last moment he veered aside and yelled 'Great fucking book!' This was the best piece of criticism that the book had had.[1]

Some crucial issues for a more regular reader's advance on Banville are couched in this dramatized encounter with the voice of public opinion in this contextually pivotal year of 1989. In tone at least, Banville's anecdote is designed to display a capacity for colloquial diversion in a writer who had gained a reputation for incorrigible seriousness. Profilers and interviewers had regularly mentioned his sartorial elegance, his furrowed brow, his owlish and po-faced demeanour, his cold *gravitas* and levelling stare, his epicurean delight in fine teas and classical music, his preference for expensive manuscript books in which to write a fine calligraphy with

equally expensive fountain pens. While such observations may be veri-
fiable to some extent, the same terms of personal description had been
used so repetitively to fatten copy that Banville's deportment often
seemed a caricatured extension of his own prose style, and the adjectives
perennially applied to him could be favourable or scornful depending
on one's own predispositions on writers: austere, aloof, urbane, hermetic, reserved, cerebral, intellectual, precious, ironic.

By 1989, the prime attendant cliché applied to the work itself was that
from the beginning it had been intentionally difficult, inaccessible to the
man – or cyclist – in the street. As Banville's own caricature pictured it, a
notion had developed 'that the Banville reader is an intellectual, probably
an academic, woolly gansey with double-strength spectacles'.[2] The publication in that year of *The Book of Evidence* would provide a reasonable
challenge to such received ideas about the kind of readers who might
most appropriately engage with a Banville book.

From even his first years as a serious writer, Banville had enjoyed
considerable official recognition. In 1967, at the age of 22 and with just
two stories to his name, he won two major prizes. Though Banville
seemed to quickly lose interest in the short story form after *Long Lankin*,
and though the collection is now often too hastily regarded as very
much the minor end of the œuvre, its stories were, even in their uncollected versions, highly regarded at the time, and one, 'Summer Voices',
was included in an anthology of stories from the distinguished
Transatlantic Review in 1970, alongside others by notables of the twentieth-
century short story. Subsequent work of Banville's formational and early
periods was similarly acknowledged, and though his first novel,
Nightspawn, attracted few plaudits as such, the following three novels,
Birchwood, *Copernicus* and *Kepler*, all won important prizes.

General popularity did not necessarily correspond with such official
recognition however. Though Banville's books were from the outset
reasonably widely reviewed, in comparative terms he did not enjoy a
broad readership either in Ireland or abroad for the first two decades of
his career. While *The Newton Letter* and *Mefisto* began to appear on university
reading lists in the late 1980s, neither novel proved broadly accessible,
neither won any major prizes, and their reception underlined at that stage
the reputation that Banville, by design or otherwise, had been gaining as
a writer's writer. A new popular appeal, however, came with *The Book of*

Evidence. The novel was short-listed for the Booker Prize and won the Guinness Peat Aviation Award. Since 1989 it has regularly appeared on lists of best-selling Irish literary fiction, and in the comprehensive 2003 'Novel Choice' readers' poll organized by the *Irish Times* and the James Joyce Centre, Dublin, it was voted to be one of the top ten Irish novels of all time. Nationally and internationally, it is Banville's most widely prescribed book on relevant courses in Irish literature in English.

Along with cyclists shouting compliments at him on the street, scholarly criticism of Banville's work had also been gathering pace, especially after an important *Irish University Review* special issue in 1981, edited by the German academic Rüdiger Imhof. Imhof's *John Banville: A Critical Introduction* (1989), the first full-length study, was published around the same time as *The Book of Evidence*, and this was followed two years later by the first relevant book by an Irishman: Joseph McMinn's *John Banville: A Critical Study* (1991). These accessible major studies, both of which have subsequently been expanded for second editions in 1997 and 1999 respectively, coincided with and helped intensify the developing general curiosity about Banville's previous and ongoing work. As well as an exponential increase in related interest from the popular media (taking the form, most usefully, of an array of in-depth interviews), the level of worldwide attention he began to attract is reflected in the extensive range of theses, articles and books now available on various dimensions of his work. It might have taken the twenty years up to *The Book of Evidence* for Banville criticism to gather evident momentum, but he now holds a position as perhaps the most written about of contemporary Irish novelists.

Extensive help is available at this stage to anyone wishing to read Banville in detail. His international profile has been abetted by the exponentially expanding range of translations of his books now available in both major and minor languages. Critical books too have underlined his present stature as a world novelist. The Brazilian scholar of Irish Studies Laura Izarra published *Mirrors and Holographic Labyrinths: The Process of a 'New' Aesthetic Synthesis in the Novels of John Banville* in 1999. Ingo Berensmeyer, another German academic, published *John Banville: Fictions of Order – Authority, Authorship, Authenticity* in 2000. Similarly using her dissertation work, Elke D'Hoker, a Belgian, published *Visions of Alterity: Representation in the Works of John Banville* in 2004. At home, Derek Hand has recently followed his *John Banville: Exploring Fictions* (2002) with his editorship of a second special Banville issue of *The Irish University Review* (2006). And just as the present book was being finished, another Irish scholar, Brendan McNamee, published *The Quest for God in the Novels of John Banville, 1973–2005: A Postmodern Spirituality* (2006).

It has not always been a matter of open-armed welcome for Banville's work after *The Book of Evidence*. While the two subsequent novels, *Ghosts* and *Athena*, have provided rich pickings for academic readers, they have often been met with confusion and frustration in general readers, who perhaps are less given to the tracings of artistic codes and patterns that such deeply self-reflexive fictions seem to demand. However, a further 'art' novel, *The Untouchable*, proved amenable to a wide readership. Shortly after publication, the opening twenty lines of this novel appeared as a set passage for the Cambridge English finals alongside such popular canonical authors as Defoe and Dickens. It wasn't simply that the subject of the Cambridge Spies in *The Untouchable* proved naturally attractive to Cambridge dons and undergraduates. Though *The Untouchable* retains the Banville hallmarks of stylistic refinement and complexity of theme, these are contained by a plot- and dialogue-driven narrative that until very recently was comparatively rare in Banville, and so the novel was a second point of relatively easy access to the œuvre alongside *The Book of Evidence*.

Over the following years, nevertheless, a second moment of hazardous exposure was impending for Banville. After *The Untouchable* came the interrelated *Eclipse* and *Shroud*, novels which tackled questions about human authenticity and morality raised in all Banville's previous books, but which also seemed so deliberately to thwart expectations after *The Untouchable* of at least a partial conventionalization of the Banville style that they turned off many of his readers anew. And the frequently reluctant critical mood slouched soon after towards Banville's greatest moment of fame. On the night of 10 October 2005, at the Guildhall in London, it was announced that *The Sea* had won Banville the Man Booker Prize. *The Sea*, one of Banville's shortest novels, had been a 7/1 outsider for the prize and, in the context of a far from unanimous approval rating from reviewers, it had been tipped by very few critics. After the prize, *The Sea* was greeted by some highly approving reviews and reassessments, but equally by some considered and constructive negative reactions that were laudably unswayed by the author's new world fame. One high-profile voice of opposition, however, sounded as though years of seething at Banville's books were finally being given release. This was from Boyd Tonkin, literary editor of The Independent, the very morning after Banville's win:

> Yesterday the Man Booker judges made possibly the worst, cer-
> tainly the most perverse, and perhaps the most indefensible choice
> in the 36-year history of the contest. By choosing John Banville's
> The Sea, they selected an icy and over-controlled exercise in coterie
> aestheticism ahead of a shortlist, and a long list, packed with a
> plenitude of riches and delights.
>
> The Dublin novelist, whose emotional rage is limited and
> whose prose exhibits all the chilly perfection of a waxwork model,
> must today count himself as the luckiest writer on the planet. This
> was a travesty of a result from a travesty of a judging process.[3]

Aside from wondering how a writer who continues in his book bio-notes to identify Wexford as his place of birth can so readily be packaged as a 'Dublin' novelist, and how 'perfection' can be so blithely dismissed merely by attaching it to a dismissive adjective, even the committed Banville reader might want to allow Tonkin his complaints, intemperately toned as they are. Potentially comprehensive inferences can be made nevertheless. Banville's books have always sat uneasily on the desks of British literary editors and reviewers, and while he has never been given to invoking stark or simplistic national differences (as we shall presently see in Chapters 2 and 3), he has remarked on this apparent unease a number of times, and in this case he was characteristically forthright in rejecting Tonkin's views as evidence of cultural 'chauvinism'.[4] Banville is a seasoned newspaperman, has worked as a literary reviewer, journalist and editor for most of his career as a writer, and is not given to over-sensitive reaction to the reception of his books, or, indeed, his prize-winnings. He knows how the book world works; he is unlikely to think it is always a nice place. While the often bruising critical style he practised as a prolific reviewer during the 1970s and 1980s has generally become much more relaxed in the intervening time, his own approach to the reviewing of his peers can still on occasion be uncompromising, and it is unlikely he would there-fore be easily discomfited when he bears the brunt in return.

In the lead-up to Tonkin's brand of post-Booker negative reaction, it is not so much that Banville may have met with widespread disapproval for a particularly damning – and by now infamous – review of Ian McEwan's novel *Saturday* in the *New York Review of Books* a few months before *The Sea* won the same prize for which McEwan's novel had been long-listed. It was more that provocative aesthetic positions that Banville has consciously and openly held since he began publishing, yet hadn't perhaps so categorically expressed in recent years, were on high display in this review. These positions, which have been widely misinterpreted as advocacy of a straightforward doctrine of art for art's sake (hence Tonkin's accusations of 'coterie aestheticism'), can be broadly character-ized as apolitical, but only in the sense that Banville staunchly opposes any displacement in literature of primary aesthetic concerns to make room for overt politicizing or moralizing. In expressing his reservations about McEwan's novel, he was dramatizing his own aesthetic first principles:

> It happens occasionally that a novelist will lose his sense of artistic proportion, especially when he has done a great deal of research and preparation. I have read all those books, he thinks, I have made all these notes, so how can I possibly go wrong? Or he devises a program, a manifesto, which he believes will carry him free above the demands of mere art – no deskbound scribbler he, no dabbler in dreams, but a man of action, a match for any scientist or soldier. He sets to work, and immediately matters start to go wrong – the thing will not flow, the characters are mulishly stubborn, even the names are not right – but yet he persists, mistaking the frustrations of an unworkable endeavour for the agonies attendant upon the fashioning of a masterpiece. But no immensity of labor will bring to successful birth a novel that was misconceived in the first place.
>
> Something of the kind seems to have happened here. *Saturday* is a dismayingly bad book.[5]

Banville's robust prioritization of artistic integrity over anything resembling propaganda in fiction has rarely met with wholehearted approval in the context of the currently dominant climate of cultural bad conscience in the West. He was a young man of the sixties and he came to maturity in a politically troubled Ireland, the argument runs; he cannot be so blind to the wrongness in the world; he should know better. And there is, it seems, especially little patience with Banville's artistic stance in the current preoccupation with the political urgencies brought on by world terrorism. In his review of McEwan's novel, he quickly underlined the public imperatives now automatically hoisted on the writer: 'If we all have a novel in us, nowadays it is likely to be a September 11 novel.' Such a withering sideswipe at simplicities of conscience in fiction was sure to infuriate; but Banville's real *coup de grâce* surely lay in subsequent comments that perhaps held up too clear a book-chat mirror to certain kinds of readers and critics:

> The politics of the book is banal, of the sort that is to be heard at any middle-class Saturday-night dinner party, before the talk moves on to property prices and recipes for fish stew ... *Saturday* has the feel of a neoliberal polemic gone badly wrong; if Tony Blair ... were to appoint a committee to produce a 'novel for our time', the result would surely be something like this ... Another source of dismay ... is the ecstatic reception which *Saturday* has received from reviewers and book buyers alike. Are we in the West so shaken in our sense of ourselves and our culture, are we so disablingly terrified in the face of the various fanaticisms which threaten us, that we can allow ourselves to be persuaded and comforted by such a self-satisfied and, in many ways, ridiculous novel as this?

The point here is that so long as Banville only skirted the brightest spot-lights,then negative reactions in books' pages to his work and his underlying aesthetic positions tended to take on more a baffled than actively hostile tone. But now that his confidence in the rare artistic value of his commercially limited fiction had resurfaced to somewhat mischievous effect in his Man Booker interviews, there appeared to be a public stiffening of attitude.

As Banville continues to become more popular during the last number of years, there appears to be an equivalent polarization of critical reception, and his third potentially hazardous exposure concerns the moment of perhaps his clearest bid for a wider readership: his recent first move into the surprisingly guarded domain of popular crime fiction with the detective novel *Christine Falls*, published under the name Benjamin Black, a pseudonym that recalls certain characters and elements of *Nightspawn*, which in itself was intended as a kind of intellectual thriller. Reactions to this most striking change of Banville's direction to date, especially from those who enjoy the Irish limelight of this brand of fiction, are worth keeping an eye on. While the reviews internationally were mixed, some master practitioners of popular mystery fiction did welcome Banville to their domain and clearly saw that there are organic stylistic and thematic affinities between his more difficult literary fiction and this new generic accessibility. There is more at stake in *Christine Falls* than the simple testing of a new literary register, however. The novel does not subvert the precise stylistic requirements of popular fiction to any overt moralizing, but, in a new move for Banville, Irish society – particularly the hypocritical Catholic climate of the 1950s – is delineated in a mood of sad outrage. The potential of Quirke, the Dublin pathologist-cum-detective of *Christine Falls*, to develop into 'a wonderful, mordant observer of this country's foibles' was recognized by John Connolly, one of Ireland's most successful practitioners of this type of fiction, but Banville is apparently not to be allowed to climb too unawares down and out into the popular world:

> Banville's use of a pseudonym to join the fray inevitably begs the question: why? There is a sense in which his adoption of the Black persona is a recognition – and it cannot be anything but conscious – that this is not a 'proper' Banville novel; it is Banville-lite, an 'entertainment' ...
>
> But the freedom offered to Banville by the pseudonym has not been matched by any great ambition, and *Christine Falls* is a very conventional, and rather old fashioned, crime novel. The result is a mystery that isn't really very mysterious, and characters that veer towards the stereotypical ... most readers will be aware of the pedigree of its creator and may feel that more was to be expected of the alter-ego of one of Ireland's finest writers.[6]

Banville will be exploring Ireland in his new popular mode for some time to come since *Christine Falls* was only the first in a planned interrelated series of novels for which he will adopt the *alter ego* Benjamin Black, and, with no intervening work published under Banville's actual name, it has been quickly followed by a second Black novel, *The Silver Swan*. While it may be that aficionados of this venerable tradition of fiction will continue to have mixed feelings about Banville's early work in his series, it is already clear that within the context of his own œuvre the potentially distracting peculiarities of these new Black books make considerable internal sense.

It is a standard in crime thriller fiction that the author should pick a recurrent signature character or narrator, and, in Banville's opting for the 1950s Dublin pathologist, Quirke, we are on familiar ground. Certainly, Banville's characteristically dense style has relaxed and there is more of an emphasis on plotting than he had hitherto practised. Certainly, Benjamin Black's novels are a departure at this stage in that, after an obsession of more than twenty years' duration with highly articulate first-person narrators, they return us to the third-person narration Banville had tried in both *Copernicus* and *Kepler*. And most certainly it is curious to think that Banville has had to significantly change direction in order to write directly about the Ireland he grew up in. But it would be a mistake both to be suspicious of Banville's motives in adopting a pseudonym to write this new kind of relatively accessible novel and, in a related way, to expect of Benjamin Black anything like conventional crime fiction. To call Benjamin Black's fiction 'Banville-lite' is to miss two points. Firstly, crime fiction, which is in any case a very diverse genre, has a long tradition of pseudonymous carry-on, with authors who write other kinds of fiction adopting new names to try their hand and sometimes with even the use of multiple names to write different kinds of narrative within the broader genre. There is a natural and surely usually conscious relationship between this slippage of names and dodging and shifting in crime fiction authorship, and the very subjects and typical characterization of the novels themselves. Secondly, as well as to indicate to his established readers that they shouldn't expect Benjamin Black to behave stylistically like John Banville, Banville's long-time reputation as a difficult author was such that potential readers perhaps usually dissuaded by the Banville name needed to also be told by a change of name that maybe they could expect something different from Black (and it should be realized that *Christine Falls* was practically finished before *The Sea* won the Man Booker and Banville's literary fiction was consequently deemed newly accessible).

Black, in any case, is only a partially cloaked Banville. Quirke, this new Black protagonist, would bear extensive comparison to Banville's typical narrator of the last twenty years. As with these others, he is a troubled soul, with a painful past that he assuages through the distractions of work and, not least, through alcohol – besides the fact that hard drinking is a staple in Black's kind of fiction, a study could be written on the extraordinary levels of booze consumption in Banville's fiction generally. Quirke is something of a self-consciously outsized man, a regular trait also with Banville's narrators. And the overall mood and incident of the two Black narratives thus far are pure Banville: paranoia, nastiness, death, claustrophobia, murk and gloom. Two sides of Black's concentration would bear particular comparison to the literary fiction of Banville's late period. Cass, the damaged daughter of Cleave in *Eclipse* who resurfaces in *Shroud*, is the most extensively drawn instance in a long line of enigmatic Banville females, and Phoebe, Quirke's very similar and equally hurt daughter in *Christine Falls*, has been similarly developed for *The Silver Swan*. Banville has indicated that he may particularly wish to develop the character of Phoebe in the next Benjamin Black instalment. There are also particularly close parallels between *Christine Falls* and *The Sea* in terms of their mutual, if very different, focus on childhood. Banville has always been good on the quirks of children and the quirks of adults in remembering their childhood, but, in keeping with his tendency in his late period to write and speak a little more about his own experiences as a child, the idealizations of childhood in *The Sea*, and the diametrically drawn horrors of an Irish 1950s childhood in *Christine Falls*, suggest that this topic, like womanhood, may become a staple of his late period.

Rather than be considered isolated experiments, *Christine Falls* and *The Silver Swan* should be read in organic relationship to Banville's other work. To simply think of this brand of 'conventional' or 'old-fashioned' mystery fiction as an inferior *alter ego* of his literary fiction would be to miss the crucial fact that in this new venture Banville is equally preoccupied with the perfectibility of a particular genre in and of its own established terms. In the same way that his first venture into theatre with his 1994 version of *The Broken Jug*, by Heinrich von Kleist (1777–1811), subsequently developed into a significant pattern with the two further Kleist adaptations of *God's Gift* (2000) and *Love in the Wars* (2005), his current attention to popular fiction is likely to establish its own set of close interrelationships with other of his writings completed beforehand, during and afterwards. Banville has repeatedly emphasized that he resists the separation of fiction into genres and argues that good novels are good novels whatever their supposed classification. Intertextual and allusive aspects continue to intrigue scholarly investigators of his literary fiction; an equal sense of reverence for stylistic forebears lies behind his approach to popular fiction, and Banville has been equally eager to defer to masters in the chosen field. As with the Kleist adaptations, certain elements of *jeu d'esprit* here should not be underestimated, but in allowing for the influence of a long list of relevant writers in the genre, Banville has also underlined a seriousness of intent with his Black books. Even when we might have expected at least a partial relaxation of his focus on form with his move into the popular novel, he has spoken of his conception of crime fiction in terms which, as we will see in Chapter 4, are distinctly reminiscent of his deeply serious conception of high literary form:

> What we get from crime novels is a sense of completion. Life is a mess – we do not remember being born, and death, as Ludwig Wittgenstein wisely said, is not an experience in life, so all we have is this chaotic middle bit, bristling with loose ends, in which nothing is ever properly finished or done with. It could be said, of course, that all novels offer a beginning, middle and an end – even *Finnegans Wake* has a shape – but crime stories do it better. No matter how unlikely the cast of suspects or how baffling the strew of clues, we know with rare certainty that when the murderer is unmasked, as he or she inevitably must be, everything will click into place.[7]

So, aside from it never having been a secret that Benjamin Black is actually John Banville, the close similarity of their respective types of fiction, at the levels both of content and underlying conception, suggests that Black is unlikely to ever be considered separately to his older twin. The overarching point to be made is that because of the Man Booker win and the new kind of publicity surrounding *Christine Falls* and *The Silver Swan*, the characteristic mood-image of Banville conjured up by profilers and interviewers has perceptibly changed. He may, we can now think, be finally coming to realize that he should, like a good Irishman, write fiction about the recent society and history of his own country. He is no longer apparently always the dauntingly bejewelled figuration of his own literary style. He is more frequently portrayed now as congenial, self-effacing, humorous and accessible – he is, as it were, now safely as worldly at times as the rest of us. This change on the one hand underestimates the frequent presence of these estimable qualities in the work and person of the earlier Banville, and on the other betrays the continued presence of difficulty, seriousness and inscrutability, at least in the work. Nevertheless, the change is clearly encouraged by the buoyant answers he currently sometimes gives to his own questions: 'And anyway, what does it matter, art or otherwise? For oh, dear, what fun I am having.'[8]

AGAINST POSTMODERNISM: THE PROBLEM OF BANVILLE'S MAJOR CONTEXT

Critiques of Banville need not be at all refracted through his own personal reflections or, for that matter, through his aesthetic judgments, even when so forcibly expressed as in the McEwan review. We may not want to insist on close parallels between his disposition and that of his characteristically slippery narrators, but he has inevitably developed a set of fluid façades in the way that most authors do who are regularly put through the publicity wringer. This is part of the fun he is currently having, and surely has always had to some degree. 'Well, I tell you what I've done', he revealed to one recent interviewer, 'I've developed a persona behind which I hide. I strap it on and stride into the world. I've developed a patter.'[9] It can be safely assumed, nevertheless, that his thoughts on certain critics and critical approaches, particularly when successively re-emphasized, reflect the seriously held aesthetic positions that inform his own work, his criticism and reviewing included. Even his later commentaries on certain thinkers can cast retrospective light on the influence some traditions of thought have had on him from the beginning.

In general, Banville has written about and reviewed what he approvingly terms 'old-fashioned' critics, and he is somewhat nostalgic for a time when literary criticism was practised by 'men of letters' rather than academics. Though he has sometimes expressed admiration for such radical contemporary figures as the French thinker, Michel Foucault (1926–84), he is far more likely to attend at length to out-of-fashion critics such as the literary journalists Edmund Wilson (1895–1972) and Cyril Connolly (1903–74). His thrust in selecting laudable critics has mainly been anti-theoretical. He approves, for instance, of the formalist brand of close reading currently practised and promoted by the American-based Irish academic Denis Donoghue, and has applauded him, especially, for meeting the challenge of apocalyptic French theory with a humanist resolve. Banville's enduring regard for older critics of literature who cannot be subsumed under any narrow theoretical banner is best voiced in a review of the American essayist and novelist Cynthia Ozick, who continues their brand of practical and broadly humanist criticism. Ozick, Banville argues, is in 'the very best sense' an 'old-fash-ioned critic: enthusiastic, adventurous, conservative (again, in the best sense), unenthralled by academe'. In her 'repeated insistence on the sov-ereignty of thought and imagination', Ozick is for Banville 'unashamed-ly unreconstructed. She will have no truck with postmodernist babble.'[10]

The terms of praise here, repeated in many of Banville's pieces on his other exemplary thinkers, are crucial in light of the most wide-ranging received critical idea about his work. In accordance with its general currency over the past two decades or so, the theoretical term postmod-ernism has been brought to bear on Banville studies to variant conse-quence. There has been much vacillation on the matter, and, in effect, the term has been applied to Banville more by way of repeated assertion than by convincing argument. In an especially misleading vein, post-modernism has often been construed as in some way an antonym for Banville's 'Irishness', and this will be redressed in Chapters 2 and 3. As is eventually said of most isms, postmodernism at this stage can mean virtually anything. A discrimination of postmodernisms is not a task for present purposes; neither will it suffice to simply accept or reject post-modernism as a totality since to do that would be to facilely homogenize a wide variety of literary, cultural and sociological trends. What is cer-tain is that it is not enough to use postmodernism as a catch-all term for a handful of fairly standard self-conscious narrative devices and strate-gies that Banville uses in common with a host of writers of the past few decades. These elements of Banville's work might be read either as the mere leavings of standard postmodern stylistics, tiredly applied, or as camouflage for some of his more distinctly traditional aspects.

If postmodernism is defined in the company of one of its principal the-orists, the American Marxist Fredric Jameson, as primarily a temporal and sociological category, dependent for its international critical existence on 'the hypothesis of some radical break' that is 'generally traced back to the end of the 1950s or the early 1960s', then Banville is in a sense as inevitably postmodern as every other writer of his generation.[11] If taken more as a sty-listic phenomenon, the term postmodernism can be used to account only for some surface aspects of Banville's work, those introverted narrative tics he might superficially have in common with the lineage of self-conscious fiction, a lineage which, even though the term postmodernist is often used to describe it, stretches back to the very origins of literary fiction.

While Banville's fiction is no more endemically immune than any other to the template of determined postmodernist theorists, and while his jettisoning of 'postmodernist babble' does not necessarily carry over into his own aesthetic practice, any relevant discussion should pay more attention than has thus far been granted to Banville's own view of the matter. All the evidence in this context points to the importance of Banville's work, not as any kind of instance of postmodernism, but as a composite of some of the more quasi-religious or hermetic strands of historical modernism, the literary movement generally taken to comprise the late years of the nineteenth century and the early decades of the twentieth. This is especially clear in the context of two of the grand theories of postmodernism, one about the position of 'metanarratives', and one about the relative value of 'high' and 'low' art.

Metanarratives, or master-narratives, are those grand systems or disciplines of thought we have inherited in the Western world which claim to comprehensively explain all human knowledge and experience. And if, as famously formulated by the French theorist Jean-François Lyotard (1924–98), our increasing 'incredulity towards metanarratives' is taken as the prime definition, then there is a fundamental sense in which Banville can be said to not be a postmodernist writer.[12] On one level, it could be argued that a radical questioning of metanarratives is enacted in Banville's work. *Birchwood*, *The Newton Letter* and *Shroud*, for example, fundamentally undermine the metanarrative of History. The novels of the Tetralogy are all designed, on an immediate level, to cast doubt on the metanarratives of Science (including Astronomy and Mathematics). The Trilogy novels, and, again, *Shroud*, involve a rejection of the oldest metanarrative of Religion, specifically its attendant codes of belief in transcendent order and moral regulation, and we will investigate some related issues here and also in Chapter 5. In the most general sense, the apparent postmodernist tricks of all Banville's books can be seen to deconstruct the metanarrative of the act of Narrative itself, especially the claim, as old as fiction, that the self can narrate itself into full being and meaning. *Nightspawn*, modelled as it is on the work of one of Banville's major Irish exemplars, Samuel Beckett (1906–89), is a glaring example of this brand of disbelief in narrative and is the only Banville work that might justifiably be described as quintessentially postmodernist in style.

Banville is thus in one sense an opponent of the *logocentric*, the all-encompassing assumption in Western thinking that everything has a definitive meaning or truth, the same assumption that is the prime target of deconstructive postmodern intellectual strategies generally. He has argued time and again that the world has, or at least potentially has, no meaning, no moral centre, and in making this argument, as we shall later see in Chapter 6, he has made increasing use, inside and outside his books, of his idolized German philosopher, Friedrich Nietzsche (1844–1900), who is often nominated as the first postmodernist. Yet, in his views of art's nature and function, Banville has never embraced anything like the full-scale socio-cultural disorder diagnosed, and sometimes in turn promoted, by some of the major postmodernists. The desire for order and form, for at least *artistic* meaning, that Lyotard, among others, has construed as modernist nostalgia misplaced in a chaotic postmodern world is one of the defining forces in Banville's work. It is true that he is thematically preoccupied with chaos and senselessness, but this is subsumed in a broader determination as an artist to satisfy the rage for order. In every Banville narrative there is a narrator or protagonist, representative of the artist *qua* artist, conferring retrospective order, if not inherent meaning necessarily, on past events and on the world's phenomena. This rage for order will be our focus in Chapter 4.

One of the most succinct statements of the modernist faith in literary art is contained in the frequently quoted phrase 'Only connect!' from *Howards End* (1910) by E.M. Forster (1879–1970), and this is an imperative that Banville's artist figures recognize and obey through the narrative act if not in the lived lives their narratives describe. One of the ultimate ironies of novels such as *The Newton Letter* and *The Book of Evidence*, as Banville sees it in retrospect – and this can be extended to all his fiction – is that 'in both you've got this very poised voice, a perfectly controlled tone relating something that's completely chaotic'.[13] Behind the thematic rejection of metanarratives in all his novels, Banville proposes, usually explicitly, a single absolute metanarrative, that of an autonomous imagination which has sufficient creative distance to confer order on experience and memory. That this effort at order is regularly admitted to be uncertain and provisional by Banville and by his narrators or protagonists does not detract from the simultaneous insistence that the effort is necessary. This is especially so in the novels of the Trilogy where, after the comprehensive deconstructions of the Tetralogy, the artistic products of the imagination are conjectured to represent a special kind of metanarrative that can even compensate for the loss of the ultimate metanarrative of the Word of God.

The second grand theory of the postmodern condition concerns the relative value of high and low art forms. A contrast is set up by this theory between the modernist preoccupation with, broadly speaking, elitist forms of culture, and the eager postmodernist embracing of all varieties of popular culture. The title of a book by the comparative literature expert Andreas Huyssen, *After the Great Divide*, is in itself symptomatic of this way of defining the move from modernist into postmodernist culture, and Banville has shown himself to be very aware of the implications of the move for literature. For Huyssen, the postmodern artistic disposition targets an older active division between high and low art. A perceptible 'anxiety of contamination' characterized the major nineteenth-century ideas about art that were combined in the early twentieth century in modernism – these were ideas taken from the artistic movements called 'symbolism' and 'aestheticism', both of which insisted that art is a higher pursuit, wholly independent or autonomous, and should therefore remain untouched by common or lowly concerns such as popularity and morality. In reaction to this broad modernist position, postmodernism is characterized by 'a plethora of strategic moves tending to destabilise the high/low opposition from within'. In light of such postmodernist strategies, says Huyssen, the modernist dogma of autonomous art has come to seem increasingly sterile.[14]

When Banville was publishing his first fiction in the late 1960s and early 1970s, major efforts were already afoot to dispense with the old division between high and low art, to, as the terminologies of the time had it, cross borders and close gaps in the world of art. But even at that stage Banville tended resolutely in the opposite direction, and he has remained an inveterate campaigner for aesthetic distinction between high and low concerns in art. In his aesthetic positions, he associates with, and has occasionally written about, a number of European writers who are considered exemplary of high autonomous art before, during and after modernism: from the nineteenth century, the French novelist Gustave Flaubert (1821–80) and his compatriot, the poet Stéphane Mallarmé (1842–98); and from the twentieth century, writers from the Germanic tradition such as Hugo von Hofmannsthal (1874–1929), Franz Kafka

(1883–1924) and Thomas Mann (1875–1955), another French novelist, Marcel Proust (1871–1922), and Banville's two countrymen, Beckett and James Joyce (1882–1941). So if postmodernism can be described as a search for a viable modern tradition *outside* of the classical modernist canon, outside of what Huyssen paradigmatically calls the 'Proust-Joyce-Mann' high tradition, then any comprehensive application of the term is nullified in the Banville context. The revivifying, not the sterilizing, of the dogma of autonomous art is Banville's project.

Most positively viewed – and this is the viewpoint Banville adopts – the aesthetic 'anxiety of contamination' in modernism is concerned with preserving the integrity of the autonomous art work so that it can conceptually counterbalance the potential senselessness and chaos of our world. Modernism always remained convinced of the traditional notion of the autonomous art work and believed in the importance of the construction of artistic form and meaning even when it was deemed equally important that the safety of such constructions be called into doubt within the same art forms. The specialized status of art in both constructing and deconstructing a belief in form is Banville's most tenaciously held idea on literature and art, and he was particularly strong on this during his formational, early and middle periods. For him, only the rigid preservation of a two-dimensional culture can protect the specialized status of the aesthetic. While there may be an ounce of mischief-making in his fondness for quoting Cyril Connolly's dictum that the only responsibility of the artist is to create a masterpiece, there is firm conviction in his view that 'popular culture is easy and immediate' and that 'it would be dangerous if popular culture came to be seen as the only kind of culture'. In Banville's view, today we are 'up to our armpits in popular culture. We're sinking in it.' Thus, people 'must continually be reminded that there is another kind of art, another kind of culture, which is difficult'. This difficulty favours the specialized status of the aesthetic: 'it's better that the high arts are marginalized. It's better for people to admit "this is not going to appeal to everybody, this is elitist"'.[15]

This argument for two artistic dimensions might be seen as one of the major reasons Banville has recently adopted his pseudonym. John Banville writes a frequently difficult type of book that does not appeal to everybody; Benjamin Black's books are deliberately written in a populist mode and are much more comfortable with a plain and accessible storyline.

What should also be remembered, however, is that even within the domain of intentionally difficult literary fiction Banville always resisted, in principle as well as in practice, what he considered to be the more obvious varieties of postmodernist narrative experimentalism which were widely popular when he was maturing as a writer in his formational and early periods. The main varieties were the *nouveau roman*, a predominantly French version of fiction which insisted that the psychologization of narrators and characters has no place in the novel, and magic realism, a version of fiction practised across the world which freely mixes elements of the real and the fantastic in single narratives. These kinds of fiction were, and usually still are, lauded as broadly continuing the development of one strand of modernism, the idea of the radical *avant-garde*, whereby revolutionary experimentalism in the arts and literature would encourage new perceptions of the world and, thereby, a new and better human disposition, new and better social and political conditions. For Banville, however, this is all to attach too direct a Utopian programme to literary fiction, and his version of a continued modernism has emphasized other functions for literary art, functions that are more oblique and conceptualist and individualist, certainly, but which are nonetheless directed at deep and collective human needs. In the process, as we shall see in Chapter 4, he has held to some traditional but complex notions about the possibilities for exploring internal human psychology in fiction and about fiction's responsibilities towards the external real world.

CONNOISSEUR OF SILENCE: BANVILLE AND BELIEF

Adherence to the modernist idea of art's autonomy is generally taken to be an advocacy of an aesthetic position usually phrased as 'art for art's sake' – the implication is that anyone who insists that art is a high and autonomous pursuit can never simultaneously suggest that art exists for society's sake or for anything else outside of immediate aesthetic concerns. While it is sometimes tempting to view Banville's position as reminiscent of those of the Irish aesthete Oscar Wilde (1854–1900), a writer with whom he has surprisingly rarely been compared, it is important to recognize that the special status Banville ascribes to art is not necessarily equivalent to the notion that all art is quite useless. The aim instead is to find an alternative operational value for an art that is freed of conventional notions of communication or instruction or any other direct utility.

The theory of the autonomy of art is closely allied to certain theories of the individual's relationship to society. The moment when the idea of individual autonomy emerged in Western thought is difficult to pinpoint, though its centrality in the development of the various theories of the social contract that makes civil life possible is undisputed. A prime moment of formulation, if not origin, was the ethos of individualism that arose between the fourteenth and seventeenth centuries during the periods of the Renaissance and the Reformation, an ethos in large part motivated against the authority and regulative beliefs of the traditional Christian church. The humanist emphasis on personal genius which emerged in these periods culminated in the extreme idealization of the artist during the romantic movement of the late eighteenth and early nineteenth centuries. In and after the voluminous treatises on aesthetics that were produced during the Enlightenment of the eighteenth century, personal autonomy and aesthetic autonomy were combined in the romantic idea that the imagination and its aesthetic judgements were laws unto themselves. The general question of the autonomy of the individual has thus been one of the central preoccupations of modern history, and the question has had a tenacious hold in aesthetics, in itself one of the defining intellectual disciplines of the West.

While nineteenth-century aestheticism, with its idea that art should exist only for art's own sake, can be regarded as the most colourful flowering of the idea of autonomy as carried over into creativity, the resultant development of modernism in the early twentieth century produced particularly complex ideas about the relationship between the personal and the universal as defined in the relationship between the individual work of art and the world outside it. Especially refined ideas about autonomy have been offered by the German intellectual Theodor Adorno (1903–69), a propagator of high-modernist ideas well into the twentieth century. Banville's general position on the nature and function of art has affinities with Adorno's. Adorno has figured both directly and indirectly in the fiction, and Banville made particular mention of him in his journalism during the middle period, when he was writing the Trilogy. Adorno's monumental *Aesthetic Theory* (1970), where his basic position is constantly re-emphasized with phrases such as 'autonomy is an irrevocable aspect of art' and 'art's opposition to the real world is in the realm of form', aimed to provide a basis for a non-moralistic assessment of what he called the 'monomaniac separatism' of the idea that art should exist only for art's sake. The 'ivory tower', says Adorno, this modernist symbol of the aggressively autonomous artist, has been dismissed since modernism by all kinds of societies, both totalitarian and democratic, but it has persevered as a valid symbol of independent creativity because it reflects the tenacity of a seemingly endemic human inclination: the 'impulse towards identity with oneself'.[16] To explain his general argument for the universality of self-identity in an essay on art and religion, Adorno used the metaphor of the 'monad', which, following other philosophers, he defined as something which 'represents' the universe but which has 'no windows; it represents the universal within its own walls':

> The relationship of the work and the universal becomes the more profound the less the work copes explicitly with universalities, the more it becomes infatuated with its own detached world, its material, its problems, its consistency, its way of expression. Only by reaching the acme of genuine individualization, only by obstinately following up the desiderata of its concretion, does the work become truly the bearer of the universal.[17]

The usefulness of this idea of the detached monad in defining the potential function of autonomous art is defined by Banville in a passage from *Athena* patently influenced by Adorno's theories and which quotes directly from *Aesthetic Theory*. 'She' in this passage most immediately refers to Syrinx, the figure from Greek myth in one of the seven closely described paintings Banville has concocted for the novel; but 'She' can also be taken as a personification of Art:

> She is the pivot of the picture, the fulcrum between two states of being, the representation of life-in-death and death-in-life, of what changes and yet endures; the witness that she offers is the possibility of transcendence, both of the self and of the world, though world and self remain the same. She is the perfect illustration of Adorno's dictum that 'In their relation to empirical reality works of art recall the theologumenon that in a state of redemption everything will be just as it is and yet wholly different'. (p.105)

As illustrated here, especially in the word *theologumenon* denoting a specifically theological statement, Adorno's theories of the nature and function
of autonomy in art have a perceptibly religious tone. Whether Adorno's
ideas have directly informed Banville's own recent formulations, or
whether Adorno is called in to illustrate an idea he always held in any
case, a similar religious tone is evident in Banville's speculations on aesthetics. The relation between autonomous art, life, death and transcendence that Adorno sets up is figured in Banville as almost a sacral code,
and there is something classically elemental in the way this code operates in the work: 'at some level', Banville allows, 'all my art is about grief
and loss and about the awareness of death.'[18]

Banville's interest in the phenomenon of death by murder became
immediately apparent with *The Book of Evidence* and has clearly been consolidated recently with *Christine Falls* and *The Silver Swan*. It is not always
noticed, however, that death and dying generally figure heavily in all
Banville's work, from the stories of *Long Lankin* (one of which is directly
entitled 'A Death'), through the hilarious and grotesque passings in
Nightspawn and *Birchwood*, through the final scenes of both *Copernicus* and
Kepler, through the central death of the mother in *Mefisto*, through the
death of the father in *The Book of Evidence* and the murders of the Trilogy,
into the suicides at the end of both *The Untouchable* and *Eclipse*, the great
public disaster of the Holocaust's death-dealing in *Shroud*, and Max
Morden's deeply felt private grief at the death of his wife in *The Sea*. Far
from being reducible to a penchant for postmodern philosophical and
narrative sophistry, Banville's deconstruction of language and metanarratives is allied to a thematic of life and death that forms part of a general
preoccupation with the very basics of human existence:

> I think modernism raised questions that were never answered, they
> were simply evaded. Postmodernism is a total evasion of the hard
> questions ... Questions raised by modernism included questions
> about being, about language, about whether we speak language or
> language speaks us, how do we express, what is expressed ... If
> discourse is suspect, then how do we live?[19]

This question of 'how do we live?' is the moral root of Banville's
aesthetics of autonomy. Banville is, in an idiosyncratic but vital way, a
religious writer. Outside of *Christine Falls*, with its directly sociological

treatment of the Irish Catholic Church in Dublin and Boston during the 1950s, his work cannot perhaps be comprehensively discussed in terms of the denominational religious criticism brought to, say, the work of the avowedly Catholic novelists Evelyn Waugh (1903–66) and Graham Greene (1904–91), both of whom have considerably influenced his style. Yet Banville is so regularly concerned with the nature of man and the possibilities of living in a post-faith age that in a broad sense he can be termed a religious writer. There are a surprising number of religious references and settings in the œuvre. In *Long Lankin*, a fat little man appears ranting about God and the Apocalypse in 'A Death'; and 'Summer Voices' has a scriptural opening. *Nightspawn* includes a retelling of the Cain story (p.47f). The first section of *Birchwood* is entitled 'The Book of the Dead', an allusion to Egyptian mortuary tradition, and later there are allusions to Dante's *Divine Comedy* (p.132). Copernicus's story, since he was a canon, inevitably contains religious elements and there is, for instance, an echo of Ecclesiastes in his enunciation of 'Vanity, all vanity' towards the end (p.240). Kepler keeps a talismanic engraving of Dürer's 'Knight with Death & the Devil' with him (p.131), and *Mefisto* refers in its second paragraph to the refrain 'Who only is escaped alone' from Job, a refrain that shows up again in *Shroud* (p.60). The Trilogy is replete with religious references, with Freddie Montgomery specifically discussing at one point his 'Search for God' (*Ghosts*, p.192f). For his single story for children, Banville adapted the foundational biblical story of Noah's Ark. One of the most dramatic scenes in this religious context occurs in *Eclipse* when Cleave travels to the scene of his daughter's suicide: he arrives at the site beside an Italian church, accompanied by a priest and by a range of biblical allusions to Golgotha and to the Psalms (pp.207–8). That scene would be worth extensive comparison with Gabriel Swan's attentiveness to the drugged-out Adele in the hospital church in *Mefisto* (pp.208–10). By the time of the writing of *Shroud*, with its central symbol of the Turin Shroud itself, the religious theme for Banville is total.

Banville's obsession with angels and ghosts, though partly attributable to the frequently discussed influence on him of the work of the German poet Rainer Maria Rilke (1875–1926) and the American poet Wallace Stevens (1879–1955), can also be taken as enduring evidence of spiritual yearning in his books. While Banville's fiction often discreetly echoes the opening line ('Who, if I cried, would hear me among the angelic / orders?') of Rilke's *Duino Elegies* (1922), such imploring invocations sometimes occur so blatantly that Banville's narrators are conferred with an extreme and despairing emotionalism that far outweighs the coldness popularly associated with them. Freddie's cry in *The Book of Evidence* is as raw as such invocations get:

O God, O Christ, release me from this place.
O Someone. (p.38)

These specific references and allusions are part of a more generalized concern in Banville's work with the possibility of religious belief. The post-religious threat under which all Banville's characters live is described perfectly, though covertly, in *Copernicus*, where, at the head of a succession of six central italicized quotations, Banville places one from the beginning of *Fear and Trembling*, published in 1843 by the Danish theologian Søren Kierkegaard (1813–55). Copernicus addresses the words to Rheticus:

If at the foundation of all there lay only a wildly seething power which, writhing with obscure passions, produced everything that is great and everything that is insignificant, if a bottomless void never satiated lay hidden beneath all, what then would life be but despair? (p.208)

Kierkegaard is now often thought of as one of the first formulators of existentialism, a predominantly twentieth-century philosophy which seeks to deal with the possibility that we are deluding ourselves if we think that a divine or transcendent meaning or destiny exists for us. And the central question of *Fear and Trembling* is what the despairing individual can do to find independent meaning and an ethical grounding in an absurd world of potentially 'bottomless void'. In Banville's way of looking at this predicament, the situation of the autonomous individual is primary. As he put it in a piece for the *Irish Times* on the last day of 1999:

It was Freud who observed that after Copernicus, belief in a God who had created the world and kept it in his care was no longer tenable ... It is hard for us in our sceptical and hard-boiled age to appreciate what a shock to the belief-system of the 16th century was the announcement that the Earth does not sit supreme and immobile at the core of the universe, but is a satellite among other satellites of the sun. Suddenly, half-way through the second millennium, Man, the *magnum miraculum*, found himself unceremoniously pushed from the centre of creation.[20]

A concern with the freedom and autonomy of the individual is natural in the context of this perception of cosmic displacement. One of Banville's sweeping generalizations indicates the impact of this sense of loss on the world-view that informs his work:

> We moderns have an unshakeable sense of individuality, our own and that of others. But the concept of the individual, as we know it, is relatively recent. Indeed, the critic Harold Bloom contends that it was Shakespeare who single-handedly invented, or discovered, human personality. This is a little extreme, perhaps, but it is true that even the most cursory study of the Renaissance will show that something profound in human beings' conceptions of themselves and who and what they are began to occur somewhere around the middle of the 14th century. With the decline of the feudal system, which was essentially the system of the beehive, and, later, the great discoveries in cosmology by Copernicus, Kepler and Galileo, European society began to fragment in ways that were not always destructive.

The predicament that results from this fragmentation is summed up by Banville in classic existentialist terms: 'Pushed out of the centre of creation, where he had believed God had set him, Man suddenly saw the possibilities of individual freedom, with all the benefits and the terrors it entailed.'[21]

Banville has repeatedly stated that in fiction he aims for psychological depth rather than social breadth, a preference reflected in the mode he has generally chosen to explore the possibilities of individual freedom: the monologue, a favourite form of existentialist writers. He has remarked that he would now find it very difficult to go back to writing in the third person, that he is 'a monologist essentially'.[22] What he has been trying to do all along 'is follow Beckett's precept, when he was writing about Proust: "in art, the only possible progression, is a progression that is in depth"'. Like Proust and Beckett, he tries 'to go right down into the well of a particular human being and find out what's down there';

he tries to 'get that obsessive, singular voice that expresses something about how it feels to actually be a single human consciousness'.[23] In view of its elevation of the solitary individual, the point Beckett builds around Proust, in his essay simply entitled 'Proust' (1930), is worth developing. Beckett promotes the artist's general removal from the world: 'Because the only possible spiritual development is in the sense of depth ... And art is the apotheosis of solitude.' 'We are alone', is the definitive position: 'We cannot know and we cannot be known. "Man is the creature that cannot come forth from himself, who knows others only in himself, and who, if he asserts the contrary, lies".'[24] This kind of impenetrable aloneness constitutes for Banville's monologists a kind of unavoidable, rearguard autonomy. As Freddie Montgomery admits in *Ghosts*, 'there is no getting away from the passionate attachment to self, that I-beam set down in the dead centre of the world and holding the whole rickety edifice in place'. And he aims to transform himself into 'a monomorph: a monad' (p.26), which recalls us to Adorno, another admirer of Beckett.

Although in one sense this constitutes the standard existential theme of human alienation, Banville persists in bringing to the problem of individuality a distinctly spiritual terminology. The recognition of alienation, isolation and meaninglessness by his protagonists is always accompanied by a tortuous desire in them for some variety of transcendent experience or reassurance. All his books, Banville says, are at an essential level 'about solitude in the face of an incomprehensible world'; but because he is a novelist and artist he takes 'great delight in what we have done with this solitude. We've invented this extraordinary world to hold up, like a talisman, a crucifix, against death. And it does all come back to death.'[25]

We will come back ourselves in Chapters 5 and 6 to other idiosyncratic aspects of Banville's focus on death. For the present, we must recognize that this aspect of Banville crosses metaphysical speculation with a socially and historically conscientious world-view with which he is not often credited. Banville most directly confronts the modern spiritual problem thematically through the Holocaust context of *Shroud*. But in more general aesthetic terms his proposed resolution to crises of faith is a conception of art as a kind of spilt religion. 'The only real spiritual prop we have', Banville believes, 'is the imagination', and he refers to the article of faith that 'art makes life' expressed by one of his major influences, the

American novelist Henry James (1843–1916). This may seem, Banville allows, an arrogant statement, but he interprets James as meaning 'that art, and the imagination which produces art, is a force of formation, that the imagination forms life, forms the incoherency of life into something manageable'.[26] James's views on fiction would bear extensive comparison to Banville's art of the novel; the context of this small reference alone is revelatory in that it points to Banville's all-encompassing faith in the specialized status of the aesthetic. James's relevant lines read:

> and so far from that of literature being irrelevant to the literary report upon life, and to its being made as interesting as possible, I regard it as relevant in a degree that leaves everything else behind. It is art that *makes* life, makes interest, makes importance, for our consideration and application of these things, and I know of no substitute whatever for the force and beauty of its process.[27]

Banville is reasonably circumspect, however, on this matter of art as spilt religion. Artists, who in any case seem to 'want to be gods in the sense that the artist is a man who is very interested in control and subjugating reality to certain, quite well-defined laws', can, he suggests, take the place of God,

> but it would be very foolish for us to imagine that this would have the same kind of effects that we imagine religion had. Art will not redeem us. It will not save us from death. But it will do other things, such as leave something after us, a mark on the world which will say: 'we've been here'. It's extraordinary to listen to a Beethoven quartet and say 'this man sat at a desk, in grief and despair and joy and wrote this music. This is a definite thumbprint on the world.' That, to me, is the most redemption we can expect.[28]

In this reduced version of redemption, the concepts of autonomy and belief are intimately linked. Banville later reaffirmed his aesthetics of autonomy in an approving commentary on a contemporary discussion of literature's interaction with religion by the Italian writer Roberto Calasso in *Literature and the Gods* (2001). Banville, who has always been fascinated by Greek myths and the pagan gods, has frequently expressed his admiration for Calasso and is fundamentally in concurrence with his mythic and religiously inclined thought. Calasso's reclamation of the Greek myths in *The Marriage of Cadmus and Harmony* (1988), which Banville read in translation in his middle period, is arguably an important influence on the formulation of the mythic scenarios that inform the seven set-piece descriptions of paintings in *Athena*. Considering Calasso on religion, Banville posed the question: 'If today our best, our only, possibility of finding the divine is through the act of reading, how must we prepare ourselves for the encounter?' The best preparation was suggested in a quotation he chose from Calasso on the concept of 'absolute literature': '"Literature" because it is a knowledge that claims to be accessible only and exclusively by way of literary composition', and 'absolute' because it is 'a knowledge that one assimilates while in search of an absolute, and that thus draws in no less than everything; and at the same time it is something *absolutum*, unbound, freed from any duty or common cause, from any social utility'. It is this last quality, Banville agreed, 'its total independence and autonomy, that marks off absolute literature from what had gone before'.[29]

The absolute idea of God and/or the gods, the transcendent autonomous realm, is transferred here into an idea of literature's autonomy and transcendence. For Calasso, the ethos of 'absolute' literature originates in romanticism, culminates in symbolism with poets such as Mallarmé, and survives thereafter in various hybrid forms. And the subsequent other writers he mentions have all been mainstays of Banville's personal tradition. There is also a characteristic literary form involved here when Calasso points to the central development in this context of the art of the monologue. By these arguments, there appears to be an intimate connection between absolute or autonomous art, the decline of religious belief, and the narrative of the modern self-obsessive individual.

In working out the partial redemption that autonomous art can provide, Banville resorts to an aesthetic of silence that has something of a mystical aspect. A mad formalist could have much fun with the frequency of the word *silence* in the Banville œuvre. Silence, and its near synonyms, *stillness* and *quietness*, are used variously, in whatever conjugations, as motif, as metaphor, as image, and, most importantly, as aesthetic model. Only Beckett has used the word with similar pattern in fiction, and while Banville's repeated use of it has been increasingly perceptible in successive books, reaching a high point in the Trilogy, it should be noted that varieties of silence have fascinated him from the outset. Even in his shortest book of fiction, Long Lankin, silence, or its near synonyms, occurred eighty-four times, sometimes repeated within single passages or pages. And even in his one major work of non-fiction, Prague Pictures, a real silence is the aspect of this city that most immediately comes to his mind: 'Perhaps it is the snow that intensifies the silence of the city in these, my earliest memories of it. Prague's silence is more a presence than an absence' (p.1).

The fascination with silence has a cohesive theoretical context in literary studies and linguistics. As a seemingly contradictory aspiration, for a writer it has been a characteristic high-modernist option. The option is a natural one when the writer in question refuses any straightforward notions of art as easily consumable communication. Banville also includes in his aesthetic of silence various aspects of a mystical and spiritual inheritance. In some cases this is tangential: Kierkegaard's Fear and Trembling, which, as we have seen, Banville uses and quotes in Copernicus, is narrated by one Johannes de silentio, and the Austrian philosopher Ludwig Wittgenstein (1889–1951), whose line on silence closes Birchwood, claimed in the same source that 'There are, indeed, things that cannot be put into words. They make themselves manifest. They are what is mystical.'[30]

On other occasions, the matter of religious belief, or unbelief, is directly allied to imperatives of silence in the novels. In Copernicus, for example, it is reported of the canon that 'Suddenly one day God abandoned him'; though he continues with a surface belief in the trappings of ceremonies and sacraments, beyond the rituals 'there was for him now only a silent white void that was everywhere and everything and eternal' (p.115). More hopefully, the Jew Wincklemann in Kepler explains to the astronomer: 'There are things in our religion which may not be spoken, because to speak such ultimate things is to ... to damage them. Perhaps it is the same with your science?' (pp.47–8). A particular moment of interest in the life of Newton is paralleled by his historian's broken confidence in instrumental language: 'He was giving himself up more and more to interpretative study of the Bible, and to that darker work in alchemy which so embarrasses his biographers' (Newton Letter, p.6). In these and many other similar moments, Banville is at least giving the nod to the possibility of crucial forms of knowledge and experience beyond the logical and the linguistic.

Beyond conceptual speculation, there is a distinctly socio-political aspect to Banville's aesthetics of silence. Crucial here is the steady impact on him of the thought and criticism of the professor of comparative literature, George Steiner. Steiner's opinions helped mould the enduring view of art's relations with society which Banville adopted in his formational period. For his part, Steiner in return has had no hesitation in suggesting that a number of ideas from his essay 'The Cleric of Treason' (1980) on Anthony Blunt were borrowed by Banville for his version of Blunt in The Untouchable.[31] Banville has written a considerable number of pieces on Steiner that testify to the overall influence, including an introduction to Steiner's The Deeps of the Sea and Other Fiction (1996). Banville's praise for Steiner, occasionally quali- fied, has been directed principally at his 'almost messianic zeal in the promotion and defence of literature, and a critical passion that is rare in these jaded, post-humanist times'.[32] Two Steiner books in particular have been vital, one in formulating Banville's aesthetics, the other in allowing him to reaffirm them. 'One of the most important books of my education', he recalls, 'was George Steiner's Language and Silence. When I was growing up he was a window on to wider things.'[33] Later, speaking in similar terms, Banville was very specific about this early educational book:

> It has been said before, but bears repeating, that for many of us growing up in the 1950s and 1960s he was a key figure. This was true especially in Ireland, as we sought for ways to break free from the parochialism and pervasive pastoralism of Irish art and letters. In books such as Language and Silence, Steiner opened a window for us into the house of European culture.[34]

While Steiner's immersion in European literatures, especially of the Germanic tradition, undoubtedly helped direct Banville's own formational reading choices, Steiner's method of literary explication has been equally important to him. He reads Steiner as fundamentally a religious writer. Any reservations he has had to express on Steiner's thought have emanated from just this aspect, as in his review of Real Presences (1989), a book that elabo- rates on issues raised in Language and Silence (1967). Applauding Steiner's persistence with older aesthetic matters such as beauty and transcendence, with the idea of the seemingly mysterious – or numinous – nature of art, Banville offered an important qualification: 'Dr Steiner argues that the numinous in the art-work has its source in the artist's desire, not to emulate the Creator, but to set himself up as a kind of anti-Creator, to *make new worlds*.' Though 'interesting' as such, Banville suggested that this idea strikes 'an oddly lame note' since 'the Creator, God the Father', is not the only 'necessary' presence: 'Nietzsche, one of the most profound aesthetic thinkers, argues that the "real presence" that we seem to feel is nothing more than the twitching in us still of a primordial reflex of fear and awe in the face of the natural world.'[35] Banville does not dismiss here the idea of the numinous 'real presence'. What is involved is a variant interpretation whereby, for Banville, the numinous, in a kind of transcendence downwards, is taken to reside not in the supernatural but in the natural phenomenal world. This has implications which we will examine in detail in Chapters 4 and 6.

In keeping with Steiner's ideas in *Language and Silence*, Banville places his narrators and protagonists in a world where consciousness cannot rely on the inherited assumptions of language. In emphasizing the positive creative implications of a reduced faith in language and a consequent retreat to silence, Steiner provides a quick digest of writers, most of whom Banville has paid direct compliment to over the course of his work in journalism, who sought to give back to language a kind of incantatory or magical power. These writers had recourse to a new musical paradigm for literature whereby the form and sound of language would strive to achieve a silent meaning superior to the plain meaning of the *content* of language. The musical analogies of *Four Quartets* (1935–42) by T.S. Eliot (1888–1965) are a typical example (and it should be remembered that Eliot's work is a distinct presence in Banville as early as *Nightspawn*): 'Words, after speech, reach / Into the silence. Only by the form, the pattern, / Can words or music reach / The stillness'.[36]

Whether strictly under Steiner's influence or otherwise, Banville's sense of prose style and its conjunction with music and silence can best be understood in the context outlined here. And the context begins to expand once it is encountered. As well as mentioning many poets, Steiner also refers in *Language and Silence* to fiction writers heavily influenced by nineteenth-century poetics: Proust, whose tone can be heard in Banville from *Birchwood* on; and Kafka and Beckett, writers for whom Banville's admiration, as we shall see in Chapter 2, approaches the evangelical. A less familiar fictional presence is also worth mentioning here to emphasize the multiplication of intellectual influence. Steiner twice claims that an Austrian novel deeply indebted to symbolist poetics, *The Death of Virgil* (1945) by Hermann Broch (1886–1951), is one of the most significant efforts in fiction to develop the music analogy and its relations with silence. Banville has expressed his own admiration for *The Death of Virgil* several times, and Broch's benign valedictory tone at its end bears considerable comparison with the end of *Copernicus*:

> ... the word hovered over the universe, over the nothing, floating beyond the expressible as well as the inexpressible, and he, caught under and amidst the roaring, he floated on with the word ... a floating sea, a floating fire, sea-heavy, sea-light, notwithstanding it was still the word: he could not hold fast to it and he might not hold fast to it; incomprehensible and unutterable for him: it was the word beyond speech.[37]

While the idea of silence that Steiner works with is often taken to be an especially introverted version of aestheticism, he also crucially develops, most notably through Kafka, a precisely political and moral angle on the rise of writers' preoccupation with silence in the first half of the twentieth century. Essentially, this concerns confrontations with barbarism during and after the world wars:

> The question of whether the poet should speak or be silent, of whether language is in a condition to accord with his needs, is a real one. 'No poetry after Auschwitz', said Adorno ... Has our civilization, by virtue of the inhumanity it has carried out and condoned – we are accomplices to that which leaves us indifferent – forfeited its claims to that indispensable luxury which we call literature? [...] It is better for the poet to mutilate his own tongue than to dignify the inhuman either with his gift or his uncaring ... Precisely because it is the signature of his humanity, because it is that which makes of man a being of striving unrest, the word should have no natural life, no neutral sanctuary, in the places and season of bestiality. Silence is an alternative.

This alternative, Steiner argues, is 'the most honest temptation to silence in contemporary feeling'.[38]

And this 'honest' alternative was adopted literally by Banville as a young writer. One of the most valuable contributions Imhof has made

31

to the interpretation of *Nightspawn* is his quotation from a Banville letter of the time to his American publisher, W.W. Norton. Luckily discovered by Imhof in a second-hand copy of the novel, the letter provides a key to an understanding of Banville's dominant aesthetics of silence. The parallels between the letter and Steiner's views are striking. 'Anyone writing today, who cares at all about his craft', Banville wrote, 'is conscious of how this half century has shifted the battleground of art':

> Fifty years ago, writing was a struggle with the raucous voice of language; today it is a struggle with the insidious whisper of silence. Total silence seems the only really honest way to speak about Buchenwald and Hiroshima; silence has now come to seem, not failure, but honesty.

The provisional, aspirational quality of silence was immediately acknowledged, however:

> All right, silence is fine; but what do you do if you have a voice and it won't stop still? First of all, in my case at least, one has to use that voice to speak about that voice; one has to build up a base which is nearest to the honesty of silence, and begin from there. NIGHTSPAWN, for me, is that base. I have written a book which ... is as near to silence as I can get, at the moment.[39]

The echoes of Steiner and Adorno, combined with the overwhelming influence of Beckett on Banville during this formational period, give something of a derivative and schematic feel to this manifesto on silence. Yet it is clear from more private moments in the drafting of *Nightspawn* that the silence project was no pose. The writing of *Nightspawn* seems to have been a difficult process for Banville in that he was eking out his basic aesthetics from what he was doing in practice: 'All the writing is an investigation into silence, and the ways of making silence profound by the addition of sound; writing is the deepening of silence with sound and vision.'[40] A restatement of the idea in his late period further indicates that the impulse to silence was deeply felt. Agreeing that there is a perceptible move in his work towards an emptying of content, his conviction is reflected in a broad generalization: 'Any writer who's honest with himself wants to go silent ... The only utterance that can be perfect is silence; it can be perfect, but it can't be eloquent, at least not for very long.'[41]

So here is the productive irony. Silence can be only a notional strategy. As with religious belief, once language and meaning are posited, any move away from these is a matter of circular negative definition. The French existentialist Jean-Paul Sartre (1905–80) put the case for the modern writer after the horrors of the Second World War plainly in his 1948 book *What is Literature?* And here it should be noted that Sartre's prime fictional treatment of the case, *Nausea* (1938), was a clear influence on the work of Banville's middle period and is quoted almost verbatim at the end of *The Newton Letter*. Sartre said:

> And since he has once committed himself in the universe of language, he can never again pretend that he cannot speak. Once you enter the universe of meanings, there is nothing you can do to get out of it. Let words organize themselves freely and they will make sentences, and each sentence contains language in its entirety and refers back to the whole universe. Silence itself is defined in relationship to words, as the pause in music receives its meaning from the group of notes round it. This silence is a moment of language; being silent is not being dumb; it is to refuse to speak, and therefore to keep on speaking.[42]

Shroud is the work in which Banville has most nakedly confronted the problematic of silence, the potential destruction of the writer's faith in cultivated language by the alignments of high culture and high crimes against humanity in the Holocaust. The narrator, going under the name Axel Vander, is a literary academic who deftly echoes the work of Steiner at numerous points when he mentions some of his work on language. Modelled on real-life émigré intellectuals such as Adorno and Thomas Mann, Vander has addressed from the vantage point of the USA the combined philosophical and political crucifixion of language in old, war-torn Europe. One of his major books, entitled *After Words*, is a concoction by Banville, but one of the book's chapter titles, 'Effacement and Real Presence', which Vander has chosen to read on his trip to Turin (pp.150–6), directly invokes Steiner's *Real Presences*, the volume Banville had earlier reviewed. A single descriptive paragraph from the opening of *Real Presences* signals the close alignment of the theme of the threatened word in *Shroud*, and indeed in all of Banville, with Steiner's thought:

This study will contend that the wager on the meaning of meaning, on the potential of insight and response when one human voice addresses another, when we come face to face with the text and work of art or music, which is to say when we encounter the *other* in its condition of freedom, is a wager on transcendence.[43]

Beyond such specific use of Steiner, it is clear that consciously or unconsciously Banville manoeuvred from his early period onwards into the spheres of intellectual exploration that Steiner repeatedly suggested were likely for writers who keenly felt the twentieth-century tension between silence and the word. These other dimensions or forms of perception (Steiner has always called them 'grammars' of perception) are Mathematics (*Copernicus*, *Kepler* and especially *Mefisto*), Art (the Trilogy, *The Untouchable*, *The Sea*), and Music (a form crucial to the overall Banville aesthetic of the novel and one we shall explore further in Chapter 4). In the broadest sense, the continuation of Banville's voice in the context of the dialectic tension between silence and the word is guaranteed by his compositional dedication to the idea of the novel and all artistic writing, and therefore of man's autonomous capacity for form, as blissful if not angelic perfection, as perfectibility not abandoned, only permanently deferred. 'When I look back over the stuff I've written', Banville said just as he was entering his late period, 'I shudder':

> I detest all my own work. I find it a deep source of embarrassment ... Somebody once asked Iris Murdoch why she wrote so many novels, and she said she felt that each new one would excuse all the ones that went before it. A lot of novelists and a lot of artists feel like that. The next work is the one that's going to justify everything [...] I still see ahead of me somewhere, maybe in ten years' time, a work of art that would be so simple, so pristine, so clear, that it would be unavoidable, even for me, that I would have to say 'Yes, I got it right there.' As it stands, I've got it right in a few sentences, maybe a few paragraphs, maybe a few scenes. Maybe I chose the perfect name for a character somewhere, these tiny things I get a slight glow from remembering. But overall, I don't think I've succeeded yet, no.[44]

So there is a prime ambiguity in Banville's aesthetics of silence and in the profound matters of transcendental belief worked out therein. The decline of faith in language is equivalent to a declining faith in a mean-ingful centre, in the supreme metanarrative of God's word. Decline of faith in God philosophically means a waning of faith in, and thus a retreat into silence from, the biblical declaration 'In the beginning was the word'. And so to remain convinced of the perfectibility of language – for Banville, language as formulated in the novel genre – is to testify to Nietzsche's suggestion that if we continue to believe in the relevance and significance of grammar in helping us make sense of our world and of ourselves as potentially autonomous beings, then we continue to believe in a god-like central significance for things. It is to testify that there may, after all, still be meaning in meaning, for us individually, for us collectively. The exam-ination of that testimony is the vital due process of John Banville's fiction.

NOTES

1. Mike Murphy, 'John Banville', *The Arts Show* (RTÉ radio) (8 February 1995).
2. Ibid.
3. Boyd Tonkin, 'The Wrong Choice in a List Packed with Delights', *Independent* (11 October 2005).
4. Liam Fay, 'Wexford's Winner', *Sunday Times* (Ireland edition) (16 October 2005).
5. All references to this review are to John Banville, 'A Day in the Life', *New York Review of Books*, 52, 9 (26 May 2005), pp.42–4.
6. John Connolly, 'Joining the Criminal Fraternity', *Irish Times* (30 September 2006).
7. John Banville, 'Personally Speaking I Blame Agatha for Turning Me to Crime', *Sunday Telegraph* (11 February 2007).
8. Ibid.
9. Tom Adair, 'Meet the Other Half', *Scotsman* (21 October 2006).
10. John Banville, 'Northern Lights and the Mystery of Mr James', *Irish Times* (22 May 1993).
11. Fredric Jameson, *Postmodernism, or The Cultural Logic of Late Capitalism* (London: Verso, 1991), p.1.
12. Jean-François Lyotard, *The Postmodern Condition: A Report on Knowledge*, trans. Geoff Bennington and Brian Massumi, foreword Fredric Jameson (Manchester: Manchester University Press, 1984), p.xxiv.
13. Fintan O'Toole, 'Stepping into the Limelight – and the Chaos', *Irish Times* (21 October 1989).
14. Andreas Huyssen, *After the Great Divide: Modernism, Mass Culture and Postmodernism* (London: Macmillan, 1988), pp.vii, ix.
15. Joe Jackson, 'Hitler, Stalin, Bob Dylan, Roddy Doyle … and Me', *Hot Press*, 18, 19 (5 October 1994), pp.14–15.
16. Theodor Adorno, *Aesthetic Theory*, ed. Gretel Adorno and Rolf Tiedemann, trans. C. Lenhardt (London: Routledge & Kegan Paul, 1984), pp.1, 7, 8, 153.

17. Theodor Adorno, 'Theses Upon Art and Religion Today', *Notes to Literature*, ed. Rolf Tiedmann, trans. Shierry Weber Nicholsen, vol. 2 (New York: Columbia University Press, 1991), p.297.

18. Jackson, 'Hitler, Stalin, Bob Dylan, Roddy Doyle ... and Me', p.15.

19. Michael Ross, 'Chaos Theory', *Sunday Times* (19 November 2000).

20. John Banville, 'Pushed from the Centre of Creation', *Irish Times* (31 December 1999).

21. John Banville, 'Are We Who We Say We Are?', *Irish Times* (4 March 2000).

22. Melvyn Bragg, 'John Banville', *The South Bank Show* (LWT/Ulster Television, 1993).

23. Joe Jackson, 'John Banville', *Hot Press*, 24, 21 (8 November 2000), p.60.

24. Samuel Beckett, *Proust/Three Dialogues with Georges Duthuit* (London: Calder & Boyars, 1970), pp.64, 66.

25. Jackson, 'Hitler, Stalin, Bob Dylan, Roddy Doyle ... and Me', p.16.

26. Michael Garvey (prod. and dir.), *Undercover Portrait: John Banville* (Orpheus Productions for RTÉ television, 2000).

27. Henry James, *Henry James: A Life in Letters*, ed. Philip Horne (New York: Viking, 1999), p.555.

28. Jackson, 'Hitler, Stalin, Bob Dylan, Roddy Doyle ... and Me', p.16.

29. John Banville, 'Summon the Gods', *Irish Times* (4 August 2001).

30. Ludwig Wittgenstein, *Tractatus Logico-Philosophicus*, trans. D.F. Pears and B.F. McGuinness, intro. Bertrand Russell (London: Routledge & Kegan Paul, 1997), p.73.

31. George Steiner, 'To Be Perfectly Blunt', *Observer* (4 May 1997).

32. John Banville, 'The Real Presence of a Passionate Mind', *Irish Times* (5 July 1997).

33. Ruth Padel, 'The Patient English', *Independent on Sunday* (27 April 1997).

34. John Banville, 'Champion of the "Real Presence"', *Irish Times* (12 May 2001).

35. John Banville, 'What do We Mean by Meaning?', *Irish Times* (1 July 1989).

36. T.S. Eliot, *Collected Poems 1909–1962* (London: Faber & Faber, 1974), p.194.

37. Hermann Broch, *The Death of Virgil*, trans. Jean Starr Untermeyer (New York: Vintage, 1995), pp.481–2.

38. George Steiner, *Language and Silence: Essays 1958–1966* (Harmondsworth: Peregrine, 1979), pp.75, 76, 71.

39. Rüdiger Imhof, *John Banville: A Critical Introduction*, 2nd edn (Dublin: Wolfhound, 1997), pp.42–3.

40. Ms. 10252.2.3. Drafts of *Blood* [*Nightspawn*].

41. Arminta Wallace, 'A World Without People', *Irish Times* (21 September 2000).

42. Jean-Paul Sartre, *What is Literature?*, trans. Bernard Frechtman (London: Methuen, 1967), p.14.

43. George Steiner, *Real Presences: Is There Anything in What We Say?* (London: Faber & Faber, 1989), p.4.

44. Clíodhna Ní Anluain (ed.), 'John Banville', in *Reading the Future: Irish Writers in Conversation with Mike Murphy* (Dublin: Lilliput Press, 2000), pp.24, 40.

CHAPTER TWO

A Man with Nothing to Say: The Irish Context

'You see the implication? I'm an Irishman, so I'm going to write books about Irish topics, the state of modern Ireland.' This quick and ironic refusal by John Banville of the presumption that there is a natural and direct bond between a writer and his national literary tradition is part of a project, adopted from his formational period, of trying to stay aloof, at least in principle, from Irish subject matter. To fulfil his own individual creative vision, the artist must be able to privately and publicly free himself from his professional surroundings: 'To think of yourself as part of a movement would be fatal.'[1] Banville's warning here from the heart of his early period must in part be understood in the context of the then emergent Field Day Company, the most concerted Irish literary and cultural organization of recent times. This warning, however, is also part of Banville's general determination to remain outside of the Irish cultural milieu in all manifestations. As he more straightforwardly put it moving into his late period: 'I'm not writing about Ireland … After all these years I can confess it. I live in exile here. I'm out of touch with other writers … I'm hopelessly ill-informed, here. People have to tell me things.'[2]

When speaking about the figuration of Ireland in his work, Banville has frequently been overly self-effacing however, and sometimes, it might be suspected, even mischievous. He has in fact written some of his most interesting fictions about his own country, and the next chapter will provide a detailed reading of some of these. For the moment, an exploration of the principal national contexts for these works will set the scene.

The position of his writing outside historical and contemporary Irish cultural preoccupations has been readily recognized in Banville criticism and Irish literary criticism generally. Regarding the artistic challenges of a country that has experienced a spate in social change, the critic Edna Longley has half-humorously but appositely suggested that we might typify this challenge as 'Bolgerism *versus* Banvillism'. Contemporary Irish novelists such as Dermot Bolger and Roddy Doyle focus on the cultural transformations in Dublin working-class life and popular culture since the 1960s. Banville's fiction draws instead 'on the version of high Modernism peculiar to Dublin. That is, it combines metafictional self-consciousness about the linguistic game and the deliquescent text, with an unshakable belief in itself as art, sentences polished to a bronze perfection.[3] We examined Banville's opting for a particular version of modernism in Chapter 1; we can continue now in the Irish context to suggest that this option's characteristic anxiety about the contamination of high art by everyday social life and popular culture produces in Banville's work a more visible and more productive dynamic than has generally been granted, even though useful suggestions have been made in the existing criticism.

The widespread early celebration of Banville in the reviews as a writer intent on avoiding Irish 'provincialism' has generally had more currency, however, and the categories of 'European' and 'international' writer are far more likely to be attached to him, usually in the curious assumption that these are mutually exclusive from Irishness. There is too simplistic an underlying idea in currency that questions of national identity run contrary to the idealization of transnational or globalized culture encouraged by postmodernism. Such an opposition in the Irish context often involves an extraordinary willingness to reduce Irish writing and culture to a stereotypical level that would be the envy of the Irish nationalist ideologues who are the targets of would-be internationalizers and Europeanizers in the first place.

Some of Banville's own comments have simultaneously rejected and encouraged a reduction to easy stereotypes of the dynamic between his high modernist option and his Irishness. 'One of the problems with writing the kind of writing that I do', he has complained, 'is that [non-Irish readers] say, "This is not Irish. Why doesn't it have shamrocks and *bejapers* and *begorrahs*, and people saying *fucken* all the time".'[4] This gross simplification by way of self-justification – not many Irish writers currently use leprechaun-speak – points to frequent discomfort or uncertainty in Banville regarding his actual situation within the country of Ireland, and, more specifically, within Irish literary tradition. Readers were especially surprised, and some scandalized, by a curiously stereotyping article on hurling he published in the *Irish Times* in August 1996 on the occasion of his native County Wexford reaching the All-Ireland Hurling Final.[5]

In opposition to any strong native allegiance, Banville has certainly set up for himself an idealized international tradition. From the outset, he has placed at the pinnacle of his own private canon those writers who strengthen his own determination to work independently of his immediate social and cultural location. An analysis of his views on two of his earliest and enduring models, Franz Kafka and the Russian émigré novelist Vladimir Nabokov (1899–1977), proves revealing in this regard. The way in which these writers' aesthetics have fed into Banville's own is formulated in his credo, repeated with variations throughout his career, that 'All literary artists in their heart want to write about nothing, to make an autonomous art, independent of circumstance'.[6] Nevertheless, while Banville has generally seemed intent mainly on having some parodic fun with his Irish milieu, there are also sincerely felt aspects to the figuration of specifically Irish culture in his work. There is, especially, a distinctly Irish self-consciousness regarding language that feeds into his prose style, and he is permanently obsessed with what he construes as a Joyce–Beckett nexus: any Irish writer intent on developing the novel, he feels, is faced with choosing between the models of one or the other of these native masters. While Banville's speculations on what it means to be an Irish writer writing in Ireland in an idiosyncratic Irish idiom should be approached with some caution, he has returned to this matter with sufficient frequency to warrant careful attention.

A basic way around any full acceptance of Banville's self-proclaimed disassociation from Irish concerns is provided by a neat distinction made by the British cultural theorist Raymond Williams (1921–88), between the 'commitment' and 'alignment' of a writer. While commitment can, as Williams puts it, be seen as the choice of an 'active consciousness', the less familiar term *alignment* rather refers to a social conditioning of the individual before there is even an awareness of conditioning. As Williams puts it definitively: 'born into a social situation with all its specific perspectives, and into a language, the writer begins by being aligned'.[7] In this sense, nationalism can be seen as a commitment, nationality an alignment. The indelibility of alignments, as we shall see here, is notably proven in Banville's perception of the English language as Irish writers use it. While he has certainly remained autonomous in relation to the commitments of any kind of Irish cultural nationalism, Banville has not, and cannot, entirely extricate himself from his nationality.

Though he has lived in Ireland for the duration of his career as a writer, Banville likes to think of himself as a kind of internal exile. In his first major interview he declared simply: 'I must say I've never felt part of any movement or tradition, any culture even … I've always felt outside.'[8] This self-described position is somewhat problematic. In practical terms, Banville has frequently been a central figure in the Irish arts establishment and, aside entirely from his long-standing performance in influencing reading tastes as a literary journalist, he has often committed himself to the public side of Irish cultural life. He spent a year as a Ted Nealon/ Garret FitzGerald appointee on the Irish Arts Council in 1987/88, during which time he proved a vocal critic of the government's underfunding of the arts. He strongly supported the plans for the Dublin Writers' Conference of 1988. He has, until recently, also been a member of Aosdána, Ireland's elite, self-elected body of artists. In an equally practical sense, however, he has never been given to facile promotion of Irish literature or culture. Though he has at some points argued for the vital importance of a native Irish publishing industry, he always insisted as literary editor of the Irish Times during the 1990s that his pages had no particular duty to facilitate native writing or publishing, and he saw his appointment as having a distinctly internationalizing rather than national function.

The extent to which we can pursue a reasonable sense of Irish defini-tion or context for Banville very much depends on degrees of compari-son. To take just one example: it has been pointed out that, in contrast to an Irish writer such as the dramatist Brian Friel, Banville seems to have rejected any notion of writing directly about Ireland. This kind of com-parison, however, will always set up an imbalanced scale because Friel, not least as a co-founder of Field Day, is one of Irish writing's most culturally concerned authors and so to use him, or any equally rooted writer, for a measurement of Banville's seemingly opposite tendencies as an Irish writer is to dispense too readily with the less direct, but nonetheless vital, impact of Irishness on his work. Almost as an illustration of the continued relevance of this point, as he moved into his late period Banville includ-ed in the amateur career of the actor-narrator Cleave in Eclipse a satirical cut at a certain kind of determinedly rooted Irish drama. In 'an echoing community hall' in his home town, and 'before an audience of gaping provincials', Cleave performs in 'one of those rural dramas that were still being written at the time, all cawbeens and blackthorn sticks and shawled biddies lamenting their lost sons beside fake turf fires'. Cleave has the part of 'the brawny hero's younger brother, the sensitive one, who planned to be a teacher and set up a school in the village' (pp.83–4).

If the nation does not feed directly into Banville's fiction, a combination of nationality (again, not nationalism), biography and place has had considerable impact. 'Fiction is never intentionally autobiographical', Banville has repeatedly argued, but he yet accepts that 'it would be disingenuous to pretend that at some deep level it is not about the self. That's always what one writes out of. There isn't any other material. There's only the self.'⁹ There is little doubt that Banville aims to be as impersonal as possible in his approach to writing, to desentimentalize the inherent autobiographical tendencies of the self and to separate the man who experiences life from the artist who creates. Yet a kind of oblique autobiography is present in the Banville works. *Mefisto* is perhaps the most personalized of Banville's works in this sense in that, by his own admission, it is suffused with the pain and grief he felt after the experience of death in his family. He has more than once pointed out that the European landscapes he conjured up for *Copernicus* and *Kepler* emanated directly from his memories of Wexford in the 1950s. He has revealed of *Eclipse* that the house he visualizes Cleave in was on the square in Wexford where he was born. The presence of a distinct mood or idea or memories of Wexford in the work is testified to by his proclivity in interviews and articles of his late period for autobiographical reminiscences of childhood, and *The Sea* would sustain some close reading in the context of these.

On another level, Banville's first two books, in their apparent move away from obviously Irish concerns, can be read as a kind of aesthetic autobiography. *Long Lankin* and *Nightspawn*, remarked Banville in retrospect, were 'very personal statements … there was a strong element of self-expression in them'. He has remarked in particular of *Long Lankin* that 'the whole thing is about personal freedom, how you win it … And what you do with it.'¹⁰ Individual aesthetic freedom at home has thus from the beginning been a preoccupation with Banville. While major writers such as Joyce and Beckett heroized their departures, he says he has never felt the need to depart as such, that he 'never cared enough about Ireland to feel I had to flee from it, or leave it'. This self-selected domestic exile is an aspect of a general sense of existential homelessness: 'I don't feel particularly at home in Ireland, I don't feel at home anywhere.'[11] His most strenuous statement of his selected distance and anxiety of socio-political contamination within Ireland, however, points up vital cultural specifics. The statement was occasioned by his review of *The Field Day Anthology of Irish Writing* (1991). In the face of the version of national tradition inscribed in this anthology, Banville complained that 'We autonomists feel like atheists debating with religious enthusiasts who see the hand of a personal god at work everywhere'. Literature, for Banville, must remain pure and autonomous from such national enthusiasm: he recommended as a suitable inoculation a rereading of Oscar Wilde's prescriptions on aestheticism and art for art's sake.[12] This is not to suggest that Banville has been mainly reactive in establishing his position as an autonomist, but so convinced is he in this position that when he sees an equal and opposite position promoted he has often tended to reach for his pen.

AESTHETIC ESCAPE: BANVILLE, EUROPE AND THE INFLUENCE OF NABOKOV AND KAFKA

When in sociological mood, Banville has situated himself among 'the new Irish bourgeoisie with lower-middle-class or peasant backgrounds'.[13] Yet he has always seemed, or wanted to seem, more middle-European than Irish middle class. While he has frequently rejected the idea of a coherent literary tradition in his own country, he has always promoted a cohesive and comprehensive tradition of European literature. He conforms to the general modernist view that existing artistic monuments, from whatever moment in history and from whatever country, form in themselves an ideal and simultaneous order. Ever since he began reading, he has felt a kinship with an ordered Europe of the mind.

Every author takes some sense of meaning or context from one or more traditions, and novels that determinedly contain extensive reference to literary history, as Banville's do, in one way ask to be read within the confines of the ideal order of that literary history rather than in relation to subject matter or correspondence with objective, extra-literary reality. Banville's Europe of the mind might be viewed as a continental alternative to an idealized Irish version of the ecumenical imagination – what was termed at the time the 'fifth province' – that preoccupied many Irish intellectuals during the 1980s. He has similarly construed his Europe of the mind as a cultural cure for other damaging nationalisms. He has regularly suggested that to the Irish cultural cosmopolitan a range of European writers should mean as much as, say, Joyce or Beckett. By his own recollection, the young Banville never read Irish writers then in popular currency and devoted himself instead to reading their English counterparts.

The importance of some of these early English models – Evelyn Waugh and Graham Greene especially – would be re-emphasized in the style of *The Untouchable*. Banville's aesthetic tradition has principally depended on a mainland Europe of the mind, however. The prime early influence was Vladimir Nabokov, about whose work he wrote a series of reviews and articles. The presence of aspects of Nabokov's own fictions in the œuvre is undeniable. The structural device and metaphor of chess in *Nightspawn* is reminiscent of Nabokov's Russian novel *The Defence*, published in translation in 1964. *Birchwood*, with its character Ada and its themes of time, memory and family, echoes Nabokov's *Ada* (1969). The works of Banville's early, middle and late periods are all to some degree influenced in such themes as madness and murder, in the motifs of the double and the stage, in the mood of demonic laughter, by Nabokov's novels *Laughter in the Dark* (revised in translation by Nabokov in 1960), *Invitation to a Beheading* (published in translation in 1959 by Nabokov), *Despair* (published in a revised translation in 1965) and *Look at the Harlequins* (1974). In particular, *The Book of Evidence* has precise parallels with Nabokov's most famous novel, *Lolita* (1955).

The Nabokov influence was by no means blind. Although Banville's reviews of his work show that he had long been a Nabokov fan, they also display a balanced and frequently combative approach to this revered precursor's ideas. Much as the high tone and rich vocabulary of Nabokov's novels find their way into the voices of Banville's narrators, his qualifying of Nabokov's influence is vital to understanding his ultimately self-questioning version of the aesthetics of autonomy. Reviewing *Transparent Things* (1972) for his first published commentary on Nabokov, Banville lamented that the 'friendly warmth' of earlier books had 'given way to ice ... the tone now is detached, falsely jocular and smug, like the voice in those repellent forewords to the translations of his Russian novels'. While, for an obituary article in 1977, Banville commented that 'few writers of any age have so enriched our perceptions of language, of beauty, and of the world of common things', he still found 'repellent' Nabokov's 'reactionary politics and "aristocratic" attitudes'. He used similar terms in a scathing review of *Strong Opinions* (1973), a book that robustly propounded Nabokov's aesthetics. Banville found the personality that emerged from the book to be 'repellent; it is vain, ill-tempered, cruel, politically amoral and artistically exclusive; it sits at the centre of an overblown prose, guffawing horribly and lashing out all round it with poison-tipped tentacles'.[14]

These qualms about Nabokov's characteristic aesthetic positions seem partly self-contradictory. If, for instance, certain choice comments from *Strong Opinions* are placed alongside some of Banville's own robust aesthetic opinions from his early period, the correspondences are striking. Nabokov: 'Nothing bores me more than political novels and the literature of social intent'; 'I have no social purpose, no moral message'; 'A work of art has no importance whatever to society'; 'Art is difficult'.[15] Banville: 'Literature is one of the few human pursuits that transcend politics, and those with an axe, or a sickle, to grind should keep their sweaty paws off it'; 'art is a cold, unfeeling brute, and simply will not have its acolytes weeping on its shoulder'; 'I like all art to be cold and pure'; 'Art is amoral ... and I'm not concerned with morality'.[16] While Banville has at no point offered the same extended commentaries on his attitude to art as contained in the compendium of *Strong Opinions*, such individual remarks recur throughout his career, and these are frequently as uncompromising as anything in Nabokov. In his middle period, for example, he insisted that he 'wouldn't want to be in the mainstream of anything ... you only get there by not being able to swim very well'.[17] While Banville has seemed, then, to reject the more extreme formulations of Nabokov's aestheticism, his generally enduring admiration for Nabokov's work is at the very foundation of his European tradition of the mind.

The developing aesthetic of Banville's formational and early periods also drew heavily on the work and thought of Kafka. As with Nabokov, comprehensive implications for Banville's style of fiction are involved here. In one of the journalism pieces of his early period, Banville included some information on the theory of the modern novel. He pointed to the importance of the Hungarian critic Georg Lukács (1885–1971) and his definition of 'the choice facing the contemporary bourgeois writer, whether to follow the methods of Kafka or Thomas Mann, that is, whether to choose realism or formalistic experimentation, social sanity or morbidity: "Ought *angst* to be taken as an absolute, or ought it to be overcome?"' This, said Banville, is 'a very big question':

> ... indeed, it is the question now which every serious artist must answer for himself. Formalism leads inevitably, as Lukacs pointed out, to the inward obsession with *angst*, while at the same time it helps to renew art and expand its frontiers. Traditional realism tends toward technical stasis, yet enables a few writers, the finest of the few, to engage the social problem of his [sic] time. Lukacs again: 'is man the helpless victim of transcendental and inexplicable forces, or is he a member of a human community in which he can play a part, however small, towards its modification or reform?'

Though commending Lukács as 'a very great critic, and therefore very convincing', Banville immediately qualified the choice between Kafka and Mann in terms that brought him down definitively on the side of Kafka. The point is, he said, that 'we cannot unlearn the lessons of modernism, that the novelist cannot go back to "realism" and write as if nothing much had happened in the period between, say, James's *The Ambassadors* and Beckett's *The Unnamable*'.[18]

Thematic elements from Mann have been essential to Banville's own work – ideas and moral problems from Mann's novel, *Doctor Faustus* (1947), are central to the Tetralogy in the middle period, and the mood and motifs of *Death in Venice* (1912) and *Confessions of Felix Krull, Confidence Man* (1954) permeate much of the work of the late period. Banville's opting for the Kafka side of the opposition, however, points to his association of a specific aesthetic of fiction with a particular view of the world and human consciousness. For Banville, Kafka's significance lies in his illustration of the idea that the modern mind has somehow been disinherited of meaning and belief and of connectedness with a whole:

> There has been a loss of certainty, of coherence ... Breadth has gone, as Beckett was among the first to recognize – the only real possibility that remains to us is *depth*. Down we must go, with Kafka down in the burrow, out of the big world and into the dark underground

of our selves. The novelist no longer pretends to be any less baffled or blind than the rest of us.[19]

Kafka's fiction represents for Banville the grand irony of mankind's simultaneous loss of belief in God and yearning for some kind of eternal godlike meaning to be revealed. He cherishes Kafka for being 'obsessed with the numinous, with the faint, infinitely faint radiance of the divine in our poor world'.[20]

The direct influence of Kafka on Banville's work is generally well hidden. Kafka's most familiar novel, The Trial (1925), is a partial presence in The Book of Evidence, and he also makes a covert appearance in Kepler in the lines of encroaching despair the scientist includes in a letter – though the lines go uncredited, Banville sets them off with italics and they are from a Kafka letter of July 1914: 'I do not speak like I write, I do not write like I think, I do not think like I ought to think, and so everything goes on in deepest darkness' (p.86). More important is an overarching idea on writing that Banville has adopted from Kafka. While Banville has written comparatively little exclusively on Kafka, he has surfaced with regularity since the early period in reviews of other writers and in interviews with regard to a single small quotation. The importance for Banville of this quotation cannot be overestimated. Kafka is first mentioned in one of the Hibernia reviews of the early period as an illustration of the point – a repeated point of Banville's at the time – that what really counts in modernist writing is not what is said as such, but the 'manner of saying'. Kafka once remarked, said Banville, 'that the writer is one who has nothing to say'.[21] Banville has returned to this idea regularly, always using it to assert the autonomy of literary art both from the socio-political world and from the artist's own self-expressive desires. The insistence that the writer is a man with nothing to say is 'very ambiguous', Banville allows, but he insists: 'it's my motto. I feel I should have it carved in stone above my desk.'[22]

For a novelist resident in a country such as Ireland, which usually expects cultural commentary and reflection in its writers, the implications of such a motto are patent. The imperative is that the writer must remain objective, autonomous from the demand that he express or analyse either society or himself, explicitly at least. The dispassionate observer of life, not he who is immersed or engaged, becomes the supreme artist. It is only by saying nothing in the Kafka sense, by staying silent on the typical issues and concerns of the day, that Banville feels he might ironically be able to say anything worthwhile, anything new, anything that will have an enduring rather than merely immediate or local relevance.

The intersection of Irish writing and the Europe of the mind represented by Nabokov and Kafka is figured for Banville in the work of James Joyce and Samuel Beckett. While Banville has argued that it is probably not very important that Joyce and Beckett were born in Ireland, his reading of these two exemplars displays some classic symptoms of an Irish anxiety of influence. Ireland, his argument runs, does not have a cohesive tradition of fiction:

> We don't really have minor writers; we just either have completely third or fourth rate writers or we have great ones ... We have these big figures standing behind us that frighten the living daylights out of us. Being a novelist in the eighties and nineties: Joyce put everything in; Beckett threw everything out. What on earth is there left for us to do? Except maybe to keep it all in and deny it at the same time ... The Irish novelist, if he has any sense of history, is constantly fighting with the past, trying to strike the father dead.[23]

Every Irish writer, Banville believes, has to take either a Joyce direction or a Beckett direction, and in his view he has headed off towards Beckett. Banville's fondness for Beckett depends largely on a view of him as the quintessential afflicted post-Joyce writer. The main difference between Joyce and Beckett is that with regard to the novel form, Joyce tried to throw everything in, and Beckett tried to throw nothing in. One of Banville's main ambitions for his novels, as we will see in Chapter 4, is to empty them of content, to throw everything out in Beckett's sense, and so he has distinctly ambivalent feelings about Joyce's legacy for writers of fiction in Ireland and elsewhere. While he has always viewed Joyce's two great experimental novels, *Ulysses* (1922) and particularly *Finnegans Wake* (1939), as dead ends for the novel form, he has also sometimes expressed doubts about the value of even the much more accessible *A Portrait of the Artist as a Young Man* (1916):

I don't believe in it, I think it's a pose ... I think that it is dishonest ... I do have great difficulty with Joyce. I find him very ... uncanny, and very ... (*very long pause*) I find him dishonest, in a strange, complicated way ... Beckett sets out to fail. But Joyce's ego is such that he has to succeed, and he has to spoil what he has done. You can see it in *Ulysses*, you can see it going wrong. The stylistic experiments for me don't work. I can admire it, I think it is a very great achievement, but I feel that there is an even greater achievement lost, an even greater book lost, by his fascination with experiment.[24]

The comment on Joyce's stylistic experiments here is crucial: while Banville has repeatedly been called an experimental writer, his style owes much more to the kind of straight, even classical prose of Beckett's work than to the spatial and formal innovations of Joyce or his postmodern imitators.

Banville's hesitation about Joyce's legacy also involves a rejection of Joyce's acceptance of life in favour of Beckett's sense of meaninglessness and absurdity. Though it is more like a prayer than literary analysis, Banville's brief contribution to an *Irish University Review* special issue on Beckett in 1984 is worth quoting here in full, not least for its alignment of Beckett with Kafka:

His work rises through the mire of our times like a buried testament. He knows, with Kafka, that so long as we can say, here is the worst, then the worst has not yet arrived. Out of such scant hopes he has built his aesthetic. To look things in the face and not flinch. To shun accumulation, valuing depth over breadth. To find forms that will accommodate the chaos. To work always out of darkness. To go on. His courage has been exemplary, his success a revelation. We stand rapt, like Sapo before the flight of the hawk, fascinated by such extremes of need, of pride, of patience and of solitude.[25]

Banville has applauded Beckett for combining the theme of metaphysical collapse with a meticulous emphasis on formal construction and for his quasi-religious redemptive faith in the power of artistic language. Beckett's 'supreme achievement', he says, was 'to have shown us that the horror and cruelty of the world, the "disaster" which is our age, can be redeemed through the beauty and power of language – language and nothing more, not progress, optimism or delusions, but words alone. It is a salutary message.'[26] The major combined aesthetic and metaphysical nuance Banville takes from Beckett, however, is an obsession with silence. For Banville, Beckett's metaphysical investigations in fiction have far more relevance for modern readers than any number of realistic novels, and the philosophical ideas of Banville's books would bear considerable comparison with Beckett's.

As he has developed as a writer, Banville has found that there is a kind of 'diminished returns' factor to reading Beckett. He might almost be said to have exhausted certain elements of Beckett in *Nightspawn*, a novel that is, he has granted, perhaps too nakedly Beckettian. Beckett's concern with absurdity, language and silence persists in the work nevertheless. In the late period, *Eclipse*, as laden with ideas of silence as all the previous books, is perhaps the closest Banville has so far come to the exact tone of Beckett's own late prose, its reductions and 'lessness'. The influence of late Beckett may not continue to manifest itself in the work in the same way as in *The Sea*, where the arrangements of tightly controlled blocks of paragraphs and the overall lessening of both length and plot are distinctly reminiscent of Beckett's own *Company* (1980) and *Ill Seen Ill Said* (1981). But it is probable that, in one form or another, for Banville's work Beckett is here to stay. He continues to read his favoured Irish model with close attention and he continues to regularly reread some of his late prose in particular:

POETIC IMPRECISION: HIBERNO-ENGLISH AND THE BANVILLE NOVEL

There is a specifically national dimension to the preoccupation with language and literary form Banville has gleaned from Beckett, and here he has tended to move fluidly between autobiographical specifics and ethnic generalization. Leading on from the admission that things become 'real' for him only when expressed in literature, he at one stage claimed that this is in fact 'a very Irish thing. The Irish are obsessed with language.'[27] Banville has identified what this obsession entails:

Irish English is a very different beast from English English or American English. Very different. The way in which Irish writers are only too happy to infuse their language with ambiguity is very different. An English writer will try to be clear. Orwell said that good prose should be like a pane of glass. The Irish writer would say: 'No no, it's a lens, it distorts everything.' You see, the odd thing is that the Irish language died in the 1840s but we still have that deep grammar inside us and it still dictates ... If you look at Joyce, or even Yeats, who seems to be making declarative statements, he's always ambiguous. Ambiguity is the essence of Irish writing, I think.[28]

Banville has always held to this theory of 'ambiguity' in the Irish use of English. Even though he rigidly disclaimed any place in Irish tradition in his formational and early periods, he suggested that a couple of things should perhaps be cleared up before the idea of an Irish national literary tradition was dismissed entirely. Clarification mainly concerned the native use of language: 'What people in Ireland do with the English language certainly has very particular traits. If you want to compare it with English literature or English writing it has, to use a short-hand term, a Celtic approach, which is very different from the English.'[29]

Banville's first extended commentary on the Irish use of English is included in a talk he gave to the Writers' Workshop at the University of Iowa in 1981. Here he sees the Irish case as symptomatic of the modern writer's problem with language generally. Speaking of a style of literary language 'in which sense is often subordinate to sound, in which meaning is shaped and directed by patterns immanent in the words themselves', he suggests there is a kind of preformed symbolist aesthetic – the kind I outlined in Chapter 1 – available in the 'poetically imprecise' idiom of 'Irish-English'. For the Irish, he claimed, 'language is not primarily a tool for expressing what we mean. Sometimes I think it is quite the opposite. We have profound misgivings about words. We love them ... but we do not trust them. Therefore we play with them.' Such a separation of articulacy from instrumentality or reference might be accused of adhering too blithely to an old colonial view of the Irishman as debilitated by an imagination that does not take for granted the empirical connection between word and world: 'What I am talking about is something subversive, destructive even, and in a way profoundly despairing.'[30]

A couple of years later, still in his early period and surprisingly motivated by lines from a poem by one of Ireland's most locally rooted writers, 'Kerr's Ass' by Patrick Kavanagh (1904–67), Banville had some fun with what he termed the 'Hibernophonic plausibility' of Irish toponymy, or place names, but also adopted a more resonant historicist approach to Hiberno-English generally. 'The language in which we work', he now suggested, 'is a source of models and reasons that are not ours. Speech for us is always, at one level, an act of mimicry: behind the cadences, someone else's history reverberates. The rhythms of our rhetoric were laid down by an imperium not our own.'[31] Later, in his middle period, while speculating on the reasons for Ireland's 'great tradition' of writing, he pointed out that the language of this tradition is 'the language of the colonist', and elaborated at length:

> The assimilation – or imposition – of the language, effectively completed after the great Famine of the 1840s was a painful but productive process which wrought deep changes both in the Irish national sensibility and in the language itself.
>
> Hiberno-English, as we may call it, is a wonderfully versatile yet often treacherous literary tool. The subtlety, richness and volatility of English as written in Ireland is the result of an alchemical fusion, as it were, between two wholly dissimilar methods of linguistic interpretation of the world and our being in it … it is this intermeshing of the two languages, with all its political, psychological and epistemological consequences, that goes a long way towards explaining the continuing extraordinary richness of Irish writing.[32]

While some misplaced examples damaged Banville's general commentary somewhat in this case, the academic accuracy of his views is not our concern here. Though he is apparently sincere in his analysis, Banville's remarks are far more crucial to an understanding of his personal views of certain aspects of the literary language available to him than they are to an accurate understanding of Hiberno-English as detailed by linguists. On one hand, Banville's sense of Irish linguistic self-consciousness seems to cater for standard views of the Irish as a nation of blatherers and dreamers. Taken as an artistic rather than a scholarly viewpoint, however, there is as much sincerity involved as in a widely quoted scene in Joyce's *Portrait* concerning the fretting of the Irish soul under the shadow of the English language. Banville is, in any case, conscious of the potential stereotyping involved:

I am well aware of the danger there is in saying these things. Shamrocks. Leprechauns. The gift of the gab. Little old men with pipes in their gobs sitting on ditches and maundering on about how things were in their fathers' time ... If I have conjured these images, please banish them at once from your minds.[33]

A deeply felt artistic motivation that is as close as Banville ever comes to straightforward national pride lies behind these speculations on Hiberno-English: 'If I write a sentence that is pure Hiberno-English, a sentence in English that no other English speaker other than an Irish person could write, then I feel a certain satisfaction and a certain love, I suppose, for what is expressed in the rhythms of Hiberno-English.'[34] It is a matter of debate whether the distancing effect involved in feeling removed from standard English is – or at least has been – an ethnic reality or, instead or in considerable part, a myth happily sustained by Irish writers in and after some of Joyce's related musings in Portrait. The recurrence of the sense of disjunction in contemporary Irish novelists suggests both that the felt remove has been important and that it may not necessarily be a myth. While the post-colonialist critics who have lately taken the disjunction for granted and have built some ambitious theories of Irish fiction around it may sometimes take some believing, other novelists of Banville's generation have at the same time offered convincing testimony. In an essay that examines Irish writing's general sense of language's relations with history, Colm Tóibín, another Wexford novelist, finds that exactly the same elements of Hiberno-English that Banville discusses are artistically important in contemporary Irish fiction. Tóibín explicates the sense of language in Beckett and Flann O'Brien (1911–66), writers who are 'modern and self-conscious, are almost hermetically sealed in the study of the possibilities of language itself, raising questions about communication and silence'. In this kind of writing, which Tóibín believes is practised even by a writer so different in style to Banville as John McGahern (1934–2006), there is a 'sense of desperation in the prose, a sense that the language is being worked for all its worth because there is nothing else, there is no world outside, nothing to lean on except the personal voice and the literary tradition'. Behind the continued linguistic obsessiveness of contemporary Irish fiction there is a 'deliberate elusiveness', a perceived gulf between word and thing, word and history.[35]

This gulf is not the sole preserve of Wexford novelists. The writer and director Neil Jordan has also referred to the Irish writer's 'dissatisfaction with the accepted and scientifically approved explanations of the world', and has suggested that there is an artistically advantageous 'inarticulacy' in the Irish approach to language. In Irish fiction there is an impression 'that the reality is too large, that it doesn't fit the language. And this awareness of the inadequacy of language is perhaps why we are so fascinated by it, so good at reworking it in new and original ways.'[36] From this view-point, there may not be so much native distance in the end between a writer like Banville and a much more culturally focused one like Friel, for there is a striking parallel between Friel's resort in his Hiberno-English themed play *Translations* (1980) to George Steiner's linguistic theories, and, as we have seen in Chapter 1, Banville's use of Steiner in the development of his general aesthetics of silence.

There are some very specific points in Banville's work, particularly in the formational, early and middle periods, where related matters con-cerning language and identity are raised. Ben White, the displaced Irish writer of 'Island' and 'The Possessed' in *Long Lankin*, illustrates the basic problem in his role as returned narrator in *Nightspawn*. When one of his Greek acquaintances asks him, 'English, are you?', he stammers back, 'Yes, no, Irish' (p.70). At one point during his fantastical trip around Ireland in *Birchwood*, Godkin, educated as a member of the Ascendancy class, min-gles with the natives in a pub but cannot make sense of his surroundings: 'Much raucous laughter tumbled out of gap-toothed mouths, and the voices and the strange macaronic talk clashed in the smoky air like the sounds of battle' (p.121). This is a contributory factor in his final decision to live an autonomous life in his Big House with his declaration: 'I do not speak the language of this wild country' (p.170). In *The Book of Evidence*, Freddie Montgomery's ultimately criminal patrician disposition is discreetly uncovered in his presumptuous dismissal of the Irish language as set against his own proficiency in English. Arriving by boat at Dun Laoghaire, known in pre-Independence Ireland as Kingstown, he remembers that his father 'never referred to the place as anything but Kingstown: he had no time for the native jabber'. Thus his attitude to the proper noun is as confused as Ben White's cultural identity: 'The charm I had felt in Kingstown, I mean Dun Laoghaire' (pp.27, 30). With this automatic preference for Ascendancy English, Freddie appears all the more unjustified in his cheap shot at 'the politicals' in his prison who insist on 'barking at each other in bad Irish' (p.5).

More important than these isolated moments, however, is the broader import of Banville's views on Hiberno-English for his approach to the novel form. The flourishing of the English novel depended to a considerable degree on the development of realism. As Banville sees it, a different native sense of language and its explanatory value has made a similar evolution of the novel impossible in Ireland. He appears to explain away the poor quality of much Irish fiction of the last two centuries in the argument that the realist genre is simply not amenable to Hiberno-English:

> artistic modes, like language itself, carry with them certain ghostly injunctions, idiosyncrasies, limitations. The novel still looks like one of those ingenious yet faintly absurd domestic contraptions so beloved of the Victorians: Mrs Eliot's Patented Self-Loading Moral Measuring Appliance, Mr Dickens's Famous and Ever-Popular Heart-Warmer. Somehow, Irish-English is not a fuel on which such gadgets can be run. The high tone of Tory rectitude or Whig good sense does not convince in the rain-sodden environs of Ballykillmuck.

This is a strikingly similar notion of developments, or lack thereof, in the Irish novel as worked out more theoretically by specialists in Irish post-colonial studies. Banville patently invokes post-colonialist ideas here in combining his sense of Hiberno-English with the development of the novel. Attentive to the idea of the empire 'writing back' through the development of new literary modes and forms, Banville has argued that 'The English language, its "models and reasons", forced us into subversion and subterfuge, elaborations of defence and attack.' And one aesthetic result of this attack was, he claims, the idea of the novel as an autonomous high-art form. The enthusiasm for the novel as an 'art form', he says, came, not from English novelists, but from 'colonials' like Henry James and Joyce.[37]

Banville's claim is arguably justified in the sense that the practice of the novel as art form in English was certainly advanced by these 'colonials'. While he relishes this post-colonial development of the autonomous idea of the novel, he nevertheless insists, lest he ever be recruited entirely for post-colonial preoccupations in Irish culture, that the empire writing back through innovative forms is no cause for nationalist gloating. In his view, something new is made possible by the imposing presence of British models against which writers of other nationalities can rebel. And in the interviews of his late period he has often continued to talk of his place, when it comes to his sense of the literary possibilities of language, within a specifically Irish tradition.

THE IRISH AUTONOMIST IN HIS PLACE: HISTORICIZING BANVILLE

While these aspects of literary tradition and literary language all underline the importance of thinking about Banville in an Irish context, it is worth asking if there are reasons, beyond the tautological one of an autonomous mentality generating its own obsessions with autonomy, why Banville, as a writer at a particular time in a particular place, became obsessed with the idea of autonomy. In his essay on the ideology of modernism, Fredric Jameson argues that by the mid-1970s 'The idea of the autonomy of the work of art – which at first seemed a proud boast and a value to be defended – now begins to look a little shameful, like a symptom into whose pathology one would want to inquire more closely.' The question that should now be asked, he says, is 'not whether literary works are autonomous, nor even how art manages to lift itself above its immediate social situation and to free itself from its social context'; rather, we must ask 'what kind of society it can be in which works of art have become autonomous to this degree, in which the older social and cultic functions of literature have become so unfamiliar as to have made us forgetful ... of the power and influence that a socially living art can exercise'.[38]

In part at least, the origins of Banville's aesthetics of autonomy and internal exile lie in the nature of the Irish society he grew up in during the 1940s, 1950s and 1960s. Banville has spoken, in vitriolic terms typical of his generation of Irish intellectuals, of an early determination to get out of Ireland at the first opportunity, to escape the cultural legacy of the mid-century, an 'unremarkable, mean-spirited time' of 'stagnation', 'paralysis' and 'intellectual isolationism'.[39] Although he has regularly recalled a happy youth, this always gives way in his reminiscences to a recollection of his eventual disillusionment with the country and a desire in his late teens to escape. In this, Banville was typical of a generation that was becoming increasingly critical of the perceived cultural and personal restrictiveness of the Irish Republic.

Accounts of the cultural situation facing the Irish writer in this period can explain this combined sense of paralysis and desire to escape in young intellectuals. For just one major example, a lead essay published in the Irish journal *Studies* half-way through the 1960s, entitled 'Inherited Dissent: The Dilemma of the Irish Writer' and written by the academic, Augustine Martin (1935–95), has become a touchstone for discussions on this subject. As Martin saw it, the historic force of tradition and the contemporary nature of Irish society were meeting in a skewed axis. The prime negative inheritance for the Irish writer was the 'hardened cliché' of the image of the writer as 'a pariah, at odds with his smug, philistine society'. The young Irish writer had his position in society 'defined, stated, ramified and laid down for him. He is above it, beyond it, persecuted by it, outcast from it. He is so much an outsider that he cannot create and sustain a character/narrator who represents that society's concept of normality! He is a freak!' One of Martin's chief dreads was that the result of this 'barrier of extraneous prejudice' between the Irish writer and his society would be to 'drive the artist into an Ivory tower', and a final admonition was that unless the 'living bond' between the Irish artist and society was constantly renewed there would be 'a real danger of art separating from life, leading to a barren aestheticism, a doctrine of *l'art pour l'art*'. The young Banville would surely have smirked at Martin's conclusion that 'such a movement is unhealthy in any situation, but the mere idea of it at this stage in our young tradition borders on the ludicrous'.[40]

Going by Martin's assessment, which has been paralleled by many other similar accounts of the period, it seems that Banville's early disgruntled attitude towards Irish society and his model of the individualist artist constituted a widespread malaise rather than an idiosyncratic choice. The popular notion that Ireland has a very strong lineage of writers is qualified by a frequently voiced critical perception that Irish writers have generally felt like solitaries rather than part of a common pursuit. It might be said, overall, that what we have in Ireland is a strong tradition of individualism in writing, and there appears, therefore, to be a close relationship between the inherited traditions of the Irish writer in the second half of the twentieth century and the Irish writer's chosen themes and modes. A self sundered from society, an interest in private over public experience, a fascination with alienation, the prioritizing of abnormality over normality: these have regularly been the chief characteristics of contemporary Irish writing.

There is nothing perhaps necessary or automatic in the reaction of Irish writers to all this. Banville's move towards a commitment to the aesthetics of autonomy out of the alignments of the Irish writer and the Ireland of the 1950s and 1960s can be taken as simply one of the more cohesive, convinced and articulate responses. His aesthetic of autonomy is one of the most striking of the depoliticized ideologies of writing to have emerged since the 1960s, but it is only de-politicized in that its exterior context and its good conscience have retreated under its own surfaces and usually remain more immanent than apparent. Even though the literary and cultural situation has changed enormously in Ireland since the years of Banville's formational period, his commitment to internal exile remains. The perseverance of certain Irish alignments alongside such a commitment, most obviously reflected in his enduring sense of the actuality of a Hiberno-English linguistic style, points to the ambiguity involved in notionally having nothing to say as an Irish writer. He ironically underlined this productive home-and-away tension as he was heading into his present late period, remarking that 'the only way to really exile oneself from Ireland now is to stay in Ireland. I'm not sure that I understand that, but I feel that it's right.'[41]

NOTES

1. Lavinia Greacen, 'A Serious Writer', Irish Times (24 March 1981).
2. Ruth Padel, 'The Patient English', Independent on Sunday (27 April 1997).
3. Edna Longley, The Living Stream: Literature and Revisionism in Ireland (Newcastle upon Tyne: Bloodaxe, 1994), p.64.
4. Liam Fay, 'The Touchable', Hot Press, 21, 13 (9 July 1997), p.45.
5. John Banville, 'Passing Beautiful in Yellowbelly Heaven', Irish Times (31 August 1996).
6. John Banville, 'Samuel Beckett Dies in Paris, Aged 83', Irish Times (25–27 December 1989).
7. Raymond Williams, Resources of Hope: Culture, Democracy, Socialism, ed. Robin Gable, intro. Robin Blackburn (London: Verso, 1989), pp.86–7.
8. M.P. Hederman and R. Kearney (eds), 'Novelists on the Novel: Ronan Sheehan Talks to John Banville and Francis Stuart' (1979), in The Crane Bag Book of Irish Studies (1977–1981) (Dublin: Blackwater Press, 1982), p.412.
9. Michael Ross, 'Chaos Theory', Sunday Times, 'Culture Ireland' (19 November 2000).
10. Rüdiger Imhof, 'My Readers, that Small Band, Deserve a Rest', Irish University Review, 11, 1 (1981), pp.10,9.

11. Clíodhna Ní Anluain (ed.), 'John Banville', in *Reading the Future: Irish Writers in Conversation with Mike Murphy* (Dublin: Lilliput Press, 2000), p.37.

12. John Banville, 'Put Up What Flag You Like, It's Too Late', *Observer* (1 December 1991).

13. John Banville, 'Portrait of the Critic as a Young Man', *New York Review of Books*, 37, 16 (25 October 1990), p.49.

14. John Banville, 'Inutile Genius', *Hibernia* (25 May 1973), p.23; 'Vladimir Nabokov', *Hibernia* (5 August 1977), p.27; 'Opinions Better Kept Private', *Hibernia* (7 June 1974), p.29.

15. Vladimir Nabokov, *Strong Opinions* (New York: Vintage, 1990), pp.3, 16, 33, 115.

16. John Banville, 'Bread or Madeleines', *Hibernia* (30 May 1975), p.20; 'Adieu Tristesse', *Hibernia* (1 April 1977), p.26; Lavinia Greacen, 'A Serious Writer'; Fintan O'Toole, 'Stepping into the Limelight – and the Chaos', *Irish Times* (21 October 1989).

17. Mike Murphy, 'John Banville', *The Arts Show* (RTÉ radio) (8 February 1995).

18. John Banville, 'Fowles at the Crossroads', *Hibernia* (14 October 1977), p.27.

19. John Banville, 'Physics and Fiction: Order from Chaos', *New York Times Book Review* (21 April 1985), p.41.

20. John Banville, 'The Legend of the Man who Fell to Earth', *Irish Times* (2 June 1990).

21. John Banville, 'Cracker-Barrel Philosopher', *Hibernia* (2 May 1975), p.19.

22. Melvyn Bragg, 'John Banville', *The South Bank Show* (LWT/Ulster Television, 1993).

23. Ibid.

24. Hedwig Schwall, 'Interview with John Banville', *European English Messenger*, 6, 1 (1997), p.16.

25. John Banville, 'Out of the Abyss', *Irish University Review*, 14, 1 (spring 1984), p.102.

26. John Banville, 'Beginnings', *Hibernia* (7 January 1977), p.32.

27. Schwall, 'An Interview with John Banville', pp.17–18.

28. Anonymous, 'Oblique Dreamer', *Observer* (17 September 2000), p.15.

29. Hederman and Kearney, 'Novelists on the Novel', p.408.

30. John Banville, 'A Talk', *Irish University Review*, 11, 1 (spring 1981), p.14.

31. John Banville, 'Place Names, The Place', in *Ireland and the Arts* (special issue of *The Literary Review*), ed. Tim Pat Coogan (Dublin: Namara Press, 1983), p.64.

32. John Banville, 'A Great Tradition', *Sunday Times* (21 March 1993).

33. Banville, 'A Talk', p.14.

34. Fay, 'The Touchable', p.45.

35. Colm Tóibín, 'Martyrs and Metaphors', *Letters from the New Island*, ed. Dermot Bolger (Dublin: Raven Arts Press, 1991), pp.51–2.

36. Neil Jordan, 'Imagining Otherwise', in *Across the Frontiers: Ireland in the 1990s*, ed. Richard Kearney (Dublin: Wolfhound, 1988), p.198.

37. Banville, 'Place Names, The Place', pp.64–5.

38. Fredric Jameson, *The Ideologies of Theory: Essays 1971–1986* (Minneapolis, MN: University of Minnesota Press, 1988), vol. 2, pp.116–17.

39. John Banville, 'The Ireland of de Valera and O'Faoláin', *Irish Review*, 17–18 (winter 1995), pp.142–52.

40. Augustine Martin, 'Inherited Dissent', *Studies*, 54 (spring 1965), pp.1, 13, 20.

41. Ní Anluain, 'John Banville', pp.36–7.

CHAPTER THREE

Novels of Their Place and Time:
Birchwood, *The Newton Letter*,
The Untouchable

One of Banville's uncollected stories from his early period, 'Rondo' (1977), consists of a monologue delivered by a narrator who is understandably obsessed with his own history since he suffers from amnesia, and he diverts himself 'by imagining possible pasts'. The struggles of this nameless, placeless and past-less Beckett-like figure to somehow root himself were revisited in Banville's screenplay *Seachange* in 1994. In *Seachange*, a neat connection is made between loss of personal memory and the unavailability of wider Irish historical knowledge of locality. Now enjoying the ear of a predominantly silent witness and dressed in the Beckett standard of ill-fitting black suit, the amnesiac babbles about the worrying inaccessibility of any real sense of the past. 'Have you visited the castle?' he at one stage asks: 'You should. Fascinating. For centuries ... [pauses in troubled thought] For centuries ... [His thinking becomes anguished and he despairs completely] Dear God'.[1]

Banville's return to this amnesiac after nearly twenty years underlines his enduring concern with the almost archetypal Beckett scenario of the individual trying to narrate, in the present, a confusing and even incomprehensible past. The preoccupation of Banville's narrators from all his periods with remembering and making sense of their private pasts is readily recognized. As with the amnesiac's poignantly exasperated attention to the local castle, however, this preoccupation also extends to the narration of certain exterior factors. Banville has written a number of works that deal with Irish history and culture, though there are distinct reasons, perhaps, why the relevant works are rarely given as much attention for Irish aspects as for elements not immediately reducible to cultural specifics. Enthusiasts of postmodern fiction or, more specifically, metafiction (fiction *about* fiction), to whom Banville's work proves so attractive, tend to be particularly fascinated with the problematic relationship between historical narrative and creative narrative that has sometimes been his apparent theme. The usual suggestion is that postmodern metafiction has been especially good at proving the argument that history is as much a creation of narrative procedures as is fiction. The trouble with such enthusiasts, however, is that in their preoccupation with the confidence trick of narrative in and of itself they sometimes provide very limited readings of historical novels; for them, as it were, history is emptied of content in advance. Many Banville critics have been busy denying the full import of his Irish themes in this way.

In denying the cultural specificity of writers, a common postmodernist's malformation is to suggest, by examples and illustration, that for any novel to deal successfully with an issue at hand it must conform to the example set down by a canon of so-called international and so-called experimental fiction. This has especially been the case with the matter of the regular examination of fiction's relationship to history in postmodern novels. It is a particularly old mistake to assume that the cultural specificity of a work of literature can be located exclusively in its subject matter, in its content, and that literary form is always and everywhere the element in literature that transcends, or can transcend, that cultural specificity. Content can be national, so the story goes; form, or at least a writer's emphasizing of form over content, is apparently more the international dimension of literature. The component parts of literary form – mode, tone, vocabulary, stylistic figures, generic treatment, and so on – may also have their precise cultural origins, may have relations with particularities of place and time that are perhaps the more important for being more implicit than the immediate significations of subject matter. In the case of the historical novel, we might say that particular pasts are not so easily sundered from the brand of artistry chosen to deal with them. This is not, as is the frequent objection, to confine the reception or criticism of literature to finite coordinates. Instead, it is to suggest that, as for instance in Banville's case, a novel's associations with time and place can be much more dynamic and complex, much more highly formulated than usually allowed for in the standard division of a work of literature into mutually distinguishable elements of form and content.

Neither is this necessarily to argue for the absolute ethnic spontaneity of literary form. It is to suggest, however, that the favouring of form over content, a split that even Banville has come to suspect, is a discursive sleight of hand that postmodernists sometimes use to either deliberately or inadvertently conjure away vital aspects of texts. For instance, such canonical postmodernist novels as John Fowles's *The French Lieutenant's Woman* (1969) and John Barth's *The Sot-Weed Factor* (1960), novels frequently invoked during Banville's formational and early periods as worthy models for writers who might have wished to address the fiction-history issue, are specifically centred on their own involved cultural histories, of Victorian England and colonial America respectively. If all historical novels have wide-ranging relevance to the general problems of communicating history, it can also be said that there is no uniform standard for testing a novel's drawing of the fiction–history axis. Despite what many postmodernism enthusiasts argue, the historical novel can deal with history in terms of the actualized past on the ground as well as, or in conjunction with, the transcendent modern intellectual anxiety about narrating history in the first place. We will cover only some of this ground here, but the overall suggestion to be made is that a comprehensive exploration of Banville's Irish dimension can provide rich possibilities of discovery.

It is not surprising that those interested in exploring the theme of history in Banville initially worked mainly with *Copernicus* and *Kepler*. As partly fictional-historical biographies, they are the natural choice. Their availability for the decontextualized side of postmodernist criticism is demonstrated in their regular inclusion by academic critics in the influential category idea of 'historiographic metafiction', fiction where the general problem of language and reference is specifically directed at the related problem of writing history. To include these novels in this category, however, is to misread the vital themes of *Copernicus* and *Kepler* and to distract attention from some of the major aspects of the Tetralogy as a whole. The two novels might provisionally be termed historical, but when compared to other works from the œuvre, they are distinctly not metahistorical. When he was still in the middle of writing the Tetralogy, Banville remarked that *Copernicus* and *Kepler* had 'misled a lot of people into thinking that I had decided to become a "historical novelist", and others that I engaged in an effort to trace the history of scientific ideas from the 16th century to the present'.[2] While there is an obvious historical dimension to these two science novels, this is subordinated to other themes, as we will see in our next chapter.

Both *Birchwood* and the somewhat similarly themed *Newton Letter* have been consistently read in terms that suggest that their real purpose is not to deal with the content of history but to parody, in ways comparable to certain strands in international postmodern fiction generally, existing fictional subgenres and forms. The focus has principally been on Banville's parody in both books of the venerable Irish subgenre of the Big House novel, where the symbolic and thematic focus would be on the typical residences of the pre-Independence ruling Ascendancy class or, more particularly, on the threatened dilapidation of these residences and this class. Banville has, indeed, retained a fascination for stereotypes in this subgenre, not least in his 1999 adaptation of Elizabeth Bowen's novel *The Last September* (1929), which included some potentially clichéd scenes with images of IRA guns and phallic symbols aimed at defining the relationship between the Anglo-Irish and the native Irish. In accordance with this predilection for both perpetuating and satirizing Irish historical solemnities and stereotypes, Banville imposed on two of his adaptations of his beloved German dramatist Heinrich von Kleist some extensively worked but hilarious Irish settings: on *God's Gift*, the scenario of Wexford during the 1798 Rebellion; on *The Broken Jug*, the Irish Famine.[3]

The wise realization of Banville's amnesiac in *Seachange* is that the past does not evaporate simply because he cannot himself remember it, but is merely 'misplaced': it is only 'shut off … it's still there, intact', only he 'can't locate it'. Or, as his prototype more emphatically puts it: 'I was, I am, heavy with the weight of my history, it is still there, the silt of years, only I cannot find it'.[4] While Banville has certainly had much fun with Irish subject matter, there is also more seriousness and depth involved here than is generally recognized. He has sometimes pointed to 'the capacity of art to maintain its autonomy while still serving as witness to social and political events'.[5] It can be particularly seen in *Birchwood*, *The Newton Letter* and *The Untouchable* that Banville's work has often paid witness in various ways to Irish history, tradition and society in accompaniment with other subjects. And a reading of Banville as historical witness need not happen subsequent to, or subordinate to, other critical approaches. As with clinical amnesia, the fact that Irish memory does not always appear on the surface of Banville's work does not mean it is not there.

ADVENTURE TIME: THE CIRCLE OF HISTORY IN *BIRCHWOOD*

The novel that introduced the Banville style as we have come to typically know it – a yearning backward look, a high tone, rich language, carefully modulated rhythms, the major themes of authenticity, identity, memory, personal downfall, moral uncertainty – is also the major Ireland-centred work in the œuvre. 'I always think of *Birchwood* as my "Irish" novel', Banville has repeatedly pointed out: 'this is my book about Ireland'.[6] *Birchwood* was generally received at the time as something of a curiosity, and this has continued to be the prevailing critical pattern. On the most immediate level, this is ascribable to the novel's idiosyncratic mix of fantasy and deliberate historical anachronism, elements that have distracted commentators from the solidities of the novel's Irish setting. Though the historical elements of *Birchwood* are patent, and only a basic knowledge of Irish history would be necessary to understand these, critics have proved wary of reading it as an historical novel proper. It has been well noted for its precarious allegiance to the Big House subgenre; further coverage of this aspect is thus not required at this stage, though additional comprehensive argument can be built thereon. Other dimensions can be identified by attending to the interaction in the novel of history with the apparently traditional structure of the *Bildungsroman*, a novel that has as its major theme the growth and education of a hero. While this is well-trodden critical ground, both in general terms and with regard to some aspects of Banville's writing, his filtering of history and the *Bildungsroman* through one particular combined motif requires elaboration. This is the motif of the circle, and the related motif of the circus.

The circle might be taken as a natural compositional motif in Banville. Circular devices, circular images and patterns, prove naturally attractive to the kind of writers who, as we saw through George Steiner in Chapter 1, feel the need to invoke other 'grammars' of comprehension (in this case mathematics/geometry). And the same applies to writers who have ambitions to create pure, autonomous, self-circumscribed fictions, as illustrated by the case of Banville's major influence in his general aesthetics of the novel, Henry James: 'Really, universally, relations stop nowhere, and the exquisite problem of the artist is eternally but to draw, by a geometry of his own, the circle within which they shall happily appear to do so.'[7]

The alliance of circle and circus provides for further nuances here. Without piling on all the available illustrations, we can trace a constant reappearance of ideas about circles and circuses in Banville's work, ideas that are related simply by a mutual etymology but which have significance well beyond this. At the end of 'The Possessed' in Long Lankin (1970), when the disgruntled Irish writer Ben White tries to accommodate himself to the world, he says: 'there are all kinds of things I could do. Join a circus maybe ... they say everything is a circle and who am I to fight the laws of the universe' (1st edn, pp.188–9). As Banville was preparing to write Birchwood, these ideas were emphasized. In an uncollected early story, 'Mr Mallin's Quest', which would be partly assimilated into Birchwood, the protagonist gazes out of a window at one stage and spies some burlesque, spectral figures parading through his demesne. 'Always, even as a child', it is reported, 'he had hated circuses, and feared them obscurely, perceiving in the lights, the glare, the dust and glitter, a ramshackle, careless frivolity which threatened the stability of things.'[8] The two important circus-circle implications suggested in these two early instances can be developed from similar moments in later work. At two points in The Broken Jug, the grotesque activities of the play's 1846 courtroom are described as a 'circus' (pp.63, 80). On this level, the circus for Banville is a direct description of frolics, a 'ramshackle, careless frivolity' that threatens social stability and personal sanity. This level should not be missed in the œuvre because it is central to the enduring sense of comedy, ironic and high-toned but nonetheless antic, which has always attracted him to the figures of the commedia dell'arte, the formalized, and indeed circus-like, ancient Italian acting troupe, the major figures of which, the doleful Pierrot and the mischievous Harlequin, have made important appearances in novels from all Banville's periods, in Nightspawn and Birchwood, and, especially, in Ghosts and Shroud.

Beyond this immediate and highly entertaining symbolic function, with its attendant provision of stock clownish figures, the general idea of circus extends into a comparatively more intellectually serious conception of circularity which has profound implications for some of Banville's major themes and characteristic narrative movements. This is perhaps best revealed in an elementary but resounding remark he made in his late period about *Eclipse*, a novel where the same circus that is at the heart of *Birchwood* makes a prolonged reappearance. The vivid and emotive remembrance of things past is one of the defining activities of a Banville narrator, but he seemed somewhat puzzled about the depth of this activity in *Eclipse*: 'I think that going back – what is it about the past? I can never understand it. Why is it so powerful? Why does it appeal to us as if it had some extraordinary pearl of meaning that we can't find in our present lives?'[9] In structural terms, Banville's fictions are circularly devised, characteristically narrated by a man who moves back in narrative time from a moment in the present, to which he returns again at the end. As an extension of this extraordinary appeal of private pasts, Banville poses, inside and outside the work, the question of what the past as a whole, or as a subject for study, means for us.

The conjoining of circle and circus is Banville's deliberate figuration of his ideas on history. The thinkers he mentions in a commentary on a book on Irish history in his middle period where he asked the question 'What is history for?' are noteworthy in this regard, especially since his own answer is more in the form of what history is *not* for: 'Certainly it is not the disinterested factual pursuit that historians would like us to believe it is. Since Nietzsche – if not, indeed, since Heraclitus – the notion has been abandoned that within the facts of history objective truth lies waiting to be excavated.'[10] We will further investigate in Chapter 6 the influence on Banville of Friedrich Nietzsche, himself deeply influenced by such ancient Greek philosophers as Heraclitus, but for the moment we can notice that, rather than accept the notion of linearity involved in the traditional conception of history as a developing objective truth, Banville much prefers Nietzsche's famous description of history in terms of circular movement. This is reflected in his frequent deference to Nietzsche's notion of the eternal recurrence of the same, as indicated by the appearance of Nietzsche's German phrase '*Die ewige Wiederkunft*' ('eternal return of the same') in *Mefisto* (p.223), and by the Heraclitus-influenced concept of history that lies behind Victor Maskell's belief throughout *The Untouchable* in the philosophies of the ancient Stoics.

Formal and thematic circularity in Banville is intimately linked with this appeal of the recurring past, and the motif does a lot of work in *Birchwood*. As he put it in some notes for 'Inheritance', an abandoned film version, this novel and its narrative structure can be seen 'as allegory: events and attitudes of the past two hundred years of Irish history find their parrallel [sic] in the story. The cyclical effect of that history is disclosed: the futility of many actions and the repetitive struggles of political factions.'[11] This 'cyclical effect' is already associated with the Godkin family's declining fortunes when the narrator, Gabriel, includes as an example of the 'silent evidence' of impending doom a memory of 'the games of musical chairs which Mama played, switching them from the front rooms to the back in a circle of increasing degeneracy until the day when, groaning and creaking, they regained their original places and the wheel ceased to turn' (p.44). When Godkin sets off on a fantastical picaresque journey round the country in part two of the novel, the metaphoric significance of his wanderings is accentuated by the fact that they take place in the company of the epitome of travelling institutions: the circus. 'My journey', he remembers, 'described a wide circle the centre of which was, unknown to me, the circus, carrying me with it toward its goal by some mysterious intangible magnetism' (p.153). The circus itself becomes a symbol for the state of the country, both in real terms as Godkin walks in a circle around Famine Ireland, and in terms of the confused sense of his environment he takes with him out of his Big House. Having learned 'befogged geography, not its facts but its poetry' from his Aunt Martha, he moves from his papa's 'kingdom' out into the 'collapsible kingdom' of the circus and of Ireland generally (pp.40, 80, 102).

The status of the circus as symbol for Ireland is ironically figured in its advertising poster (p.99) where the traditionally royal 'We were amused', in the context of nineteenth-century Ireland, assumes more significance than usual:

PROSPERO'S MAGIC CIRCUS
by appointment to the
CROWNED HEADS OF EUROPE
magicians actors
acrobats clowns
wild beasts

THRILLS!

SPILLS!

EXCITEMENT!

Admission 6d

CHILDREN 2d

for one week only

'WE WERE AMUSED'

HRH

The Queen

The vocabulary of Banville's similes is also occasionally loaded in this context, and Godkin's view of himself collating his memories with the circus 'like an archaeologist mapping a buried empire' has obvious import for a journey round nineteenth-century colonial Ireland (p.5).

By taking Godkin out on the Irish roads in Birchwood, Banville triggers a structural device essential to the picaresque system of encounters that lie behind the Bildungsroman. In this kind of novel the emphasis on temporal and geographical movement is total and the focus on personal development in relation to society is intense. The circus in Birchwood is the symbolic figuration of a distinct time and movement pattern, or what the Russian narrative theorist Mikhail Bakhtin (1895–1975) called a 'chronotope'. This is Bakhtin's account of the uses of the road 'chronotope':

> On the road ... the spatial and temporal paths of the most varied people – representatives of all social classes, estates, religions, nationalities, ages – intersect at one spatial and temporal point. People who are normally kept separate by social and spatial distance can accidentally meet; any contrast may crop up, the most various fates may collide and interweave with one another.[12]

As with one of the original versions of this chronotope, Cervantes' Don Quixote (1605, 1615), with whose hero Godkin is identified in his determination to be a 'knight errant', the democratic tendency of the picaresque chronotope leads the hero of Birchwood away from the frozen time of the Ascendancy Big House and out into the surrounding country, resulting in adventures with the nationalist enclave in the circus and meetings with the lower orders, particularly in the form of an encounter with the archetypal tenant, Cotter (p.154f.).

Despite its connections with the rise of realism, the on-the-road chronotope enjoys a broad freedom in the presentation of time. In the 'travel' novel, Bakhtin observed, temporal categories are 'extremely poorly developed ... time in and of itself lacks any significance or historical coloring'. The only version of time developed in this type of novel, he says, is 'adventure time, which consists of the most immediate units – moments, hours, days – snatched at random from the temporal process'.[13] A fundamental purpose of the Bildungsroman is identified here. A Bildungsroman always sets up some kind of tension between the external world of real experience and the internal potential of the individual imagination to reflect on and give meaning to this experience. This tension produces a recognition on behalf of the Bildungsroman hero that the practicalities of living and operating in the communal world necessarily limit one's sense of absolute freedom and therefore that one's sense of self develops, not in a vacuum, but in the context of some regulation of the private imagination by forces beyond its control.

The Bildungsroman is closely associated with the emergence of national consciousness in the modern era. This brand of novel not only tells stories of individual growth and development but, by extension, can also capture a country's general sense of its own emergence and progress. The Bildungsroman characteristically contains a narrative whereby individuals try to make sense of their relationship with a particular environment and whereby the country to which these individuals belong tries, through the representative author, to make sense of the relationship between its past and its present. If the Bildungsroman structure is to be fulfilled, the individual hero must in some way capitulate to, or at least be reconciled with, the forces of history, modernity and nationality. A proper Bildungsroman hero is above all else supremely adaptable.

The patterns of Birchwood move considerably against this standard Bildungsroman structure. Godkin apparently rejects the idea that independent intellectual authority can be claimed for his own narrative of his country's history, in that he gives up in the end on the possibility of ever gaining meaningful knowledge. But he is simultaneously busy in asserting, outside of all this, an absolute autonomy and a supreme narrative of self. His main intent is aloofness: 'Outside is destruction and decay ... I shall stay here, alone, and live a life different from any the house has ever known. Yes' (p.170). When the absolute autonomy of the hero is asserted in this way over the world he meets in his adventures, the traditional Bildungsroman structure begins to fall apart. Rather than reach a point of mutual recognition with a complexly political and violent Ireland, Godkin transforms his country into a metaphor for his own self and his position of asserted autonomy. He demands that 'The future must have a locus!' (p.132). He is set to abandon his adventures abroad amongst the people of the country and to opt instead for the individualizing locus of his own imagination, as represented by the supremely autonomous figure of Prospero (p.168).

This position is allied to the displaced ideology of the artist-as-outsider, encouraged historically in Ireland and further accentuated by Banville, as we have seen in Chapter 2. In a mix of politics and aesthetics, the heroic artist-outsider surrounded by the philistine hordes has long been one of the major aristocratic images of this ideology. And the classic scenario of this transposition, recurrent in twentieth-century Irish fiction, is the Big House surrounded by the equal and opposite smallness and meanness of the peasantry or the vulgar middle classes. Godkin's assertion of autonomy at the end of Birchwood is a refusal to have his horizons widened and his self socialized by his adventures among the surrounding populace.

This has autobiographical import in aesthetic terms, beyond the simple trick Banville performs of inserting himself into the narrative via an anagram of his name (Johann Livelb), which Godkin adopts while with the circus. In the midst of writing the Tetralogy, Banville asserted that 'a novelist has no business taking actual historically recorded fact'. Though this suggested a distinction between an actual historical reality (fact) and those operations the novelist performs on it, he quickly adopted a different standpoint. 'Since I've started writing novels based in historical fact', he said, 'I've realized that the past does not exist in terms of fact. It only exists in terms of the way we look at it, in the way that historians have looked at it.'[14] This position on history is best contextualized in light of developing historical debates in Ireland during Banville's formational and early periods.

Usually assembled under the broad category of Revisionism, new Irish attitudes to history and to history writing are part of the general rise of the ironic mode in historical thought during the second half of the twentieth century. Broadly speaking, this ironic mode denies the claims to authority and truth that History as a discipline has traditionally made and suggests instead that History is potentially just one more faulty metanarrative, one that is even more faulty when it claims special privilege in establishing the official story of a country's emergence and development. By Banville's formational and early periods, a whole new generation of Irish scholars had moved away from what they saw as an older reverential approach to Irish history writing, and a range of reconstructive historical texts had been published which challenged popular perceptions of the major moments in Irish history.

For novelists, this developing position on History as a discipline provided grounds for a new sense of narrative freedom when dealing with Irish history in fiction. This is only a paradoxical freedom, however. On one hand, the extraordinarily inventive treatment of Irish history in a novel such as *Birchwood* suggests a triumph of the imagination whereby the *Bildungsroman* hero asserts, in a gesture of rejection, his autonomous position above historical events and major political consequences which he cannot properly interpret, let alone control. On the other hand, such free play with the past may be taken as evidence of a sense of impotence towards the actualities of history – the lack of a sense of agency out in the world of historical happenings is transformed into a virtual agency which feels that if it cannot control history as such it can at least control the narrative *representations* of history.

Godkin's position at the end of *Birchwood* is tantamount to this kind of assertion of creative freedom from history. While he set out to trace and give pattern to his memories, in the way an archaeologist might seek to map a 'buried empire', he now dwells in the 'collapsible kingdom' of his ancestral house, of geographical and historical Ireland. And the autobiographical parallel is absolute. 'The only direct statement I've *ever* made in any book', says Banville, 'is at the end of *Birchwood* where the protagonist says: "I'll stay in this house and I'll live a life different from any the house has ever known". And that is my statement. I stay in this country but I'm not going to be an Irish writer. I'm not going to do the Irish thing.'[15] If on-the-road adventures with Irish history in *Birchwood*, with everything from bottomless Famine coffins, to Molly Maguires, to historical figures parading in costume and in the dance of death called Tötentanz, do not produce meaning of any kind, then history and society can be notionally collapsed in the autonomous imagination. It is often remarked that a total collapse of faith in historical narrative and meaning is a natural negative development when the ironic approach to history is taken completely to heart, and this development is a major context for the silence of Godkin in his very last word: 'whereof I cannot speak, thereof I must be silent' (p.171).

Fundamentally, this silence and the asserted autonomy from nation and history it encapsulates in Birchwood, is only ostensible. Ireland's situation at the time of the writing of Banville's free-play novel is vital here. Birchwood in fact emerges as a very deft contemporary Irish Zeitroman, literally a novel 'of its time', something Banville had apprehended by his middle period: 'When I think about it now, and I hesitate to say it, I realise that it is quite political in a curious way.'[16] His entire native background impinged on the novel more than he had thought at the time of writing, and in it, he says, there is a lot of the atmosphere of Ireland in the early 1970s. The political Troubles in Northern Ireland, which had established their pattern of tragedy and violence during the years when Banville was writing his first novels, are clearly figured in Birchwood through its thematic treatment of confusion, cruelty and resentment. More important, perhaps, in mind of Banville's own frequently expressed view that literature best reflects its social and political context in discreet or covert ways, is the more oblique performance of Birchwood as a Zeitroman through its narrative tone, atmosphere, imagery and vocabulary. The description of the birch wood that gives the novel's Big House its name can serve as a prime illustration:

> Our wood was one of nature's cripples. It covered, I suppose, three or four acres of the worst land on the farm, a hillside sloping down crookedly to the untended nether edge of the stagnant pond we called a lake. Under a couple of feet of soil there was a bed of solid rock, that intractable granite for which the area is notorious. On this unfriendly host the trees grew wicked and deformed, some of them so terribly twisted that they crawled horizontally across the hill, their warped branches warring with the undergrowth, while behind them, at some distance, the roots they had struggled to put down were thrust up again by the rock, queer maimed things. (p.23)

The impressive litany of related words and suggestions in this short passage (cripples, worst, stagnant, intractable, unfriendly, wicked, deformed, terribly, twisted, crawled, warped, warring, struggled, maimed) describes the demesne from which Godkin decides to escape and it also represents the Ireland of the early 1970s from which Banville tried to escape through obliquity of style and theme and the assertion of an aesthetic of autonomy.

When he finished *Birchwood*, Banville came, he says, 'to something of a dead end, because I said: what do I do now? ... Do I keep writing this kind of book, keep writing Irish books, or do I try something else?' He dedicated himself for a period to reading modern European classics. He thought for a while that he would give up fiction in favour of writing 'some kind of fictionalised history'. Primarily, he wanted 'to get away from Ireland ... to find a way of exploring the novel form in ways that would not require me to make comments on what was happening in my own life, my own town'.[17] While he retained his interest in history with the two novels that followed, *Copernicus* and *Kepler*, these are more transcendentally concerned with the theme of the autonomous imagination than with either historical fiction or fictionalized history. Though Banville did move on after *Birchwood* to further explorations of the relationship between the past and narrative, it should always be noted that he first combined a treatment of actual history and speculation about history-as-narrative in *Birchwood*, his fundamentally Irish novel. The theme of Irish history, and the position within it of the notionally autonomous individual, remains the site of Banville's most involved investigation of the imperious and seemingly irresolvable tension between self and world, between native and nation, between writer and tradition. The epigraph to *Birchwood* from the ancient Roman poet Catullus thereby has its resonance for Banville's Irish context: 'I hate and I love; ask how? I cannot tell you / Only I feel it, and I am torn in two'.

HISTORY AND CATHOLICS: THE NEWTON LETTER

After *Birchwood*, Banville's most important book on Irish themes is the novella *The Newton Letter*, the third instalment of the Tetralogy. Even before the admitted resort to closely autobiographical data in some details of his fiction in his late period, Banville metaphorically went home in *The Newton Letter*. 'I was born down there, in the south', says the narrator near the opening: 'The best memories I have of the place are of departures from it' (p.11). This brief dismissiveness, tallying with Banville's youthful attitude to his native County Wexford, refers to the locale of Ferns in the county where the narrator, an historian, has gone to try to finish a book on Sir Isaac Newton. Unlike *Birchwood*, the narrator here is nameless. In *Reflections*, the film version of the novella, the narrator is given the name Willie Meister (played by Gabriel Byrne), and this is a further acknowledgement of the German writer Goethe (1749–1832), whose novel *Elective Affinities* (1809) provided Banville with elements of his scenario, particularly with regard to character names and the encompassing theme of the clash between reality and romantic idealism. In view of the typical pairing of *Birchwood* and *The Newton Letter* in critical assessments, it is worth noting here that one of the earliest instances of the *Bildungsroman*, the brand of novel so crucial to the shape of *Birchwood*, was Goethe's *Wilhelm Meister's Apprenticeship* (1795–6). While the parallel is not explicitly indicated in *The Newton Letter*, this suggestion that its narrator can be thought of as a version of Goethe's compromised hero Wilhelm Meister suggests that we should also approach the novella as a story of personal formation. As with *Birchwood*, the implication is that the narrator will undergo his development in the context of his country and immediate surroundings – hence the early reference to his place of birth and his attitude towards it.

An important related matter concerning the autobiographical aspect of the novella and the location of the historian at the time of his narration should be cleared up here. *The Newton Letter* is dated at the end: 'Dublin – Iowa – Dublin / Summer 79 – Spring 81' (p.81). This has led to an ambiguity – always a potential problem with a first-person narrator in any case – about the distinction between author and narrator. The date is not part of the historian's narrative proper. As with James Joyce in *Ulysses*, it refers to Banville's period of composition (he visited the University of Iowa in 1980/81). The distinction is vital if the symbolic significance of the historian's location at the time of narration is to be appreciated. The historian has lived in Dublin, but he is writing about these events that happened in County Wexford, not from Iowa, but from somewhere in the broader Scandinavia, most likely Finland. The initial clues to this are not definitive: his journey through snow is mentioned in the second sentence, and he refers soon after to the 'campus postman, an asthmatic Lapp' at the university where, we later understand, he is on a one-year contract (pp.1, 8). We can accept, for the sake of argument, that a Laplander could be a postman anywhere in the world. However, though they remain somewhat hidden, the coordinates to the narrator's current location in Scandinavia are provided towards the end. As dawn comes up and he realizes that his life at Ferns is close to an end, the historian remarks, seemingly apropos of nothing: 'In northern countries they call this the wolf hour' (p.75). This turns out to be a portent of his future dwelling, and he writes a few paragraphs later:

> Was I crazy to come? My surroundings are congenial ... Spring is a ferocious and faintly mad season in this part of the world. At night I can hear the ice unpacking in the bay ... And I have heard gatherings of wolves too, far off in the frozen wastes, howling like orchestras. The landscape, if it can be called that, has a peculiar bleached beauty, much to my present taste. Tiny flowers appear on the tundra, slender and pale as the souls of dead girls. And I have seen the auroras. (p.77)

Though this oblique information on locale (tundra, the aurora borealis) is only provided at the end, it is clear that the new surroundings the historian finds so much to his taste reflect his state of mind at the time of writing. His story about his time in Ferns concerns, as with the other novels of the Tetralogy, the emotional coldness and potential aloofness of intellectual man and, most importantly, the resultant inability of such a man to understand his own surroundings. The concluding parts of this historian's narrative emphasize his feelings of isolation and loss. Thus, the historian's freezing geographical location turns out to be a deft illustration of his own mood through a pathetic fallacy, a deep association between climatic conditions and his remembered conditions at Ferns.

Through his reflections on his period in Wexford, the narrator scrutinizes his stereotyping of the people who have rented him the lodge on their Ferns estate. The fact that an academic residing at a gate-lodge has an affair with a member of a dilapidated Ascendancy family has suggested parallels with another Big House novel, Langrishe, Go Down (1966), by Irishman Aidan Higgins, but any similarities between the two works are superficial. Unlike Higgins's novel, and many other Big House novels published in contemporary Ireland, Banville's is no straight account of the Big House residents. He is not concerned with evoking a Big House period or setting in any conventional sense. In keeping with the classic placement of the four works of a Tetralogy, Banville intended this third instalment to be a satire. Thus, while *The Newton Letter* can certainly on some level be compared to any other Big House novel, the proper instances of comparison would be the relevant works that emphasize this genre's satirical possibilities, possibilities that lie not just within the clichés of generic literary treatment but also within the inherent nature of the Big House class itself, as particularly seen in one of the genre's true classics, *Troubles*, by the Anglo-Irish novelist J.G. Farrell (1935–79), which was published at the very beginning of Banville's career in 1970 and by a neat coincidence is also set somewhere on the coast of his own County Wexford. A recent reissue of *Troubles* was accompanied by an introduction by Banville, and his remark that this classic is marked by 'an air of permanent, pallid bafflement before the mundane mysteries of Irish life' might be taken as the quintessential mood he too wishes to achieve in his own Big House fiction.[18]

Much attention has also been given to Banville's satirical treatment of his narrator's loss of faith in language and narrative. Since the very first sentence of the narrator's opening ('Words fail me, Clio') is addressed to the classical muse of History, the implications for any faith in the writing of history are obvious. We know from the beginning that the narrator has lost faith in words and therefore in historical narrative. The encompassing irony is that he is relying on the communicative power of words to tell us about the failure of this communicative power. The satire is also directed specifically at the stereotyping involved in the Big House subgenre. Even if his biographical subject of Newton has no relevance to the nation as such, the fact that the narrator is an Irish historian living in Ireland – for the duration of the period recollected in the narrative at least – has further resonance. More than has been allowed in the criticism, *The Newton Letter*, though on one level given to older established material, is, like *Birchwood*, a *Zeitroman*, a novel of its specific time in recent Irish history.

While Big House fiction continues to be popular with both novelists and critics in Ireland, its perseverance is arguably testament to the enduring influence of the grand symbols of W.B. Yeats (1865–1939) and other figures of the Irish Literary Revival of the early twentieth century. That the Big House continues to be used as a setting or symbol in the context of Irish social arrangements that have drastically changed might be seen as evidence of the limited tradition available to the contemporary Irish novelist. Whatever its present social relevance, in fiction the Big House is particularly anachronistic, and Banville illustrates this at length. He even includes two explicit echoes of Yeats's poetry. In the grounds of the novella's Big House there stands a chestnut tree, referred to, in memory of Yeats's 'Among School Children', as 'that great rooted blossomer'. And Charlotte, one of the women of the Big House, is twice compared to a 'gazelle', as are the women of Yeats's 'In Memory of Eva Gore-Booth and Countess Markiewicz' (pp.19, 39–40). We as readers are treated to ironic moments in this regard that the narrator isn't necessarily aware of, as with the moment when he simply remarks that Edward 'began unceremoniously to piss against the trunk' of the chestnut – we can assume that, symbolically, the whole Yeatsian Big House symbolism is being disrespected here along with the tree itself (p.33).

In his determination to praise and idealize, the narrator mythologizes in Yeatsian fashion the residents of his Big House:

> I had them spotted for patricians from the start. The big house, Edward's tweeds, Charlotte's fine-boned slender grace that the dowdiest of clothes could not mask, even Ottilie's awkwardness, all this seemed the unmistakable stamp of their class. Protestants, of course, landed, the land gone now to gombeen men and compulsory purchase, the family fortune wasted by tax, death duties, inflation. But how bravely, how beautifully they bore their losses! Observing them, I understood that breeding such as theirs is a preparation not for squiredom itself, but for that distant day, which for the Lawlesses had arrived, when the trappings of glory are gone and only style remains. All nonsense of course, but to me, product of a post-peasant Catholic upbringing, they appeared perfected creatures. Oh, don't accuse me of snobbery. This was something else, a fascination before the spectacle of pure refinement. (pp.12–13)

The structural progression of the Big House theme in the novel is built around a gradually souring of such romanticizing. The process is sometimes discreet and cumulative, as with the patterned use Banville makes of a hurley stick. As a symbol of the traditionally Catholic and nationalist game of hurling, the hurley, on the narrator's first sighting of it in the umbrella stand at the Big House, is designed to illustrate the fact that he is so busy idealizing the occupants as stylish Protestants that he doesn't recognize clues to the contrary (p.17). After this first mention, the hurley is referred to a further seven times, six of these within eight pages (pp.31–8, 55). The hurley is thus a symbolic measuring stick of other occasions when the narrator is abruptly shocked out of his presumptions, as when he discovers one day that his 'Protestants' are in fact mass-going Catholics, and his 'entire conception of them had to be revised' (p.54).

Misplaced stereotyping is more powerfully deflated through Banville's reference to an actual political event in Ireland two years before publication of The Newton Letter. Bunny Mittler, a visitor to Ferns whom the narrator also assumes to be a Protestant, drinks a toast to 'August the twenty-seventh' and the following exchange takes place:

> 'Mountbatten?' I said. One of their dwindling band of heroes, cruelly murdered. I was charmed: only they would dare to make a memorial of a drawing-room tea party. 'Terrible thing, terrible.'
>
> I was soon disabused ...
>
> 'And don't forget Warrenpoint: eighteen paras, and an earl, all on the one day.'
>
> 'Jesus, Bunny', Edward said.
>
> She was still looking at me, amused and glittering. 'Don't mind him', she said playfully, 'he's a West Brit, self-made. I think we should name a street after it, like the French do. The glorious twenty-seventh!' ...
>
> 'It's dead men you're talking about', Edward muttered, with the sour weariness of one doing his duty by an argument that he has long ago lost.
>
> 'There's nothing wrong with this country ... that a lot more corpses like that won't cure.' She lifted her cup daintily. 'Long live death! Is this your cake, Charlotte? Scrumptious.' (pp.37–8)

Capped with its distinct touch of bathos, this scene incorporates into the wry tone of the novel a moment of seriousness that has usually been glanced over in Banville criticism. The lesson on stereotypes presented to the narrator here has significance far beyond the parody of a subgenre. It is the cruellest of ironies that the family taken to be Protestant and Anglo-Irish turns out to have an IRA supporter among its extended members. It is important to realize here that Bunny Mittler is Edward's sister, and this compounds the narrator's confusion as to the family's religious and political allegiances. The event Bunny celebrates is one of the most notorious IRA attacks of the contemporary Troubles when, on 27 August 1979, a land-mine killed eighteen British soldiers in County Down and a bomb killed Lord Louis Mountbatten and a number of others in a boat off County Sligo. *The Newton Letter* is the only contemporary Irish novel to incorporate this event in such a thematically resonant way, and attention to its inclusion is all the more requisite given Banville's usual avoidance of such obvious political content. It also renders somewhat irresponsible the suggestions some Banville commentators have made that the Irish content of the novella is of only secondary significance.

Banville himself is aware of the implications of the Irish content of the novel. On the one hand, he has admitted that the Big House theme 'has been done to death, not only by critics but also by fiction writers', that it is 'the most clichéd thing in Irish fiction'. Yet he also acknowledges the affective nature of the historical baggage that comes with it. He sees the subgenre as 'a huge museum of the past' which raises 'hackles' and 'expectations' by which no Irish person can remain unmoved'.[19] Because of its isolation in context, Banville's use of the Irish political events of 1979 might be thought of as a potentially awkward political reference. But it is inserted so organically into the style and themes of the narrative that its role in providing more than theoretical reasons for the narrator's declining faith in his own perceptions and in history can be easily missed. The misinterpretation of real political events is one of the prime implicit catalysts for the historian's onset of despair. At the opening of his narrative his depreciating faith in his professional endeavours is 'what the doctors call a vague general malaise' (p.6); by the end, his hubris is completely deflated precisely because of his misreadings of Catholic and Protestant relations with the Big House and of associated recent political events in the country. If he cannot correctly interpret the history-in-process around him, then he feels even further disqualified from attempting a history of Newton. Clio will come to his aid as invoked muse, it seems, only when he has recognized the truth about the Catholics of Ferns.

MORE ENGLISH THAN THE ENGLISH THEMSELVES: *THE UNTOUCHABLE*

To add emphasis to the culturally specific assertion of autonomy he made in his 1991 review of *The Field Day Anthology of Irish Writing*, Banville quoted a famous section from a long work, *Autumn Journal* (1939), by the Northern Irish poet Louis MacNeice (1907–63):

> I hate your grandiose airs,
>> Your sob-stuff, your laugh and your swagger,
> Your assumption that everyone cares
>> Who is king of your castle.
> Castles are out of date,
>> The tide flows round the children's sandy fancy;
> Put up what flag you like, it is too late
>> To save your soul with bunting.

Lest any ambiguity remain regarding his own position on MacNeice's dismissal of national allegiance in these lines, Banville concluded with a laconic 'Just so'.[20]

For Irish poets of a succeeding generation, MacNeice has sometimes equalled W.B. Yeats as a prime focus for attempting to resolve felt dilemmas of national identity, particularly when the feeling is that there may ultimately be no resolution of such dilemmas. Despite the apparent finality of many of MacNeice's lines, it is widely recognized that his attitude was anything but decided. His work is marked equally by an outlining of the problem of Irish nationality and an inability to solve it. While it is hardly surprising that a whole series of poets and other writers from MacNeice's native Northern Ireland should be mindful of their forebear's positions, it is more unusual that Banville, a writer from the Republic of Ireland who has never published poetry, should use MacNeice as a reference point. Both MacNeice's abrupt assertions of independence from any imposed sense of nationalism and his equally frequent uncertainty on the matter, prove naturally amenable to Banville, however. It is not coincidental that Catullus's conflicted love–hate line, '*Odi et amo*', alluded to by MacNeice in the line following those quoted above, also forms the imposing epigraph to *Birchwood*.

This conflicted sense of national identity is figured in Victor Maskell, the narrator of *The Untouchable*, a novel that leans more heavily on the life and times of MacNeice than has generally been recognized. While Maskell lives in London, he is Irish-born and considerable parts of the earlier sections of the novel focus on his visits home. The Irish aspect here, and its resonance for Banville's own perceived relationship with Ireland, is vital to understanding the persistence well into his middle period of Irish themes more usually associated with his early books.

Maskell identifies early on in the novel the 'ambiguous, ecstatic, anguished' forces in his life: the 'obsession with art', the 'murk and slither of sex', and the 'tricky question of nationality, that constant drone-note in the bagpipe music of my life' (p.47). The first two forces, characteristic Banville preoccupations, emanate in this case from the life of the infamous Cambridge spy Anthony Blunt (1907–83), on whom Maskell is ostensibly based. The third force, with its pointed allusion to one of MacNeice's best-known poems ('Bagpipe Music'), indicates the second biography that forms Maskell's character. Banville's use of the life of Blunt is patent in the design and detail of the novel; thus the various points at which Banville moves away from biographical fidelity to Blunt have confused many readers and critics. Far from being incidental, the added Irish dimension given to this virtual Blunt for The Untouchable is central to Banville's purpose. At the very least, it should be spotted that, along with books on Blunt and the 1930s period which is the setting, Banville acknowledges at the end the 'help' of a major biography, Jon Stallworthy's Louis MacNeice, which was published in 1995 during the early stages of the writing of The Untouchable.

Combining Blunt and MacNeice like this in a single narrator is somewhat natural since the two were, from quite a young age, close acquaintances. Though their friendship faded in later life, they were much together after their initial meeting as schoolboys and they particularly shared an interest in the visual arts and leftist politics, both of which are principal concerns in The Untouchable. More important, however, are the symbolic sympathies Banville has found in MacNeice. A surprising allowance for cultural inevitability is involved here. He has explained that he felt he 'had to make [Maskell] into an Irishman, or at least a man with an Irish background' because he 'couldn't pretend to be an Englishman'. He has readily admitted that he has in fact 'stolen great bleeding chunks of MacNeice's life and given them to Maskell'.[21] Banville also read much of MacNeice's own work as the project of The Untouchable was being formulated.

Some common denominators for Maskell and MacNeice may be quickly noted: a Protestant clergyman father with Home Rule sympathies and with west of Ireland ancestors; Catholic as well as Protestant affinities; left motherless when young; a mentally deficient brother with whom a guilt-ridden relationship is conducted. The more important encompassing similarity between Banville's part-model and his narrator is their mutually conflicted sense of identity, what might be called their Irish-Englishness. MacNeice's frequently voiced dissatisfaction that he couldn't seem to feel quite at home in either Ireland or England transfers literally to the novel. Maskell's talents for treason and mutability are somehow inevitable because, as he melodramatically recalls, a variety of treachery was practised by his ancestors, those 'mysterious autochthons stepping out of the mists of the western seaboard, the mighty O Measceoils, warriors, pirates, fierce clansmen all' who 'just in time to avoid the ravages of the Famine had changed their religion and Anglicised the family name and turned themselves into Yeats's hard-riding country gentlemen' (p.77). Maskell's experience of class and religious stratification in Carrickdrum (substituted for MacNeice's Carrickfergus in County Antrim), site of his 'bourgeois beginnings', establishes, in a distinct parallel with MacNeice, a perpetual sense of outsidedness:

> When I was a boy in Carrickdrum I often ventured at night into Irishtown, a half acre of higgledy-piggledy shacks behind the seafront where the Catholic poor lived in what seemed to me euphoric squalor. There was a pub in every alleyway, low, one-roomed establishments ... I would creep up to Murphy's Lounge or Maloney's Select Bar and stand outside the shut door, my heart beating in my throat – it was known for a fact that if the Catholics caught a Protestant child he would be spirited away and buried alive in a shallow grave in the hills above the town – and listen to the din inside, the laughter and the shouted oaths and jagged snatches of song ... Ah, the romance of forbidden, brute worlds! (pp.144–5)

Despite his insistence that 'one isn't a snob of course', this kind of stereotyped contrast of Catholic and Protestant is designed to suggest that Maskell is as much a conscious dissembler in this memory of cultural definition as in everything else.

Maskell's consuming sense of inauthenticity, most immediately ascribable to his career as a Soviet spy, is exacerbated by his awareness that he is a social interloper in London, a city he insists on calling his capital instead of Belfast. On his move to England, Maskell reinvents himself as an aesthete, talking of his 'entire remaking of the self, with all the dedication and unremitting labour that such an exercise would entail' (p.63). Subsequently, Maskell finds himself a simultaneous insider and outsider, a curious combination of Englishman and Irishman. This, he feels, forms a large part of his acute faculties of perception and he finds himself to be an excellent analyst of English society. When he tries to inform Moscow about how to 'distinguish between form and content in English life', he thinks parenthetically: 'trust an Irishman to know the difference' (p.152). To his annoyance, his peers constantly remind him of his Irish origins. 'You're the Irishman' is a refrain established early in the novel, a label that produces in Maskell 'a momentary gloom: the Irishman' (p.10). His visits home are sullen, particularly when he is accompanied by one of his upper-class friends. While a visiting Englishman finds Carrickdrum, complete with its Ulster fry, to be something attractively exotic, Maskell is impatient to return to England and, most pointedly, aborts a trip to Connaught and the Irish west, a region frequently idealized by MacNeice – while MacNeice's ancestors originated in Galway, Maskell's are said to come from Mayo (p.62f.). Yet, when English society presumes that he is not Irish, Maskell insists: 'I'm not English' (p.24). In an echo of Ben White's similar conflict of identity in Nightspawn, the characteristic effect of Maskell's uncertainty is his hesitant answer to the imputation of a 'conflict of loyalties': '"You're Irish, aren't you?" "Well, I ... Of course I ..."' (p.177).

Banville effectively combines this identity conflict with the general haughty tone he attributes to the young intellectuals of Maskell's time, and deploys some stereotyping along the way. When Querell, the potential spy scout, attempts to discover, by mentioning a nationalist friend of his, whether Maskell might be suitable for recruitment, this exchange takes place:

> 'He'd interest you ... He's a red-hot Sinn Feiner.'
> I laughed.
> 'I'm from the other side of the fence, you know', I said. 'My

people are black Protestants.'

'Oh, Protestants in Ireland are all Catholics, really.'

'Rather the opposite, I should have thought. Or we're all just plain pagans, perhaps.'

'Well, anyway, the place is interesting, isn't it? I mean the politics.' (p.37)

The political offhandedness here is later emphasized when this Sinn Féiner, who berates Maskell for his 'lack of patriotism' and calls him 'a dirty Unionist', becomes evasive when Maskell questions him on Irish socio-political specifics (pp.53–4). The sense of ambiguous identity is maintained by Banville to the end of The Untouchable. In testimony to the situation in London at the time of Blunt's public 'unmasking' by the prime minister, Margaret Thatcher, in the House of Commons in 1979, which is the moment from which Maskell narrates, Banville has Maskell make comments such as 'The Irish are not popular these days, with IRA bombs going off in the city every other week'; and 'Another IRA bomb in Oxford Street tonight. No one killed, but a glorious amount of damage and disruption' (pp.18, 232). Though these precisely contemporaneous references can seem somewhat overdetermined in that they are dropped into otherwise unconcerned passages, Banville's intent is presumably to accentuate the offhand tone and to dissuade the reader from holding any simplistic views about Maskell's Irishness and general politics.

Banville's admission that he had never tried to write social comedy prior to The Untouchable is an indication that it was written as something of a departure. He has often remarked that the straightforwardness of this novel, in comparison to his previous fiction, was something of a watershed for him. Partly, he takes the tone of ambiguity he brings to this foray into social comedy from Henry James, whom he was clearly following in the style of Maskell's voice. There is more patent humour involved than in James, however. The kind of comedy Banville tried to achieve owes more to the novelists he read in his formational period: it is 'that very brittle, bleak humour of the English novelists whom I admire, like Evelyn Waugh and even P.G. Wodehouse, this kind of despairing, elegant, verbal humour'.[22] There is also a sense, however, in which this brand of humour is regulated by the kind of Irish character Maskell is. Commenting on how he finds 'bracing and admirable' the 'sceptical humour' of Ireland's tradition of exile writing, Banville seemed pleased that one or two reviewers pointed out the similarity between Maskell and writers such as Oscar Wilde and George Bernard Shaw (1856–1950), who went from Ireland to England and became 'more English than the English themselves' by adapting so brilliantly to their adopted society:

> The relationship between England and Ireland is still very strange, and it's not just bombs and bullets. Geographically it's strange in that Ireland is a post-colonial nation with the former colonists living only seventy miles across the sea. If they were halfway around the world, I'm sure we wouldn't be as obsessed with the English as we are. Although I didn't set out consciously to do this, I think *The Untouchable* is a commentary on that aspect of our relationship.[23]

The conscious working with MacNeice in *The Untouchable*, then, is further allied to a sometimes unconscious adherence on Banville's part to a peculiarly Irish tradition of a sense of cultural displacement. Maskell's inability to get away from Ireland, either in society or within himself, is a parallel for what appears to amount to a similar inability in Banville. Exile from native surroundings and culture can be a commitment in physical and declarative terms, but Irish alignments, as in MacNeice, steadily come to the surface. These home alignments are perhaps all the more important in Banville's work for the determination with which he has frequently negatively defined himself in terms of attempted distance from them.

NOTES

1. John Banville, 'Rondo', *Transatlantic Review*, 60 (1977), p.181; *Seachange*, dir. Thaddeus O'Sullivan (RTÉ television, 1994).
2. Rüdiger Imhof, 'Q. and A. with John Banville', *Irish Literary Supplement*, 6, 1 (1987), p.13.
3. See John Kenny, '"Appallingly Funny": John Banville's *The Broken Jug*', in *Beyond Borders: IASIL Essays on Modern Irish Writing*, ed. Neil Sammells (Bath: Sulis Press, 2004), pp.83–103.
4. Banville, 'Rondo', p.182.
5. John Banville, 'Living in the Shadows', *New York Review of Books*, 40, 13 (15 July 1993), p.23.

6. Melvyn Bragg, 'John Banville', *The South Bank Show* (LWT/Ulster Television, 1993).

7. Henry James, 'Preface to Roderick Hudson', in *The Critical Muse: Selected Literary Criticism*, ed. and intro. Roger Gard (London: Penguin, 1987), p.452.

8. John Banville, 'Mr Mallin's Quest', *Transatlantic Review*, 37–8 (autumn/winter 1970–71), p.32.

9. Anonymous, 'Oblique Dreamer', *Observer* (17 September 2000).

10. John Banville, 'Micks on the Make Find True Selves in Exile', *Observer* (3 October 1993).

11. Ms. 10252.3.15. Notes for the filming of *Inheritance* [*Birchwood*].

12. Mikhail Bakhtin, 'Forms of Time and Chronotope in the Novel', in *The Dialogic Imagination: Four Essays*, ed. Michael Holmquist, trans. Caryl Emerson and Michael Holmquist (Austin, TX: University of Texas Press, 1981), pp.243–4.

13. Mikhail Bakhtin, 'The *Bildungsroman* and its Significance in the History of Realism/Toward a Historical Typology of the Novel', in *Speech Genres and Other Late Essays*, ed. Caryl Emerson and Michael Holmquist, trans. Vern W. McGee (Austin, TX: University of Texas Press, 1986), p.11.

14. M.P. Hederman and R. Kearney (eds), 'Novelists on the Novel: Ronan Sheehan Talks to John Banville and Francis Stuart' (1979), in *The Crane Bag Book of Irish Studies* (1977–1981) (Dublin: Blackwater Press, 1982), pp.415–16.

15. Hedwig Schwall, 'An Interview with John Banville', *European English Messenger*, 6, 1 (1997), p.19.

16. Bragg, 'John Banville'.

17. David Hanly, 'Interview with John Banville', *Bookside: Writer in Profile* (RTÉ television, 1992).

18. John Banville, 'Introduction', in *Troubles*, by J.G. Farrell (New York: New York Review of Books, 2002), p.xi.

19. John Banville, 'At the Manor', *Irish Times* (23 May 1992); Schwall, 'Interview with John Banville', p.19; Ciaran Carty, 'Out of Chaos Comes Order', *Sunday Tribune* (14 September 1986).

20. John Banville, 'Put Up What Flag You Like, It's Too Late', *Observer* (1 December 1991).

21. Andy O'Mahony, 'John Banville', *Off the Shelf* (RTÉ radio, 24 April 1997).

22. Clíodhna Ní Anluain (ed.), 'John Banville', in *Reading the Future: Irish Writers in Conversation with Mike Murphy* (Dublin: Lilliput Press, 2000), p.28.

23. Ron Hogan, 'The Beatrice Interview: John Banville', 1 June 1997, <www.beatrice.com/interviews/banville>.

CHAPTER FOUR

The Science of Imagination and the Art of the Novel: The Tetralogy and its Surrounding Ideas

BOOKS OF EVIDENCE: BANVILLE'S WORDS AND THINGS

In his first major televised interview, given while still enjoying the critical aftermath of *The Book of Evidence*, Banville went to some lengths to explain an added significance he sees in that novel's title. It was, he suggested, the best title he has ever devised, because 'in a way, all my books are Books of Evidence. They say here is the world, a strange place, what strange objects these are, and the strangest of all are the two-legged objects that walk around in it.' Opposing artists who seem able to accept the world against those 'who simply don't know what to do with the world at all', he identified himself as one of the confused. He is the kind of writer who can only 'stand aghast in front of this extraordinary world and say: Look, all I can do is give you some evidence about this, is present the evidence, but I can't present any explanation or acceptance of it.' In a resounding phrase, he summed up the artistic project that follows from this sense of general puzzlement: 'all my books are sort of phenomenological exercises'.[1]

The philosophy of phenomenology concentrates on existence as the experience of external reality. Rather than wondering whether things have an objective solidity, a *thereness*, the important question for a phenomenologist is: what is our conscious experience of these things that exist outside of consciousness? Banville's exploration of the power of consciousness to establish its own potentially autonomous reality or meaning can be readily recognized in his work. Yet his sense of himself as a phenomenologist means that he also wishes to explore the possibility that, on the contrary, it is the external world of phenomena that is the truly autonomous dimension in our experience of existence. In Banville's work, the existential position is combined with the phenomenological position to dynamic effect.

The general premise for both the existential and phenomenological philosophies is that the world outside our consciousness is found by our consciousness to be somehow alien or strange. Synonymous terms for this foundational sense of puzzlement recur in Banville's work, and the characteristic vocabulary was established in the formational and early periods. In *Birchwood* Godkin concludes: 'I find the world always odd' (p.171). In *Copernicus* the scientist finds 'that the world is absurd' (p.103). In *Kepler* even such things as oranges are 'uncanny in their tense inexorable thereness' (p.7). In *Mefisto* Gabriel Swan laments that 'the simplest things baffled me' (p.21). This is not just a flirtation with the standard existential idea of man's alienation from nature; it is a totalizing and essentially autobiographical viewpoint.

Banville has allowed that one of the nearest times he has come to speaking in his own voice in his work is in *The Book of Evidence* 'when I wrote that I have never got used to living on this planet. It's a cosmic blur.'[2] This is the relevant passage:

> I have never really got used to being on this earth. Sometimes I think our presence here is due to a cosmic blunder, that we were meant for another planet altogether, with other arrangements, and other laws, and other, grimmer skies. I try to imagine it, our true place, off on the far side of the galaxy, whirling and whirling. And the ones who were meant for here, are they out there, baffled and homesick, like us? (pp.26–7)

Though he has no specific theoretical allegiance to philosophical phenomenology as such, Banville's deeply felt predicament of existential homelessness is related to his ambiguous sense of exile within Irish culture, and is also related to two basic phenomenological principles. The first of these is this postulation that all objects of consciousness, being outside of consciousness, are enigmatic (in Banville's terms: strange, absurd, uncanny, baffling, odd) and thus that the world resists explanation.

A second principle provides a way out of the silence potentially induced in the investigative author by the impression that the world in itself makes no sense. The phenomenologist aims to define the nature of the object world through analysis of the processes of consciousness that assimilate that world. Banville's definition of his work as phenomeno-logical exercise is a version of this second fundamental move. At their root, his books seek to identify the processing patterns by which the mind, especially the creative mind, grasps reality. This self-analytical project accepts a subject/object and mind/reality divide. A famous ver-sion of this dualism was formulated by the French philosopher René Descartes (1596–1650), and, in the early period, Birchwood opens with an inversion of it. Importantly, however, the novels thematically recog-nize the interdependence of the two sides of the dualism. They acknowl-edge the presence, even precedence, of such a thing as reality alongside describing the mind's grappling with that reality.

As phenomenological exercises in this sense, Banville's books attend to the idealisms of the mind. As books of evidence, they equally set out to keep the exterior world within sight, to exhibit it. In contradiction of the frequent critical supposition that Banville's aesthetic is overwhelm-ingly a postmodernist one, a precise realist motivation is involved here. The basic impulse of all artists, as Banville sees it, is to 'actually portray it as it is ... how it looks, what it feels like to be alive, what it tastes like, how the world smells, what flesh feels like, what clay feels like ... just to get this on paper, to communicate this'.[3] This insistence on the solid-ity of the sensory is far removed from the underlying postmodernist assumption that our predominant contemporary experience of the world is a mediated or virtual one.

Such a plain statement of communicative intent by Banville contradicts any assumption that in his work all faith in language has been lost. While Banville's fiction does deliberately bruise language, this is counterpointed by a faith in specifically literary language. Banville's thematic self-decon-struction of language is a set-up for the ultimate reassertion of the value of words, especially as figured in the art of the novel. His views about the strangeness of the world, and the incapacity of language to dilute this strangeness, form the basis for claiming a supreme value for the evidential exercises of the articulate artist.

At the opening of the Tetralogy, Banville deals with, as he sees it, one of the prime moments in the development of a sense of homelessness in modern man. Copernicus literally and metaphorically decentres mankind when his new science removes planet Earth from the centre of the universe. Such a conceptual shift is accompanied in Banville's treatment by more contemporary reflections on a related decline of faith in language. When, in Copernicus's context, the inherited world-view crumbles, the prime knowledge system of language also breaks down. This 'language theme' in Banville has been well documented. What has not been sufficiently emphasized is what might be termed Banville's geocentric standpoint, his particular commitment to an elemental, if complexly developed, sense of realism.

All the novels draw a comparison between the world's silence and man's seemingly inherent need to talk. Yet they also celebrate the potential triumphs of the imagination as figured in literary language. The nature of the creative imagination is Banville's grandest theme. The theory of the imagination he has developed both inside and outside the work is informed by a strand in post-romantic poetics, mainly as articulated by Rainer Maria Rilke and Wallace Stevens.

The Tetralogy is the main site for the development of the idea of the imagination as man's prime home-making faculty in a strange world. In these four novels, Banville employs science as a paradigm to display his faith in imagination. Banville merely uses the biographies of his scientists as props – in large part, they are adapted from *The Sleepwalkers* (1959) by the Anglo-Hungarian novelist and intellectual Arthur Koestler (1905–83). Consequently, some commentators have overplayed the science-biography aspect. Banville's science is very much quasi-science and is only a means to entirely different ends. His science stories are above all else analogies for the artistic process. This confers on them the status of the *Künstlerroman*, a novel that deals with art and artistry in a general sense. The Tetralogy books are Banville's version of aesthetic autobiography in his early period.

Banville's view of the interrelationship of language and the imagination, and of this relationship as reflected in science, is informed by diverse philosophical and poetical influences. He has had to find very particular ways of accommodating these to the structures of the novel genre. In Banville's sense of its formal promise, the genre can perfectly deliver his views on the way language and imagination work in the world. Paradoxically, he turns the novel into a book of evidence by intentionally complicating its realist modes and by redirecting it towards a pure, self-enclosed or autonomous art.

A vast predicament seems to be involved in reconciling Banville's sense of the exteriority and independence of the object world with his generic view of the novel as a vitally autonomous art form. Various literary categories have been bandied about when attempts have been made to reconcile such opposing tendencies in Banville, primary among them the terms 'romantic' and 'postmodernist'. As we saw in Chapter 1, an investigation of Banville under the broad rubric of modernism can often prove more productive than other categorizations, and here we can develop the application of a term we mentioned then in the context of early modernism. Banville's particular combination of deep linguistic doubt, poetic optimism, imaginative concentration and stringency of generic practice justifies the application to his work of the term *symbolist*. (To avoid outright anachronism, the better term might arguably be *neosymbolist*.) We will see here that a symbolist aesthetic, occasionally adopted from the source and sometimes filtered down through post-symbolist writers, has allowed Banville to solve his philosophical predicaments and establish a productive relationship between the two autonomous realms of world and art.

A CONTEMPTUOUS SILENCE: THE RELATIONS BETWEEN SELF AND WORLD

When he outlined his aesthetic for the first time in article form in 1981, Banville quickly got down to basics: 'We begin with language. The literary artist, like the infant he once was, must learn how to speak in order to assimilate the world.' He compared the writer's linguistic self-consciousness to the formational problems of a child: 'The writer will feel a pang of sympathy for the child struggling among the great stone words that, with baffling arbitrariness, name the things around him ... baby learns the essential lesson, which is to leap the chasm between the name and the thing named — to leap *and not look down*.'[4] The inception of this 'essential lesson' is familiarly outlined at the opening of *Copernicus* in a passage often noted to be reminiscent of the tone of the opening of James Joyce's *A Portrait of the Artist as a Young Man*. The young Copernicus looks out at the world:

> At first it had no name. It was the thing itself, the vivid thing. It was his friend ... It was a part of the world, and yet it was his

friend ... Tree. That was its name. And also: the linden. They were nice words. He had known them a long time before he knew what they meant. They did not mean themselves, they were nothing in themselves, they meant the dancing singing thing outside ... Everything had a name, but although every name was nothing without the thing named, the thing cared nothing for its name, had no need of a name, and was itself only. (p.3)

Banville has spent his entire career looking down philosophically into the chasm between name and the thing named. This has involved a persistent nostalgia for a pre-linguistic innocent perception of the world. The pattern in the novels is for the protagonists or narrators quickly to forget the childish state where the primacy of the external world over the internalizing system of language is naturally acknowledged. Copernicus, for instance, soon forgets about 'these enigmatic matters, and learned to talk as others talked, full of conviction, unquestioningly' (p.4). At some stage in each narrative, there is a recognition of the potentially damaging idealism of language, and this recognition is the premise for a re-examination of the possible relations between name and thing named, between word and object. Crises of language occur so that, even if retrospectively, lessons can be learned. When Gabriel Godkin picks up a book in Birchwood, the words for him lie 'dead in ranks, file beside file of slaughtered music' (p.71). When Copernicus puts his ideas into words, they become 'gross ungainly travesties of the inexpressibly elegant concepts blazing in his brain', and, at the end, he decides that the book he gave his life to writing is useless: 'A hundred thousand words I used ... and yet I said nothing' (pp.49, 235). Kepler cannot communicate the 'speechless uproar in his heart' (p.89). For Swan in Mefisto, the esoteric language of mathematics represents language generally, and the breakdown in his communicative system is especially intense, represented metaphorically as a descent into hell:

Always I had thought of number falling on the chaos of things like frost falling on water, the seething particles tamed and sorted, the crystals locking, the frozen lattice spreading outwards in all directions. I could feel it in my mind, the crunch of things coming to a stop, the creaking stillness, the stunned, white air. But marshal the factors how I might, they would not equate now. Everything

was sway and flow and sudden lurch... I built up walls of number, brick on brick, to keep the pain out. They all fell down.
Equations broke in half, zeros gaped like holes. Always I was left
amid rubble, facing into the dark. (pp.109, 127)

On the one hand, language fails because these principals feel that it
cannot capture the silent sublime notion they individually have of the
meaning of things. More importantly, the equal and opposite force of the
actual, that which refuses to yield its autonomy, breaks in on language.
Banville has the phenomenal world reassert its enigmatic nature for these
idealists who have forgotten the young Copernicus's knowledge that
things have no need of names and exist in and of themselves. From the
outset, Banville has so repeatedly stressed the strangeness of the objective
world that his characters and narrators are portrayed as dizzy in the face
of it. There is a precise illustration of this from the formational period in
one of the interiorized moments of panic in *Long Lankin*. The story is 'A
Death'; the character is Stephen:

The things around him as he looked at them began to seem unreal
in their extreme reality. Everything he touched gave to his fingers
the very essence of itself. The table seemed to vibrate in the grains
of its wood, the steel of the sink was cold and sharp as ice. It was
as if he were looking down from a great height through some
mysterious spiral. In the corner behind the stove a blackthorn stick
leaned against the wall. When he saw it he stepped forward and
put out his fingers to touch it, but halted, frowning. He stared at
the knots, and they seemed to be whirling in the dark wood, each
one a small, closed world. He moved back uncertainly, and
dropped his hand. (pp.32–3)

Resignation and confusion subsequently characterize such experiences in the œuvre. The idea of an ineluctable separation of man from
nature, a petrifying sense of homelessness in face of the physical, is
stressed again and again by Banville in his formational and early periods.
'If only the world would imitate us once in a while', Ben White yearns
in *Nightspawn*: 'That would be something, wouldn't it? But the world
maintains a contemptuous silence.' He observes that 'The wind lifts the
waves, and the waves pound the shore', but feels 'Whatever I did, or

might do, the world went on, with or without me, always, and I was but a small part of an eternal confluence which I could not understand' (pp.102, 223–4). 'I believe the world is here', Canon Wodka advises Copernicus, 'that it exists, and that it is inexplicable' (p.23). The world sometimes afflicts even the more optimistic Kepler and he is assailed by 'all that which is without apparent pattern or shape, but is simply there'. In the process of losing faith in his schemes, he decides that 'we are the flaw in the crystal, the speck of grit which must be ejected from the spinning sphere' (pp.31, 134). In Mefisto, while Swan feels at home with pure mathematics, physical objects prove resistant to his schemes: 'if a sum had solid things in it I balked, like a hamfisted juggler, bobbing and ducking frantically as half-crowns and cabbages, dominoes and six-pences, whizzed out of control around my head' (p.21).

This would continue into the middle period where the narrator of the Trilogy, Freddie Montgomery, is especially articulate on man's apparent alienation from the natural world. One moment from The Book of Evidence stands out in this regard, where Freddie recalls and interprets a dramatic moment from a childhood walk:

> The trees above me swayed and groaned in the wind. Suddenly there was a great quick rushing noise, and the air darkened, and something like a bird's vast wing crashed down around me, thrashing and whipping. It was a branch that had fallen. I was not hurt, yet I could not move, and stood as if stunned, aghast and shaking. The force and swiftness of the thing had appalled me. It was not fright I felt, but a profound sense of shock at how little my presence had mattered. I might have been no more than a flaw in the air. Ground, branch, wind, sky, world, all these were the precise and necessary co-ordinates of the event. Only I was misplaced, only I had no part to play. And nothing cared. (pp.186–7)

And again, in Ghosts, Freddie comments on the world's indifference: 'I mean the way the world does not care about us, about our happiness, or how we suffer, the way it just bides there with uplifted glance, murmuring to itself in a language we shall never understand' (p.65).

In the late period, Cleave's declaration in Eclipse is symptomatic of Banville's enduring attachment to this idea of man's alienation from his surroundings: 'Everything is strange now. The most humdrum phenomena fill me with slow astonishment' (p.52). Thus, within individual novels, and from novel to novel and period to period, the feeling of astonishment towards the external world is relentless.

With a narrator who begins with the phrase 'Words fail me' and who is puzzled by the 'non-complicity' of things in man's affairs, The Newton Letter is perhaps Banville's prime site for working through these issues. Of all the Tetralogy books, this novella deals most concisely with the pervasive crisis of language and in a way that contextualizes this aspect of Banville generally. Here, also, the way out of the predicament of alienation from nature is signalled most clearly in philosophical terms that have deep implications for the aesthetic Banville developed in and after his early period.

An intertextual moment, where Banville directly and extensively uses the work of an earlier writer, has uniformly been identified as the core of The Newton Letter. Returning hesitantly to his abandoned script on Sir Isaac Newton at one stage, the narrator discusses what he calls 'the second, and longer, of those two strange letters to Locke'; this letter, he says, 'seemed to me now to lie at the centre of my work' (p.50). An extensive piece of self-reflexivity on Banville's part, his narrator goes on to quote this letter in italics. In his 'Note' at the end of the novella, Banville reveals the source of his centrepiece: 'The "second" Newton letter to John Locke is a fiction, the tone and some of the text of which is taken from Hugo von Hofmannsthal's Ein Brief ("The Letter of Lord Chandos")'. Hofmannsthal is vital to an understanding of Banville's early period. He first mentioned the Austrian writer in one of his early reviews when dealing with the general predicament of the writer after modernism. He ambivalently commended the deconstructions of language and literature by modern writers and philosophers. To emphasize his point on the wasteland potentially facing the contemporary writer, he turned to a fairly obscure early modernist essay: 'As long ago as 1902, Hofmannsthal in "The Letter of Lord Chandos", a great and neglected testament, set out the problem clearly: language is a fragile scaffolding, held up by faith and little else, and when the rivets go, the whole thing collapses.'[5] Hofmannsthal's essay, written when he was suffering a professional crisis, masquerades as a letter from one Philip, Lord Chandos, to the English philosopher and essayist Francis Bacon (1561–1626), in which he apologizes for his 'complete abandonment of literary activity'.[6]

(Banville's invention of a letter from Newton to the English philosopher John Locke (1632–1704) is thus entirely in keeping with the spirit of Hofmannsthal's original literary ventriloquism.) Hofmannsthal's narrator in the letter sets out to reveal to his addressee 'a peculiarity, a vice, a disease of my mind', a crisis whereby the writer has lost all faith not only in literary language, but in all common language: 'My case, in short, is this: I have lost completely the ability to think or to speak of anything coherently.' For this erstwhile writer and lover of words the sense of desperation is total and resembles existentialist loneliness: 'Single words floated round me; they congealed into eyes which stared at me and into which I was forced to stare back – whirlpools which gave me vertigo and, reeling incessantly, led into the void.'

On one level, there is nothing new in the ideas on language Hofmannsthal proposes here. He is writing in an identifiable post-romantic vein and echoes the crises of poetic language felt by a range of romantic writers. The difference, however, lies in the total despair attached to the modernist variation on the crisis. The Chandos Letter suggests an agonized pessimism about the possibility of ever re-animating language. The implication is that until some kind of ideal language can be found, silence is the only option.

Interpretation of Hofmannsthal's piece is principally a matter of emphasis on one of two sides: on its deconstruction of language, or on the note of hope it intermittently sounds. Essentially, the concern is with the loss of a sense of organic unity between man and nature, between man's language and the object of that language. Lord Chandos looks back with nostalgia on the days when he 'conceived the whole of existence as one great unit: the spiritual and physical worlds seemed to form no contrast … and in all expressions of Nature I felt myself'. His breakdown in language is caused by his due recognition of the separateness of self from the physical world. And, as suggested in the way Banville has his Newton narrator adopt the words of Hofmannsthal, the only way to recover from this breakdown may be to embrace freely the silence of the commonplace or inanimate world of nature and objects.

In reflecting the breakdown, Banville employs the standard romantic awe of nature's power and movement. He pays close attention in his work to the seasons and thus the atmospheric conditions in which his people move. He has described nature as 'that stealthy, innocently garish, tender background that seems always to be in the process of trying to tiptoe away from the impossible going-ons of humankind'.[7] His classic use of this background is identified in the formational period in Nightspawn where Ben White thinks of 'that four-letter word of which Heraclitus was so fond. Things fluctuate, merge, nothing remains still' (p.112). The dominant motif in Banville's use of the idea of flux, this key word from Heraclitus, is spring.

Spring imposes itself with seasonal regularity on most of the narrators, illustrating for them the relentlessness of the natural world. Again in the formational period, in Long Lankin both 'Lovers' and 'The Visit' open in early spring (pp.16, 35). The early period consolidated this aspect: 'Spring has come again, St Brigid's day, right on time', Godkin laments in Birchwood at the end of a story that perpetually mentions spring: 'The harmony of the seasons mocks me' (p.171). 'I feel the spring around me', remarks the Newton narrator at the end: 'the banality of it, the heedless power' (p.80). In the middle period the tendency continued. 'It is spring' is the beginning of Freddie's final paragraph in The Book of Evidence (p.219). It seems that when he returns in Athena Freddie had hoped he might actually be able to impose some kind of mind control on nature: 'yes, spring has come', he says resignedly at the end, 'despite my best efforts' (p.233). As soon as April appears for Maskell in The Untouchable he quickly complains: 'I do not like the springtime' (p.388). There has been no lessening of the fascination with seasonal movement in the late period. April provides the backdrop to the onset of Cleave's breakdown in Eclipse (p.3). And as Quirke wraps things up in the epilogue to Christine Falls (2006), we hear simply, in an echo of Freddie Montgomery: 'It was spring' (p.389).

A point regularly made thematically by Banville, however, is that nature and its Aprils are oppressive only when resisted, and that the solid thereness of nature can provide its own comforts. The point is plaintively put by Rheticus in Copernicus, in a passage repeated with variations, when evaluating Copernicus's theories: 'Beloved Earth! he banished you forever into darkness. And yet, what does it matter? The sky shall be forever blue, and the earth shall forever blossom in spring, and this planet shall forever be the centre of all we know' (p.180). The most obvious manifestation of this more optimistic approach to the natural world is the lyrical portrayal of the rejuvenation of the sensibility in 'De Rerum Natura', the new story Banville added to the second edition of Long Lankin, which he published in 1984 while writing the Tetralogy. In this hymn-like story, On the Nature of Things (De Rerum Natura) by the ancient Latin poet and philosopher Lucretius provides the basic theme of a young man's relearning of the simple delights of a direct sensual involvement with nature. The closing tone is euphoric, the mood contented:

> Glorious weather, days drenched with sun and the singing of larks, a lavender haze over the sweltering meadows ... He spent his time in the garden, tending the roses, the vegetables, the hives. Sometimes he took the hose and sprayed the parched plants, the trees, the earth, and then sat for hours studying the surging life around him, the spiders, the birds and flies, his beloved bees. A swarm of them settled in a corner of the drawing room, under the ceiling. That was fine with him. Life everywhere. (pp.88–9)

This direct embrace of nature and the accompanying motif of the garden would figure strongly in Banville's subsequent middle period (it would be especially interesting to trace related instances in Ghosts and The Untouchable).

The stark opposition of the human rage for order and natural disorder, at least as envisaged by Hofmannsthal and developed by Banville, is a foundational one for symbolist aesthetics. Central to any understanding of this opposition as Banville works with it is a rejection of any simplistic notion of 'art for art's sake'. In a recent introduction written for a new selection of Hofmannsthal's writings, Banville discusses these matters of potential synthesis and union between man and nature. He points out that poetry for Hofmannsthal was 'not ... a secret language known only to a blessed few, but a way of mediating between the life of the spirit and life in the world'. Hofmannsthal's project was 'the melding of the self with the objects of reality'.[8] For Hofmannsthal, and thus for Banville, literary language is elementally functional in finding some sort of accommodation between subject and object, between world and self.

So the intentions of artists, from this point of view, are, or must be, democratic. For a true symbolist, the aim is not to subordinate all exterior moments to the control of an aristocratic interior subjectivity. The recognition is that the world of things does not depend for existence or significance on man's idealizing systems, be it language or otherwise. On the contrary, the symbolist suspects that it is the outside world, as an autonomous entity, that gives man a meaningful context and significance and that can animate his interior faculties. It is therefore more than a pun to suggest that the material world provides the imagination with its material. The imagination realizes that it is far from autonomous with regard to the grounds for creativity.

In this de-privileging of self-regarding subjectivity, the idea of autonomy is challenged. An initial despairing estrangement of art from the phenomenal world ends up in homage to that world. In the kind of symbolism Hofmannsthal encourages, man will discover his true significance not by descending into an obsession with the self but by remaining firmly in the outside world. It is this hopeful emphasis on the regenerating power of external surroundings that Banville takes from the Chandos Letter, rather than the initial attitude of linguistic despair. This is indicated in the narrator's decision at the very end of *The Newton Letter* to return to writing his book.

In the Tetralogy generally there is the same sense of the death of the ideal organic connectedness between man and his natural surroundings which was documented by Hofmannsthal. But there is an equal progression in Banville's narratives, especially those of the Tetralogy, towards the renewed animation the natural world can offer to subjectivity once its essential separateness and autonomy have been sufficiently acknowledged. The final lines of the last instalment of the Tetralogy are exemplary in this. Gabriel Swan in *Mefisto* has an early desire to discover an almost paradisal meaning for things through the higher reaches of mathematics. But he progresses towards what is presented as a positive descent, a simple acceptance that chance may be the governing principle of the universe: 'It will be different this time, I think it will be different. I won't do as I used to, in the old days. No. In future, I will leave things, I will try to leave things, to chance' (p.234). Chance, the uncontrollable principle of phenomena, is the first word in the novel and the last; it is the everything.

MAKING HIMSELF AT HOME: THE PURPOSE OF IMAGINATION

Banville's thematic recognition of the autonomy of man's surroundings does not imply a demotion of the order-making faculty of imagination. The case might be described as a provisional autonomy encountering another definitive autonomy. The decision of the narrator at the end of *The Newton Letter* to 'Begin afresh ... learn how to live up here, in the light', points to his reconstituted sense of purpose for the idealizing systems of the imagination (p.80). Despite the postmodern deconstructions usually attributed to him, Banville's faith in the imagination is absolute. 'Things', he insists, are 'nothing in art until they are passed through the transfiguring fire of the Imagination'.[9] At the conclusion of his first major interview, published when he was in the middle of the Tetralogy, he set out a specific aesthetic stall and quoted a poet who would remain one of his mainstays:

> Whenever I'm asked why I write ... I always think of lines from Rilke's *Duino Elegies* in which he asks are we here just for saying 'jug, tree, possibly pillar, tower?' He says 'but for saying, remember ... oh for such saying as never the things themselves hoped so intensely to be'. That really sums up why people engage in Art. You take something and you give it an intensity which in its own life in the world it doesn't have. Say you describe something very, very well. You really catch it. The thing has a kind of surprised sense. A chair is standing there looking at you saying 'goodness, I never realized that about myself' ... You get [things] so perfectly and so vividly that they exist with an intensity which they didn't have in real life. That is what Art is for.[10]

Rainer Maria Rilke's lyric poetry presents a striking treatment of the nature and function of literary language and its relationship with the imagination. While it would be unfair to accuse Banville of facile imitation, he has used Rilke so extensively to explain his own view of language's relationship with the imagination and art that it would be difficult to draw a line between the total influence of the poet and the use of his work for illustrative purposes. It would be equally difficult to segregate the impact of Rilke from that of Wallace Stevens, who held very similar ideas about literature. Stevens is one of the great modern speculators about the imagination, and by combining some of his theories with Rilke's aesthetics Banville developed his own views on language into an idiosyncratic theory of imagination.

Banville widely used epigraphs and quotations from both these writers in his work of the early period. He first brought them together discursively, however, in 1983. Banville was theorizing on the nature of language as figured in art. 'The nominative', he said, 'is the case of art.

The poet wields the name as the wizard his wand and the statues stir and speak. To name is to cast a spell':

> Further, to name is to lay claim: to assert the community of things. It is our task. Are we here, asks Rilke, just for the saying of names?
>
>> ... but for *saying*, remember,
>> oh, for such saying as never the things themselves
>> hoped so intensely to be.
>
> Mute things have a challenging yet somehow poignant thereness; we have the gift of speech. Wallace Stevens:
>
>> From this the poem springs: that we live in a place
>> That is not our own and, much more, not ourselves
>> And hard it is in spite of blazoned days.
>
> So we say out the names, attempting thus hieratically to assimilate to ourselves all that which is not us.[11]

Though Banville has written little in extended terms on either Rilke or Stevens, he has repeated these quotations and comments, with some variations, in numerous articles, always with relation to this idea of the nominative, man's imaginative assimilation of his surroundings by naming things through language and, at a further level, by artistically describing and appropriating things through *literary* language. One of Banville's more sweeping statements on his intentions as a writer is perhaps the best place to start in investigating the combined influence of these two poets. Art, to his mind, he says, 'has to take the commonplace, the quotidian, and transfigure it into something else'. Here, he explains, he is 'not talking about transcendence or even about pursuit of the sublime ... when reality is pushed through the surface of the imagination it comes out as something very different'. Banville's characteristic view of art's relation to the world, equivalent to the Hofmannsthal view, is evinced here. The imagination transforms the world into art but at the same time it does not seek to transcend that world. A surprising realist motivation informs this sense of balance. 'I value the novel', Banville continued, 'because it can in its way be transcendent, it can in its way be sublime, but always is in touch with reality, with the ground itself':

> I came across a phrase of Wallace Stevens's ... which I felt won-
> derful. He said: The only poverty for an artist is not to live in a
> physical world. And I know exactly what he means ... Even the
> most transcendent artist has to keep feet, literally, on the ground,
> in the mundane, because otherwise his art becomes entirely insu-
> lated and vague, and I like the *solidity* of fiction.[12]

The dominant theme of Stevens's poetry was just this sense of the
autonomous solidity of the real world, the independence of man's surroundings from his consciousness.

While Stevens's sense of the separation of the imagination from its
surroundings was celebratory, Rilke's version is more impassioned and
awestruck, as illustrated in his essay 'Worpswede' (1903), where he outlined many of the ideas that would feed into his *Duino Elegies*, the set of
poems that have proved so essential for Banville:

> It is not the least and is, perhaps, the peculiar value of art, that it is
> the medium in which man and landscape, form and world, meet
> and find one another ... and in the picture, the piece of architec-
> ture, the symphony, in a word, in art, they seem to come together
> in a higher, prophetic truth, to rely upon one another, and it is as
> if, by completing one another, they become that perfect unity,
> which is the very essence of a work of art.
>
> From this point of view the theme and purpose of all art would
> seem to lie in the reconciliation of the Individual and the All ...[13]

The close correspondence between this view of art's mediating function,
and the lines from Stevens quoted above, is patent. For both Rilke and
Stevens, as for Hofmannsthal, literature – all art – springs from man's
need to reconcile himself to the felt distance between his surroundings
and his sense of self. For Banville, so deeply influenced as he has been
by these three literary thinkers, art performs in exactly the same way.
Thereby, the divide between self and world, or word and object, that is
initially a thematic problem for him, is resolved.

In furthering this idea of art as reconciliation of individual and world,
Banville has had recourse to a seemingly opposing idea of art's 'estrangement' effect. In one of his more extended and difficult articles on literary aesthetics, occasioned by James Joyce's work, he had this to say:

Far from allowing us to know things with any immediacy, art, I believe, *makes things strange*. This it does by illuminating things, literally: the making of art is a process in which the artist concentrates on the object with such force, with such ferocity of attention, that the object takes on an unearthly – no, an *earthly* glow … This is not such a mystical, not such a high-falutin process as it may seem, this interiorisation of things, this taking into us of the world, of all that stuff out there that is not ourselves. It happens all the time, continuously, in art. And its result is a different order of understanding, which *allows* the thing its thereness, its outsidedness, its absolute otherness. Such understanding is wholly individualistic, yet profoundly democratic. Every thing has its own place, its own space, which it inhabits utterly.[14]

The democratic phenomenology of art is thus facilitated for Banville by the imagination's active interiorization of the outside world. While recognition of the solid thereness of things is the initial motivation, the 'making strange' that takes place in art's efforts to celebrate that thereness also enacts a necessary transformation. The prime reason he seems fascinated with Rilke is the tension the poet recognized between an approach to creativity which democratically acknowledges the independence of the phenomenal world, and an approach which insists that to be exhibited in art the world must be internalized and transformed.

In Banville's view, this transformation is a deeply rooted human need. Elaborating at one stage on the Rilke lines, he suggested that the artist transforms things first into inwardness and then gives them back to outwardness through style: the artist's speech 'becomes song. Thus he makes a home for us, as Heidegger would say, of and in the world.'[15] Banville in fact owes much of his optimistic sense of language and art, developed out of an initial sense of crisis, to the theories of this German philosopher, Martin Heidegger (1889–1976). Points of comparison could especially be found with Heidegger's major essay on aesthetics, 'The Origin of the Work of Art' (1960). This is somewhat organically determined for Banville because Heidegger allowed that his work was all a philosophical translation of the ideas Rilke had already expressed in poetry.

For Heidegger, and by extension for Banville, the appeal of Rilke is the poet's offer of a complete solution to the decline of traditional metaphysical explanations of man's existence. In the scenario of man's perceived existential homelessness on the earth, Heidegger believed Rilke to have propounded the useful idea of art as what we might call a domesticating force. According to Heidegger, it is poetry that 'first causes dwelling to be dwelling. Poetry is what really lets us dwell ... Poetry does not fly above and surmount the earth in order to escape it and hover over it. Poetry is what first brings man onto the earth, making him belong to it, and thus brings him into dwelling.'[16] Though Banville has never discussed Heidegger at length in the context of his work, there are signs that Heidegger's mystical philosophy has had significant influence on his theory of the imagination. A passage in one of his major articles of his middle period, where he makes explicit use of the term 'phenomenology', clearly echoes Heidegger:

> Even the most abstract art is grounded in the mundane ... Life will keep breaking in. However, 'life' here means life in its *appearance*, that is, both in the way it looks, and in the way it makes itself manifest in the world. The phenomenological breath that wafts from that sentence makes me think that the word I should be using in this context is not *life*, but *being*, or even − I whisper it − Being.[17]

This mystic side of phenomenology points up a preference for a benign rather than aggressive variety of nominalism. A benign nominalism neither merely itemizes phenomena in an effort to obliterate the idealizing imagination, nor does it accept that the object should be swallowed whole by the subjective sensibility. It therefore presents Banville with a workable resolution of the combined philosophical predicaments of not feeling at home amid his natural surroundings, while also not wishing simply to deny these surroundings by retreating into an autonomous interiority. Encouraged by the theories of Hofmannsthal, Stevens, Rilke and Heidegger, he can pay deference to exterior phenomena, both in his aesthetics and thematically within the work, without capitulating to the vertigo of silence felt by his narrative counterparts in the face of the natural world. His sense of the central role of imagination and art aims for the home-making terrestrial salvation of existential man.

IDEAS OF ORDER: THE SCIENCE PARADIGM

As with phenomenology's simultaneous attention to the processes of consciousness and the objects of consciousness, there is wide scope in benign nominalism for aesthetic self-examination. The lives and work of Banville's narrators and protagonists in the Tetralogy can in part be taken as direct analogies of the self-regarding imagination. Stevens, says Banville, is

> constantly coming back to this notion that the imagination is the real power of the world. And this is what Copernicus and Kepler were saying: it is not the world 'out there' that matters, it's the world 'in here', it's what I make of it, it's what we make of the world by the power of imagination, the way that we mould the world into our own image. That's what's powerful.[18]

It is Banville's work with the theme of imagination, rather than his elements of minor postmodernist narrative trickery, that forms the vital self-reflexive side of his art.

Self-reflexive fiction that performs as a kind of parable about writing, or art in general, has a venerable history in the tradition of the Künstlerroman with its artist figures and themes. The chief function of the artist figures that Banville includes in his Tetralogy is to provide him with the opportunity for a brand of aesthetic autobiography. As fictions about the very notion of knowledge, Copernicus and Kepler have sometimes been associated with other contemporary novels, by authors such as Toni Morrison, Salman Rushdie, D.M. Thomas and Thomas Pynchon, which challenge older ideas about the primacy of scientific knowledge and which investigate the role language can play in the exercise of power. There are two problems with placing Banville in the context of this kind of fiction. While his novels do examine the nature of language and knowledge, they do not have the same legislative thrust with regard to the deconstruction of power relations as these and other novelists usually mentioned by way of comparison. Most importantly, it would be plain mistakenness to suggest that Banville in any way 'challenges' science. The 'hidden theme' of the Tetralogy, he has insisted, is 'the similarity between the workings of the artistic mind and the scientific mind; indeed, I sometimes feel that one could substitute the word "identity" for "similarity"'.[19] Banville's aim has always been to show the affinities and interdependencies of the scientific and poetic faculties, not to show them in any kind of antagonistic light.

Ever since the Enlightenment of the eighteenth century, it has been argued that mankind operates within two distinct cultures: that of science and that of 'poetry' as taken to denote man's imaginative products generally. Widespread disagreement between romantic writers and utilitarian philosophers in the early nineteenth century about the relative value of fact and fiction was later followed in the Victorian period by frequently heated debates about the relationship between science, literature and culture generally. The twentieth century took up the discussion under the heading of the 'two cultures' debate, and so it has continued, sometimes dismissively, sometimes constructively, to the present day. Some of Banville's articles have underlined his active fascination with related scientific matters. While professional scientists would no doubt see his general strategy of levelling the stark distinction between science and imaginative activity as a lowering of the discourse of science rather than an elevation of that of literature, he has persistently, and sometimes avidly, applied himself to a resolution of the two-cultures divide.

Even when *Copernicus* was still in its early stages of composition, Banville had already decided that 'Science, like art, merely constructs a paradigm of reality', and he succinctly announced the affinity between scientific and artistic genius: 'The equation $E=MC^2$ is in its way as beautiful and fascinating a feat of human intellect as *Hamlet*.'[20] Similarly, discussing in his middle period the work of the most widely read of contemporary physicists, Stephen Hawking, he argued that 'Modern physics is one of the most beautiful, moving and poetic enterprises man has ever devised.'[21] This amalgamation of art and science vocabularies by Banville has sometimes been criticized as an eccentric misreading of the nature of contemporary science, particularly of physics. He takes considerable poetic licence with his layman's theories and he has sometimes presented them outside of the bounds of his fiction.

But to demand that Banville respect the specialized definitions and vocabularies of scientific disciplines would be to miss the point. Verifiability and accuracy of interpretation are not necessary concerns when a creative writer assimilates, consciously or unconsciously, a philosophy or a theory or any form of academic knowledge. Arguably, it is the strength of individual misinterpretation of these things that distinguishes an author's vision and style. This should be extended to Banville's inter-pretations of science and scientists since, as suggested by his 'Acknowledgements' in Copernicus, he has never aimed for academically correct depictions of his scientists and is aware that 'factual errors' and 'questionable interpretations', whether 'willed or otherwise', appear in the books.

The scientists of Banville's Tetralogy provide structures for the writ-ing of a kind of collective Künstlerroman. They are, especially, a way of avoiding the more hackneyed postmodern devices that writers have employed to reflect self-consciously on their own processes. The Tetralogy, says Banville, was a way of writing about the creative process 'without writing about a man who is writing a book, about a man who is writing a book, about a man who is writing a book'. It was 'a way of looking at the artistic process from a different angle, because I regard people like Copernicus and Kepler as artists'. These scientists' schemes of fitting the phenomena to their forms rather than vice versa, he avers, is 'a perfect analogy for the artistic process'.[22]

Banville sees the imaginative identity between his scientists and all artists as lying in a mutual search for a sense of order. Two of his major non-review articles have provided important elaborations on this idea. The first is 'Physics and Fiction: Order from Chaos', which was pub-lished in the New York Times in 1985 when he was still writing the Tetralogy.[23] In this article, he specifically dealt with the fiction/physics axis and incorporated a version of a famous theory, the Uncertainty or Indeterminacy Principle, formulated by the German physicist Werner Heisenberg (1901–76), a theory which would later be directly discussed in the late period in Eclipse (p.103). Banville began with a phrase from a book entitled The Nature of the Physical World (1928) by Sir Arthur Eddington (1882–1944), the same phrase he had included amid other related quotes in Copernicus: 'Science aims at constructing a world which shall be symbolic of the world of commonplace experience' (p.208).

As Banville was aware, the scientific community of the 1980s would not have lent much credence to Eddington's views, firmly rooted as these were in the Renaissance tradition of Natural Philosophy. Through an acknowledgement of the rapid twentieth-century changes in science however, Banville managed to level the field between fiction and physics:

'The dream of certainty, of arriving at a simple, elegant, and above all concrete answer, has had to be abandoned. Experiments now produce not "yes" or "no", but a sort of drift of possibilities.' The relationship between science and literature has, at least in the modern age, been uneasy, and it seems that 'Finding itself in the same lifeboat as science has not made the novel any more accommodating toward its cold companion.'

From his commentary and the examples from fiction he mentions in this article, what Banville appears to have always wanted in science novels is not any kind of detailed scientific content, but rather a portrayal of the cerebral efforts of science and a recognition of the affinities between such efforts and all artistic endeavours of the imagination. His more combative remarks came towards the end of 'Physics and Fiction', and were designed to establish the identical powerlessness of science and fiction in certain circumstances. Rejecting the idea that science can successfully 'interfere' with things, he turned to Heidegger's 'The Origin of the Work of Art' and quoted:

> Color shines and wants only to shine. When we analyze it in rational terms by measuring its wavelengths, it is gone. It shows itself only when it remains undiscovered and unexplained. Earth thus shatters every attempt to penetrate into it. It causes every merely calculating importunity upon it to turn into a destruction.

Banville affirmed the philosopher's central views about the inscrutability of the phenomenal world and worked these into the points he was try-ing to make himself about fiction's relationship with physics:

> It is a statement, with a moral extension, as it were, of Heisenberg's principle of indeterminacy, which, put simply, says that we cannot investigate darkness by bathing it in light – a seemingly innocent observation, but one which, in the world of atomic physics, has enormous consequences. Surely not only the scientific, but the artistic mind as well, will find such ideas exciting. For the scientist, the significance of indeterminacy will consist in the nature of the limitations it imposes. For the artist, the interest will be esthetic.

This is the appropriate philosophical accompaniment to Banville's belief that the world is unexplainable, that we can be presented with evidence but no transcendent meaning.

Banville had recourse in 'Physics and Fiction' to Wallace Stevens in arguing that the situation Heidegger describes need not be desperate. With typical anthropological sweep, Banville argued that

> somewhere in our head or heart, there exists another version, a separate reality, which has shape and significance, which we think of as some sort of truth, and which is endowed with a beginning, a middle and an end. It is the desire to see this inward reality made manifest in the world that gives rise to what Wallace Stevens calls our 'rage for order'. Amid disintegration we yearn for synthesis.

He built his illustration around 'Anecdote of the Jar', one of Stevens's key poems on 'synthesis':

> In art, the only absolute criterion is shape, form, ratio, harmony, call it what you will. Call it order ...This is what art does, or seeks to do: impose a synthetic order upon the chaos ... The word synthetic perhaps requires definition. I intend it to mean not *false*, *artificial*, but, as the dictionary says, 'of, pertaining to, consisting in, combination of parts into a whole; constructive'. A principle even so severe and seemingly negative as Heisenberg's law of indeterminacy seems to offer, in its simplicity, in its calmness, above all in its beauty, a means of imposing order upon the wilderness.

Banville concluded 'Physics and Fiction' with a statement that might particularly rankle with scientists. As science 'moves away from the search for blank certainties', he said, it takes on 'more and more the character of poetic metaphor, and since fiction is moving, however sluggishly, in the same direction, perhaps a certain seepage between the two streams is inevitable'.

In a more recent article, Banville has sought to clarify his attraction to analogies between science and fiction. Though he had left the Tetralogy far behind and was moving into his late period, the highly regarded *Science Magazine* published his article on science as metaphor, entitled 'Beauty, Charm and Strangeness', in 1998.[24] Banville began on this occasion in the knowledge that his is a thesis 'which, were they to take note of it, the academies would decry as scandalous':

> My thesis is that modern science, particularly physics, is being forced, under pressure of its own advances, to acknowledge that the truths it offers are true not in an absolute but in a poetic sense, that its laws are contingent, that its facts are a kind of metaphor. Of course, art and science are fundamentally different in their methods, and in their ends. The doing of science involves a level of rigor unattainable to art. A scientific hypothesis can be proven – or, perhaps more important-ly, *disproven* – but a poem, a picture, or a piece of music, cannot. Yet in their *origins* art and science are remarkably similar.

Essentially, Banville believes that science (which he makes a point of dis-tinguishing from 'Technology') has as its impetus the same appropriative desire as all art towards our surroundings: 'The human race cannot abide nature's indifference, and uses the physical sciences to attempt to wring from it a word of acknowledgement.' It seems that scientists too must agree to Banville's consistently held view of the inscrutability of the world: 'to my mind the world has no meaning. It simply *is*. Leibniz's thrilling question, "Why is there something rather than nothing?" is significant not because an answer to it is possible, but because out of the blind, boiling chaos that is the world, a species should have emerged that is capable of posing such a question.'

Through the reference here to the famously elemental philosophical question posed by the German philosopher Gottfried Leibniz (1646–1716), the crux of Banville's view of science is that to him it is simply a variant manifestation of man's general need for order. The key similarity between art and science lies in their mutual, endlessly ongoing nature: 'This is a truth that both clear-sighted artists and scientists – that is, those not blinded by hubris, or a cramped imagination, or both – have always acknowledged: There is no end to the venture.' It seems that science is 'not *making*' a new landscape, but '*discovering* it'. There is more than enough here to disturb the pure scientist, but it should be pointed out that Banville's argument is mainly reflective of his depiction of the frequent hubris of his scientists and narrators in the Tetralogy. As with his sense of history, the endeavours of art and science move in eternally ongoing circles.

After Banville bluntly suggests that at the level of metaphor 'art and science are both blithely inutile', his conclusion via yet another reference to his beloved lines from Rilke and Stevens is almost inevitable:

The critic Frank Kermode has argued, persuasively, I believe, that one of art's greatest attractions is that it offers 'the sense of an ending'. The sense of completeness that is projected by the work of art is to be found nowhere else in our lives. We cannot remember our birth, and we shall not know our death; in between is the ramshackle circus of our days and doings. But in a poem, a picture, or a sonata, the curve is completed. This is the triumph of form. It is a deception, but one that we desire, and require.

Banville has never wavered from this conception of the psychiatric function of form. This is his own conception of why he became a writer. Equally, it is a conception discussed thematically in his work, and the Tetralogy is its grandest figuration. Usually built around his quotations from Stevens and Rilke, this definition of the humanizing purpose of art has continued to motivate his work after the Tetralogy. Going by his views in 'Beauty, Charm and Strangeness', all artists are embarked on the one project: 'to subject mundane reality to such intense, passionate, and unblinking scrutiny that it becomes transformed into something rich and strange while yet remaining solidly, stolidly, itself. Is the project of pure science any different?' The answer is that the task of both is the nominative and the evidential: 'Art and science are alike in their quest to reveal the world.'

THE NOVEL AS ONE OF THE FINE ARTS

Banville's thoughts about the interrelationship of science and art are vital to an understanding of the design of the Tetralogy novels as analogies for the creative process and purpose. His related general sense of all order-making endeavours of the human mind has further relevance to his aesthetic of the novel. Banville's attraction to Kepler, for instance, lay in 'the fact that he was prepared to say, "I'm wrong"'. Kepler worked for nine years on the orbit of Mars: 'He worked and worked and worked, and filled folio after folio of calculations, and one morning he woke up and said, "No, that's all wrong. I've got to start again."' The point about this was 'the intellectual excitement. Most people would say, "What a tragedy! What a disaster! Nine years of work gone for nothing." Kepler rubbed his hands and said, "Now we start really working."'[25]

This amounts to an evocation of the work ethic Banville brings to his chosen genre of the novel. A grand image of this applied ethic was famously proposed by the French novelist Gustave Flaubert. Picture the ideal writer: permanently dissatisfied with his work, sweating over single words and sentences, searching for the right words, constantly beginning again. In this scenario, the novel, at least in Banville's hope for it as form-making and language-making deployed at their finest, becomes the ultimate order-making tool of man. Banville suggests that 'Novels give us the sense of a closed world ... we want to impose a notion of order on this open-ended world that we exist in ... certainly what I want is order.'[26]

Having completed a conventional apprenticeship with a volume of stories, Banville has, as regards fiction, devoted himself almost exclusively to the novel. By his early period he was already suggesting that, compared to the novel, the story is 'an easy form'. Though a 'splendid' form, with 'a far higher success rate than the novel', it would, he argued, 'be foolish to expect to derive from short stories the same satisfaction to be had in the novel'.[27] As he developed in his early period, he demonstrated an intense concern with the general future direction of his chosen genre. In part, this involved a version of the standard call from bright young novelists of the time that the English novel needed to cast off its Victorian baggage: 'The novel up to now has been concerned primarily with manners and morals, but it has ... gone as far along that road as it is possible or profitable to go, and must change or die.'[28]

He continued into his middle period to be somewhat dramatic on this: 'I think the novel is now coming into a position like the early Christians: we'll have to go back into the catacombs and hide for a while and be, at the very best, a minority sport and at the worst a kind of persecuted religion.' To be driven underground, however, would be a good thing for the genre it seems: while poetry will continue to be important, the novel 'will become an anachronistic thing that strange people do, in sealed rooms. I think that would be quite good for it.'[29]

Banville has sometimes been ambivalent in explaining his sense of the value of the novel genre. He esteems the novel, he says, because although it is firmly rooted in reality and the physical world, it can also be 'transcendent' and 'sublime'. Yet, he also distrusts the genre because as a form of writing it can be both 'vulgar' and 'shambling'.[30] This is a

genuinely felt ambivalence and Banville has repeatedly provided variations on such comments: 'I'm being honest when I say that I really don't
like fiction as a form. I'm lumbered with it, I can't do anything else. I find
it rather clumsy and rather constricting ... no, not constricting: it's too
loose. There's too much freedom in fiction. I find the freedom of fiction
constricting.'[31] Clearly it is not the idea of the novel itself he dislikes so
much as the great tradition of the sprawling novel handed down by the
nineteenth century. Banville's determination, though humorously delivered, has nonetheless always been sincerely motivated: 'My modest
ambition in life is to change the novel entirely!'[32]

The inherited idea of the novel as formally free and endlessly extend-
able is Banville's main cause of annoyance in this regard. From the
beginning, he tended to be particularly suspicious of cultish American
novelists who have been overly influenced, he says, by the poet Walt
Whitman (1819–92), an 'undisciplined scribbler' and 'the worst thing
that ever happened to American literature'. He has instead campaigned
for what he takes to be an equal and opposite school of disciplined writing as represented by the relatively short novel *The Great Gatsby* (1925) by
F. Scott Fitzgerald (1896–1940). This, in his view, is the 'only real
American masterpiece of this century'.[33] He has continued to campaign
for the *Gatsby* school of the novel and his reason is precise: 'from the
point of view of a novelist, one is struck by the firmness and unity of
tone ... Tap the book at any point and the note that comes back will be
perfectly harmonious ... This is less a novel than a lyric poem, for it has
the delicacy and the iron hardness of poetry.'[34]

The lyrical and controlled aesthetic of the novel for Banville begins
with Henry James. Despite his recollection of coming late to James, by
the early period the admiration had well set in. He became sufficiently
enamoured of the James style to write a full-scale screen adaptation of
The Spoils of Poynton (1897), though the project never came to fruition. The
mark of a great novelist like James, says Banville, is that 'he teaches us
how to read, trains us, as it were, to perceive the particular and unique
rhythm of his thought and style'. With James 'the lesson is hard, but
once we have learned it from the master we can never again look at the
novel form without, unconsciously perhaps, measuring it against the
yardstick of his achievement'.[35] For Banville, James is, above all other
novelists, a 'pure artist'. In turning the novel into 'an immensely subtle,

dense and poetic art form', James has proved to be 'the greatest novelist who has ever lived'.[36] James was largely responsible for turning the genre into a high art form (it can be assumed that Banville means here the genre in English):

> I suppose the novelist, the pure novelist that I admire most of all is Henry James ... James, it seems to me, really was a pivotal figure in that he took the nineteenth-century novel, a novel which was becoming more and more realistic, more and more like documentary, more and more journalistic, and said: let's see if we can make a polished artefact out of this form, and he did ... I admire James so much because he transcended the form.[37]

In James's case, length, it seems, is not an issue: *The Portrait of a Lady* (1881), a long narrative by any account, is 'as near to perfect as the novel form is ever likely to get'.[38]

Considered the father of novel criticism, James carried over into the English-speaking world the nineteenth-century French preoccupation, especially as exhibited by Flaubert, with transforming prose into a poetic form. James was especially close to Flaubert in his rejection of romantic inspirationalism and his emphasis on form and craft. This theory of fiction stresses the organic nature of perfected art. 'A novel is a living thing, all one and continuous, like any other organism', James argued in his major essay on the genre, 'The Art of Fiction' (1884), and 'in proportion as it lives will it be found ... that in each of the parts there is something of each of the other parts'.[39] This aesthetic of the novel reverses the traditional conception and insists that form is more vital than content. In affirming that in art subject hardly matters, Banville has often lamented the fact that Flaubert is sometimes reviled for his wish to write about nothing. Flaubert, in Banville's view, was simply suggesting that all art surely aspires to the condition of a pure style. The central passage on this idea is from a Flaubert letter of 1852:

> What I find beautiful, what I'd like to do, is a book about nothing, a book with no external attachment, which would hold together by the internal strength of its style ... a book that would have almost no subject at all or at least one in which the subject would be almost invisible, if that were possible. The most beautiful works

are those with the least matter ... I believe that the future of Art lies in this direction ... one could almost establish it as an axiom that, from the point of view of pure Art, there is no such thing as a subject, style being solely in itself an absolute way of seeing things.[40]

With his concentration on the sentence, followed by the paragraph, as the primary units of composition, Banville's aesthetic bears considerable comparison. 'To someone like me who can labor for an entire morning over a sentence, still doing that Joycean, Flaubertian thing', he has quipped, 'it's remarkable to see someone like a Philip Roth or a Saul Bellow just letting fly ... I don't see how English as we use it in Europe can be revivified. It's like Latin must have been in about AD 300, tired and used up. All one can do is press very hard stylistically to make it glow.'[41] This stylistic assault on novelistic prose has direct compositional implications. Banville sees the first paragraphs of his novels as especially vital: 'It's very important, the first paragraph of a novel, because what you're doing is teaching the reader how to read. You're saying to the reader: Look, this is not a story you're going to rattle through. You've got to stop. You've got to read this in a different way.'[42] As an apt illustration, he has often likened the first paragraph of his novels to the effect of the large ornate letters at the top of pages of medieval manuscripts such as the Book of Kells.

Particularly intense rewriting of the initial stages of the novels is demonstrated in all Banville's manuscripts from his early period. At the opening of an abandoned novel, The Song of the Earth, for instance, the same first paragraph is rewritten twenty-seven times before any progress is made, with variations, erasures, reductions, and sometimes only single words changed. Even when he had begun to divert in this notebook towards writing the material that would eventually become Copernicus, the first paragraph is again recomposed twelve times. A third attempt at a beginning took sixteen redrafts. Every time a new section is begun, the same pattern is evident: numerous revisions are carried out before moving on. By his own admission, Banville has often spent months writing the first paragraphs of his novels, and a humorous exasperation with his own exacting standards is captured in one of his notes to himself in this notebook: 'It has taken 3 months to write 2 paragraphs, one of which might or might not stand. At this rate we shall be here for centuries.'[43]

The similarity between Banville's compositional approach and the writing of poetry is clear. Banville thinks of himself as something between a novelist and a poet because what he really wants to do in the novel genre is produce work with the same levels of texture and linguistic concentration as poetry. He has always wanted, in effect, to create a more opaque variety of stylized novel that will demand the same total attention as a poem. He likes to think of the novels he produces out of this commitment to the high crafting of paragraphs as sonnet sequences, and The Newton Letter is one of the high-points of this prose-poetry. Banville is well aware that this intended poeticizing of the novel potentially runs contrary to the general perception of the vital freedom of the genre, and he allows that 'maybe the novel shouldn't be turned into something that could have the same density and concentration that poetry strives for'. His commitment is absolute nevertheless: 'But I'm not interested in writing anything else.'[44]

It is a quintessentially symbolist move to pronounce on the value of literary art by reference primarily to the quotient of work expended on perfecting it as a lyrical entity. In the history of the genre, a lyrical conception of the novel has always been available as an alternative to other earlier forms like the adventure novel, the novel of manners and the mystery novel. The lyrical novel draws at least as much attention to its own formal design as to its content. The lyrical novelist's transformation of the realist fictional world through a poetic sensibility, through highly controlled language and imagery, mark him off as a symbolist. While there are vast differences between Banville's typographically traditional forms and the often extreme rearrangements of the page in historical symbolism, some root similarities are perceptible. Speaking of one of the major symbolist novels, Petersburg (1913) by the Russian author Andrei Bely (1880–1934), and of symbolist writing generally, Banville commented in the midst of writing the Tetralogy that art is not 'about' reality as such but 'about ways of looking, of comprehending, of making reality comprehensible'. He suggested that the 'symbolist project', which had sought these ways with particular determination, had somehow remained incomplete.[45] Any contemporary investigation of whether that symbolist project has been completed or otherwise, via the novel genre at least, would properly have to take considerable account of Banville.

Symbolism tended to see as a major but productive problem the tension between the two seemingly autonomous realms of the imagination and its surroundings. The prime symbolist solution for combining the imagination's capacity to embody a world with the realization that the actual world does not depend on the imagination's projections was to resort to the paradigm of music. The Tetralogy period, in retrospect, is clearly when Banville was working out many of the related issues. 'I do not equate poetry with imprecision', he said when he was halfway through the Tetralogy. 'What I am trying to communicate is the notion of a language in which sense is often subordinate to sound, in which meaning is shaped and directed by patterns immanent in the words themselves. Mallarmé would have understood.'[46]

The reference here to Stéphane Mallarmé, the French poet who might be termed the high priest of symbolism, is all the more notable for its singularity. Though this seems to be the only mention Banville has made of this particular literary mentor in his self-examining articles, certain mutual ideas can be identified. In his reaction against naturalism, the version of realism which insisted that literature should clinically record life in minute detail, Mallarmé concentrated on the evocation of private moods through highly personalized symbols and wanted all writing to strive towards the condition of music. He propagated, in a development of ideas already present in Flaubert, an absolute version of the hermetic and aristocratic interpretation of the artist's stature. Mallarmé went so far as to argue that the literary word, if deployed at full intensity, could even surpass music:

> [We] are now precisely at the moment of seeking, before that breaking up of the large rhythms of literature, and their scattering in articulate, almost instrumental, nervous waves, an art which shall complete the transposition, into the Book, of the symphony, or simply recapture our own: for, it is not in elementary sonorities of brass, strings, wood, unquestionably, but in the intellectual word at its utmost, that, fully and evidently, we should find, drawing to itself all the correspondences of the universe, the supreme Music.[47]

The paradigm of music is bound to accompany the aristocratic idea of the artist because it is the most easily autonomous art form. It can avoid the imperative of reference and any potential divide between form and content. Banville has frequently used musical structures in his work. He has described the second section of *Copernicus*, for example, as an analogue of musical theme and variation. As with his general dedication to the Flaubert imperative of extreme craft, the import of the aesthetic model of music for his work is most obvious in the compositional context. Trying to find an individual novelistic style after the success of his stories, Banville chose in his formational period to progress through the music paradigm. The second draft of 'Blood', the work-in-progress that would become *Nightspawn*, contains this typed endnote: 'A sentence, that line let fall into the black mysteries of silence, can be built just as melody is built, note upon note.' And certain notes to himself revealed an already robust conviction that to ask what a work of literature means may be as foolish as to ask what a symphony means.[48]

The notebook where the aesthetic of the early period was worked out is also crucial here. One note runs: 'Instead of "connections" in a literary sense, one can have "harmonies" – although not to get carried away by it – ignorance of musical theory helps. i.e. instead of the notion of a linear plot, can substitute fugal themes, theme-and-variations, rondos etc. All this, of course, in the spirit of music – the laws cannot be applied to prose, foolish to think they can.'[49] The title of the uncollected story, 'Rondo' (1977), is an obvious gesture to this general compositional law.

This belief in the *spirit* of music in prose (as opposed to any rigid application of the precise laws of music in the devising of novels) combines Banville's sense of the existential home-making function of literary art with his dedication to style above content. Using his familiar lines from Rilke as support, he argued during the early period that the artist intent on transfiguring phenomena through the imagination gives things 'back to outwardness' through style: '*Gesang ist Dasein*.'[50] This German phrase ('Song is existence') was Rilke's poetic motto, and it also encapsulates Banville's sense of the appropriate relations between the external world of phenomena in which man needs to feel at home and, on the other hand, the interiorizing force of mellifluous words.

The symbolist aesthetic thus provides for Banville's wish to present in the lyrical novel the evidence of the world. A curiously ambiguous but profound realism is at stake here. In the absence of any traditional adherence to the directly mimetic function of the novel, a complex and philosophically intense idea is developed of the artistic mind's relation with the exterior life it seeks to describe. The idea, as in symbolism, is that the more particularized and individualized the language the artist gives to an object, the more he might succeed in communicating its actuality, its 'thereness'. Simply put, nouns can perform only in a very basic manner unless they are surrounded by illustrative and beautifully arranged adjectives and adverbs. So rather than just attempt a basic reflection of the real, symbolist writing such as Banville's attempts to create or conjure up a complex *sensation* of the real in the sensibility of the reader.

This peculiarly formalist version of realism is what Banville has in mind when he refers to his novels as his books of evidence. Formalist realism, as he sees it, is vital in making man at home in his potentially absurd and meaningless surroundings, and it is his enduring compositional and, importantly, thematic preoccupation. The continued urgency, as he sees it, of the symbolist writer's dedication to evoking a sensation of the real through lyrical language is perfectly reflected within the work of his late period in *Eclipse* where Cleave has a heightened sense of responsibility, a heightened awareness of his surroundings, at the time of his daughter's death. 'All these things I noted with avid attention', he says: 'as if a record of them must be kept, for evidence, and the task of preserving them had fallen to me' (pp.193–4).

NOTES

1. David Hanly, 'Interview with John Banville', *Bookside: Writer in Profile* (RTÉ television, 1992).
2. Harry McGee, 'Freddie's Back as Banville Grapples with Alien Planet', *Sunday Press* (28 March 1993).
3. Melvyn Bragg, 'John Banville', *The South Bank Show* (LWT/Ulster Television, 1993).
4. John Banville, 'A Talk', *Irish University Review*, 11, 1 (Spring 1981), p.13.
5. John Banville, 'It Is Only a Novel', *Hibernia* (11 November 1977), p.23.
6. All references to 'The Letter of Lord Chandos' are from Hugo von Hofmannsthal, *Selected Prose*, trans. Mary Hottinger et al., intro. Hermann Broch (New York: Pantheon, 1952), pp.129–41.
7. John Banville, 'Travelling Light in Foreign Parts', *Irish Times* (9 October 1993).
8. John Banville, 'Introduction', in Hugo von Hofmannsthal, *The Lord Chandos Letter and Other Writings*, selected and trans. Joel Rotenberg (New York: NYRB, 2005), p.viii.
9. John Banville, 'Winners', *New York Review of Books*, 38, 19 (21 November 1991), p.27.

10. M.P. Hederman and R. Kearney (eds), 'Novelists on the Novel: Ronan Sheehan Talks to John Banville and Francis Stuart' (1979), in *The Crane Bag Book of Irish Studies* (1977–1981) (Dublin: Blackwater Press, 1982), p.416.

11. John Banville, 'Place Names: The Place', in *Ireland and the Arts* (special issue of *The Literary Review*), ed. Tim Pat Coogan (Dublin: Namara Press, 1983), p.63.

12. Hanly, 'Interview with John Banville'.

13. Rainer Maria Rilke, *Where Silence Reigns: Selected Prose*, trans. G. Craig Houston, foreword Denise Levertov (New York: New Directions, 1978), pp.9, 10.

14. John Banville, 'Survivors of Joyce', in *James Joyce: The Artist and the Labyrinth*, ed. Augustine Martin (London: Ryan Publishing, 1990), p.78 (emphasis in original).

15. John Banville, 'Silent in Several Languages', *Sunday Tribune* (16 October 1983).

16. Martin Heidegger, *Poetry, Language, Thought*, trans. Albert Hofstadter (New York: Harper & Row, 1971), pp.215, 218.

17. John Banville, 'Making Little Monsters Walk', in *The Agony and the Ego: The Art and Strategy of Fiction Writing Explored*, ed. Clare Boylan (London: Penguin, 1993), p.109.

18. Bragg, 'John Banville'.

19. Rüdiger Imhof, 'Q. and A. with John Banville', *Irish Literary Supplement*, 6, 1 (1987), p.13.

20. John Banville, 'Essays into Sanity,' *Hibernia* (2 November 1973), p.16.

21. John Banville, 'Master of the Universe', *Irish Times* (1 February 1992).

22. Hanly, 'Interview with John Banville'.

23. All references are to John Banville, 'Physics and Fiction: Order from Chaos', *New York Times Book Review* (21 April 1985), pp.1, 41–2.

24. All references are to John Banville, 'Beauty, Charm and Strangeness: Science as Metaphor', *Science Magazine*, 281, 5373 (3 July 1998), pp.40–1.

25. Clíodhna Ní Anluain (ed.), 'John Banville', in *Reading the Future: Irish Writers in Conversation with Mike Murphy* (Dublin: Lilliput Press, 2000), p.30.

26. Bragg, 'John Banville'.

27. John Banville, 'A Sense of Proportion', *Hibernia* (30 January 1976), p.26.

28. John Banville, 'Heavenly Alchemy', *Hibernia* (4 February 1977), p.28.

29. Bragg, 'John Banville'.

30. Hanly, 'Interview with John Banville'.

31. Mike Murphy, 'John Banville', *The Arts Show* (RTÉ radio) (8 February 1995).

32. Joe Jackson, 'Hitler, Stalin, Bob Dylan, Roddy Doyle ... and Me', *Hot Press*, 18, 19 (5 October 1994), p.16.

33. John Banville, 'An American Monster', *Hibernia* (14 December 1973), p.22.

34. John Banville, paperback review of *The Great Gatsby*, *Irish Times* (8 May 1991).

35. John Banville, 'Monument to H.J.', *Hibernia* (27 January 1978), p.24.

36. John Banville, 'The Master and the Madness of Art', *Irish Times* (9 January 1993).

37. Hanly, 'Interview with John Banville'.

38. John Banville, Article on favourite books of 1991, *Irish Times* (30 November 1991).

39. Henry James, *The Critical Muse: Selected Literary Criticism*, ed. and intro. Roger Gard (London: Penguin, 1987), p.196.

40. Gustave Flaubert, *Selected Letters*, trans. and intro. Geoffrey Wall (London: Penguin, 1997), pp.170–1.

41. Richard Bernstein, 'Once More Admired than Bought, a Writer Finally Basks in Success', *New York Times Book Review* (15 May 1990), p.13.

42. Hanly, 'Interview with John Banville'.

43. Ms. 10252.4.6. Notebook for *Doctor Copernicus*, with drafts of *The Song of the Earth*, an abandoned novel.

44. Fintan O'Toole, 'Stepping into the Limelight – and the Chaos', *Irish Times* (21 October 1989).

45. John Banville, 'Masterfully Manic', *Sunday Tribune* (20 November 1983).

46. Banville, 'A Talk', p.14.

47. Quoted in Arthur Symons, *The Symbolist Movement in Literature*, intro. Richard Ellmann (New York: E.P. Dutton, 1958), p.73.

48. Ms. 10252.2.3. Draft of *Blood* [*Nightspawn*].

49. Ms. 10252.4.6.

50. Banville, 'Silent in Several Languages'.

CHAPTER FIVE

Scenes of Crime: The Trilogy and Banville's Moral Fictions

Banville is a resolute high modernist in his insistence since his formational period that literature, if it is to warrant the status of art, must necessarily be locked off from the interrelated domains of direct self-expression, politics, ethics and social commentary. The separation of the aesthetic from other orders of discourse has often seemed total in his critical writings and articles. Yet the essentially humanist aesthetic at the heart of the work has involved a continuous and increasingly deft return to themes that are moral in an immanent and vital sense.

One of the chief triumphs in Banville's maturation as a novelist has been to internally examine, as he has gone along, the implications of his staunch aesthetic credo. Inside and outside the work, he has usefully complicated the simplified dichotomy between art's asserted autonomy and the exterior world in a way that has a distinctly theological import. The position of autonomous art in Banville represents the position of the existentially free individual in modernity. His emphasis during the years of writing the Tetralogy was clearly on the idea of the purity of art, on the rigid separation of form and content especially. Yet the intermittently moralistic concerns of those four books materialized into the outright thematics of good and evil of the Trilogy. This in turn developed in the novels of the late period, particularly in *Shroud* and *The Sea*, towards attention to the fundamental question of what to do with the knowledge of death.

Banville has a grand conception of man's fall from transcendent order. 'In our arrogance', he says, 'we long ago – perhaps as long ago as Eden – lost sight of our true place in the natural order.' Hence man's cruelty to himself and others: 'As a result, we range across the world, destroying and polluting as we go, the most dangerous species the world has ever known.' As support, he concurs with Friedrich Nietzsche's view that 'the animals regard man as a creature of their own kind which has in a highly dangerous fashion lost its healthy animal reason – as the mad animal, as the laughing animal, as the weeping animal, as the unhappy animal'.[1] In Banville's middle period, this perception of the loss of man's 'natural' primeval place in the order of things involves a resort to the specifically existentialist notion of the ethics of authenticity. He has, for instance, remarked that *Ghosts* is about a man 'who is yearning for ordinary life, a man who has lost everything … In that sense you could call it an existentialist novel, if that term weren't so debased.'[2]

In his middle and late periods, Banville's people are 'all playing at being themselves. Since my so-called scientific books, my characters have all been people who are trying to discover some kind of authenticity.'[3] This in itself is reflective of the human condition: 'All my characters are people who wear masks. Human beings wear masks all the time … This is not a discovery that I've made, it's as old as Freud at the very least, it's as old as Henry James. The masked man is the man. Man is masked.'[4] He uses the extended metaphor of the profession he gives Cleave in *Eclipse* to emphasize inauthenticity in his other principals: 'All my people are actors.'[5] This theme of authenticity is allied to Banville's general preoccupation with ideas of order. All his books, he says, are 'about people who are obsessed, who have what Wallace Stevens called "a rage for order" … I saw a certain pathetic beauty in their [his scientists'] obsessive search for a way to be in the world, in their existentialist search for something that would be authentic.'[6] Banville did not set out in the subsequent Trilogy to write 'about' a murderer as such, but had in mind 'identifiable themes and ideas, which however loose and vague as artistic themes and ideas always are, could perhaps be grouped under the general heading, *The Search for Authenticity*'.[7]

The problem of authenticity has figured in the œuvre mainly through the idea and problem of evil. Even in his first works, Banville displayed an interest in the related subjects of violence, viciousness, transgression and immorality. He has frequently voiced a negative, though not exactly cynical, view of humanity and its potential for destruction. In his middle period, he turned his attention to the specific act of murder, thus thematically crystallizing the pervasive, though often seemingly indiscriminate, atmosphere of menace in the earlier books.

Two approaches to transgression are crucial here. One is primarily existential, the other aesthetic. The figure of the outcast or criminal has often been taken in theories of literature to be an enactment of the meta-physical homelessness of man. Criminal and insane acts can be seen to betray an unawareness of, or a disbelief in, the social and/or religious regulation of behaviour. In some kinds of writing, however, we find criminal behaviour idealized, making transgression less a reflection of the general state of man than an element of aesthetic distinction *between* men. In the tradition of purist literary aestheticism, to which Banville's work and aesthetics belong at least in part, there is generally an ethos of dis-tance. The figure of the boastful aesthete asserts the separation of his high taste from the lowly everyday concerns of the scorned commonality. The argument runs like this: Because the aesthete can process experience at a more deeply conscious level, he can be allowed to countenance trans-gression of one kind or another as a pretext for especially deep experi-ence and a subsequent deep self-reflection. He is regulated, not by con-ventional morality, but by individual high taste.

Both approaches to transgression are combined by Banville in Freddie Montgomery of the Trilogy, slightly less so in Victor Maskell of *The Untouchable*, and with a new socio-political intensity in Axel Vander of *Shroud*.

In *The Book of Evidence* Freddie, the well-educated but dissolute middle-aged narrator, has needlessly bludgeoned a young woman to death with a hammer, and now, in the present of writing, he mulls over his crime in his prison cell. Appearing under different guises in the following two books, the newly released Freddie probes the possibilities for reparation in *Ghosts* and, after a first failure, achieves in *Athena* a kind of settlement with his conscience.

Freddie's inaugural story in *The Book of Evidence* constitutes the most forceful of Banville's moral narratives since it is here an actual murder is detailed and it is here that he is most patently set up as an almost textbook existentialist anti-hero, complete with a bored personality driven only by a search for a creditable authenticity. With a distinguished literary and philosophical lineage as a type, Freddie is honed for the probing of received post-romantic ideas about the individual's entitlement to his own private ethics of being and authenticity. Freddie appears to be Banville's quintessential creation since he has been more than usually revealing about this literary murderer's conception and function. Freddie does enjoy individuality as a narrator, but he principally serves to represent a character type to which Banville is permanently attracted: characters, as he has described them, who are 'in despair, who are desperate ... People who have reached the end of their tether'.[8] Freddie, faced as he is with the realization that morality is an invention rather than a divine ordinance, is an impressive version of this fascination of Banville's with humanity in extremis.

The problem of finding a method of coping with the void that opens up in human relations once the transcendental system of values has at least notionally collapsed is an intense variation on the opposition of chaos and form that was Banville's philosophical and stylistic concern in the Tetralogy. The direct analogy in those four books between the activities of intellectuals seeking explanatory metanarratives, and the activity, at Banville's own level, of the author devising his own system through literary narrative, is carried through into the Trilogy. The imagination is brought low in The Book of Evidence, to a depth that is all the more profound for its polar opposition to the stellar heights reached by the Tetralogy's theories of creativity. The Trilogy, in contrast to the Tetralogy, and to its own theme of painting which we will examine in the next chapter, is on this level a kind of negative analogical device to point up the potential irresponsibilities involved in the idealism of the artistic imagination.

Banville's ethics of authenticity directly implicate the figure of the representative artist. Artists especially, he feels, have 'manufactured themselves ... I think artists are all self-made.'[9] This self-making is on one hand portrayed as necessary in the work, particularly in light of Banville's increasing use, in the middle and late periods, of Friedrich Nietzsche's insistence that life is only justifiable as an aesthetic phenomenon. Yet, while they could hardly be said to be simple moral fables, the novels of Banville's middle and late periods tell of the inattentiveness that can result from both a certain excess, as well as lack of, imagination. Banville's principals of his recent novels are an illustration of the possibility that unreconstructed aestheticism can prepare the way for barbarism of the soul.

While Banville's preoccupation with extreme transgression appears newly fledged in The Book of Evidence, an interest in the subject was evident in his earliest work. The cerebral coldness of the typical Banville narrator or principal is easily noticed. Less immediately noticeable is the frequency with which, even before the middle and late phases, such coldness was predicted by a tenacious and much less intellectualized variety of viciousness.

One of the effects of Banville's almost complete adoption of the first-person confessional narrator in and after his first novel (*Kepler*, *Copernicus* and his Benjamin Black novels are the only exceptions) is an underlining of the singularity and mysterious air of his first volume, *Long Lankin*. Once the tone of *Birchwood* is taken up again in *The Newton Letter* and *Mefisto*, his narrators become increasingly intense in their quest for elucidation through their own autobiographies. They explain much, despite their characteristic stumbling and prevarication. In the uniformly third-person stories of *Long Lankin*, however, little is explained. The volume has the powerful effect of opacity Banville likes in fiction, but this is achieved in an equal and opposite fashion to the intellectualism and baroque prose of all the subsequent books. These bare, elemental stories are ritualized variations on a single structure, the origin of which has mythic import. The collection's title and thematic unity is taken from an old English–Scottish folk legend and ballad called 'Long Lankin' which, as glossed by the histrionic Jacob in the book's novella, 'The Possessed', was a reworking of the superstition that a leper could be cured if he caught the blood of a murdered victim in a silver cup (1st edn, pp.132–4, 174–5). In this tale, Long Lankin, a mason intent on avenging a refusal of payment for work, murders his Lord's child, quickly moving on to the Lady of the castle:

> My lady came down, she was thinking no harm
> Long Lankin stood ready to catch her in his arm.
> Here's blood in the kitchen. Here's blood in the hall.
> Here's blood in the parlour where my lady did fall.[10]

Informed by this embodiment of cruelty and evil, these related stories are the rawest and eeriest figuration of the obsession with transgression, guilt and angst present in all Banville's fiction. They establish the recurring atmosphere in his fiction of isolation, desolation and barely controlled horror.

Each story has a scenario with two principals whose relationship, as Banville has explained, is radically destroyed or shaken by the presence of an interloping Long Lankin-type character. These interlopers are often mere shadowy presences in the stories and the mood of creeping violence does not depend on them exclusively. Horse, the feral 'strange wild creature' of the initial and most powerful story, 'Wild Wood', is Banville's first and rough-hewn archetypal transgressor, a kind of ur-outsider. Accompanied by 'sounds of destruction', with an axe dangerously wielded, Horse lives threateningly outside of the firelight of his companions. 'You're getting dangerous with that hatchet', one of the boys complains, 'Some day you'll go rightly off your nut and brain somebody'; and it soon emerges, via a mysterious 'queer guy' who does not appear in the story proper, that 'there was a woman killed in town last night. Her head was battered in' (pp.9–15).

The imagery of blood, bone and death in 'Wild Wood' is carried through, though to less effect, in the rest of the collection. 'Admit that everywhere you look is desolation' demands the crazed interloper figure of 'A Death': 'The hand of a spurned god has touched the world and still we ignore it. I tell you, that same hand will touch us with only death' (p.29). In 'Nightwind' the interloper is a murderer, on the run in the background, who has killed his girlfriend and hangs himself before he is apprehended. In 'Summer Voices' two children find a rotting corpse washed up on a beach, and in 'Island' a woman decides she is 'too innocent' for her lover because she has never killed anyone (p.80). Equally, in one of Banville's unpublished stories from this early period, 'Sea Sequence', a bloody ending is provided in a scene where a hand is skewered to a table with a knife.[11]

In the first edition of Long Lankin, all these disturbing savage elements are developed in the more philosophically inclined novella, 'The Possessed', though incompletely and to an extent that displaces the threatening elemental effects of the preceding stories. This may in part explain Banville's omission of the novella from the second edition in 1984. Flora, the narrator's sister in 'The Possessed', plays the part of the lady victim of the Long Lankin ballad, though she is in the end only metaphorically killed. This piece's ineffectively fey obsessions with 'beautiful pain' and 'sweet torment', with 'rituals of guilt and atonement', comprise a spooky parable of existentialist psychology rather than a cohesive narrative (1st edn, pp.159, 167, 176). The whole thing serves mainly as an elongated variation on some sub-themes of good and evil gleaned from The Devils, or, in other translations, The Possessed (1872), by the Russian novelist, Fyodor Dostoyevsky (1821–81), a major name in the history of fiction about transgression.

Banville's novella is also a kind of illustration of his epigraph, taken from the closing lines of The Immoralist (1902) by the French novelist André Gide (1869–1951). The epigraph reads: 'Take me away from here and give me some reason for living. I have none left. I have freed myself. That may be. But what does it signify? This objectless liberty is a burden to me.' The peculiar conjunction of transgression, ennui and freedom in Gide's novel would figure heavily in Banville's subsequent work: in Copernicus where Gide's line is paraphrased (p.58), and especially in the Trilogy where Gide's exclamation resurfaces to tremendous effect (Ghosts, p.195). The specific act of notional existentialist freedom that Banville would come to refine is already, if awkwardly, identified at this early stage. Ben White, the chief 'unhuman creature' of 'The Possessed', who is distinctly reminiscent of the overwhelmed squirmers in Franz Kafka's fiction, twice whines a variation of Gide's line: 'I thought I could get away but they followed me. They brought me back. Always they bring you back to where you started. Like a murderer. A murderer is what they want to make of you. Kill and you will be free they whisper. Free. I want to be free' (1st edn, pp.108, 142).

When White reappears as the narrator of Nightspawn, the potential reso-nance of the demand for psychological freedom is temporarily cancelled, ridiculed rather than developed. It is as if Banville recognized that in its unformulated state at that time the subject was potentially a dead end. He seemed to realize this at the compositional stage. In an earlier form, Nightspawn was entitled 'Blood', and at one point in the drafting a hand-written note simultaneously points up both the bloody design and the humorous sense that this design was perhaps not quite working: 'Infused from here on with copious quantities of blood, and a few spare ribs or bone; a little marrow'.[12] Nevertheless, when Nightspawn eventually emerged from 'Blood' the elemental notion of the absolute freedom from the com-monplace world of man and his morality reappeared in mythic form in White's relaying of a variation on the story of Cain and Abel wherein Cain is given Gide's line, 'And what shall I do with freedom?' (p.49).

The biblical story's illustration of the idea of man's dual nature, and the refusal to condemn his potentially evil side that is part of Banville's version, proves vital to various manifestations of the dualistic nature of man in his subsequent work. As with the parody in Nightspawn of the thriller elements of shootings and killings amidst a coup d'état in Greece, however, any seriousness the subject of transgression had in 'The Possessed' is dissolved in the determinedly deconstructive fictional spoof that is the encompassing programme of this novel.

His interest in an intangible sense of evil, malignity and melancholia having been established by his first two books, Banville abandoned for the time being any attempt at a cohesive fleshing-out of this subject in convincing dramatic situations. While extreme violence pervades Birchwood, it emanates, as we have seen in Chapter 3, from very specific matters of troubled Irish politics and history. And though the Tetralogy investigates the involvement of inscrutable demonic forces in man's scientific and intellectual activity, a renewed and thorough examination of good and evil, and their relative provisions for transcendental freedom, would have to await the descent of Freddie Montgomery in The Book of Evidence.

FAITH IN NOTHING: BANVILLE AND RELIGION

Banville's early thematics of blood-spilling foundered once he moved away from the generally symbolic method of his stories, and it languished in the indiscriminate decadence of 'The Possessed' and Nightspawn. This was because it was then more a matter of the unformulated literary influence of such writers as Gide and Dostoyevsky than an element assimilated into some kind of organic vision or philosophy. The continued importance of certain bookish presences in Banville's imaginative disposition towards the world needs no reiteration; intertextuality is one of the most noted aspects of his work and thought. Less frequently remarked is the general impact his reflections on extra-literary factors might have had on the world-view that came to inform his philosophical fictions.

It has often been argued that in literature a writer's philosophy has primacy, that an attitude to the world determines style and subject rather than the other way round, as some subsequent linguistic theories might suggest. Banville's eventual return to the subjects of evil and transgression, where his earliest versions would be replaced by a vigorous examination of the ethics of authenticity, is intimately connected with an identifiable philosophic ferment. Political and historical sensitivities he is usually not granted are involved here. Having outlined the problem with the 'social morbidity' of modernism, and commending certain books that he described as 'parables of evil', Banville referred in his early period to a 'dark strain of sentimental evil which runs throughout history, never itself fully surfacing but pushing up to represent its real and all too visible monsters'.[13] An abiding interest in the damage wreaked by the Second World War, particularly its psychological implications, is reflected in the considerable number of reviews and articles he wrote during his early and middle periods on authors who had experienced it first-hand.

In this context, Banville has particularly recommended the work of the German-Jewish poet Paul Celan (1920–70). For an anthology of poetry in his middle period he chose – if not quite as a 'favourite' work, then as a cherished 'beautiful' poem – Celan's devastatingly negative piece called 'Psalm' (1963). This short poem is a despairing religious declamation with a total emphasis on nihilism and nothingness. It begins:

> No one moulds us again out of earth and clay,
> no one conjures our dust.
> No one.

While Celan's intense, involuted style would in any case recommend his poetry to Banville, such an ironic prayer to a dead God proves resonant to him as a distillation of a quintessential existential attitude that is mindful of, and even directly motivated by, actual events (Celan's parents were victims of the Holocaust).[14]

The idea that God is dead, or has been replaced by a malevolent opposite, as in the 'spurned god' of 'A Death', recurs with striking regularity in the middle and late periods. The god in one of the paintings in *Athena*, for instance, is 'not our Father who is in Heaven, our guardian in the clouds; this is the *deus invidus* who kills our children, more Thanatos than Zeus Soter' (p.130). With its seemingly direct autobiographical access to the young Banville growing up in Wexford in the 1950s, *The Sea* is frequently good on this God: 'As a boy I was quite religious. Not devout, only compulsive. The God I venerated was Yahweh, destroyer of worlds, not gentle Jesus meek and mild. The Godhead for me was menace, and I responded with fear and its inevitable concomitant, guilt' (p.119). This inverse theology is a vital motivational factor in Banville's design for his narrators and principals. The search for 'supreme fictions' which lies at the heart of the Tetralogy is a direct response to the idea that intellectual man, faced with a chaotic and formless world unassuaged by transcendental belief, has to create his own order through feats of imagination. His interest in Copernicus was in large part directed by the familiar but resounding fact that it was this scientist who exploded the earth-centred comprehension of the universe, thus undermining contemporaneous Christian dogma and largely ushering in the Renaissance rethinking of divine order. While the subject of science is most obviously employed as the Tetralogy's paradigm for imaginative acts generally, the relationship between scientific endeavour and the death of belief and essential humanity is foremost in Banville's construction of his scientists as modern existential heroes. Copernicus's agonized predicament encapsulates this: 'It was not the sufferings of the maimed and dead that pained him, but the very absence of that pain ... he felt nothing, nothing, and this emptiness horrified him' (p.44). As the historian of The Newton Letter reports it, Newton's petrification after all his papers are burnt in a fire is caused not by this immediate empirical loss but by the thought of 'the simple fact that it doesn't matter': 'Newton's mouth opens and a word like a stone falls out: Nothing ... The fire, or whatever the real conflagration was, had shown him something terrible and lovely, like flame itself. Nothing. The word reverberates. He broods on it as on some magic emblem' (pp.22–3).

This version of Newton is informed directly by one of the major figures of existentialist fiction, Roquentin, the narrator of Nausea (1938) by Sartre. The philosophical ideas of absurdism and nothingness which Sartre employed in his novel are clearly echoed by Banville and he takes some lines almost verbatim from Roquentin's mouth to close his own narrator's story. The Newton historian's final rhetorical lines read: 'Shall I have to go off again, leaving my research, my book and everything else unfinished? Shall I awake in a few months, in a few years, broken and deceived, in the midst of new ruins?' (p.81). Roquentin's equivalent sentences read: 'Shall I have to go away again, leaving everything behind – my research, my book? Shall I awake in a few months, a few years, exhausted, disappointed, in the midst of fresh ruins?'[15]

The nameless crisis Freddie suffers in The Book of Evidence is a direct development of the general existential crisis of the Newton historian. In one of his most revealing essays on his own work, with the Mosaic title 'Thou Shalt Not Kill', Banville compares Freddie's predicament to the complaint of Hofmannsthal's Lord Chandos: '"My case, in short, is this: that I have utterly lost the ability to think or speak coherently about anything at all." My Freddie Montgomery can think, yes, and he can speak – by golly, how he can speak – but what is gone is coherence. Meaning has fallen out of his life like the bottom falling out of a bucket.' As illustrative quotation, Banville chooses what he considers the 'central moment' where Freddie has a near epiphany on the way back from his Spanish island:

> A washed-blue dawn was breaking in Madrid. I stopped outside the station and watched a flock of birds wheeling and tumbling at an immense height, and, the strangest thing, a gust of euphoria, or something like euphoria, swept through me, making me tremble, and bringing tears to my eyes. It was from lack of sleep, I suppose, and the effect of the high, thin air ... I was at a turning point, you will tell me, just there the future forked for me and I took the wrong path without noticing – that's what you'll tell me, isn't it, you, who must have meaning in everything, who lust after meaning, your palms sticky and your faces on fire! But calm, Frederick, calm. Forgive me this outburst, your honour. It is just that I do not believe such moments mean anything – or any other moments, for that matter. They have significance, apparently. They may even have value of some sort. But they do not mean anything.
> There now, I have declared my faith. (pp.23–4)[16]

This is Freddie's sweeping paradoxical belief: nothing has meaning. In keeping with the paradox, matters of belief are not merely dispensed with in or after Freddie's profession of negative faith. Philosophical rumination on nothingness and the absence of transcendent meaning develops into pronounced theological speculation. Recollecting his embarkation for his penitential isle in Ghosts, Freddie, now an ex-prisoner, abruptly diverts to one of his many prolonged asides, this time on God. This amounts to a testament of the deflated belief system that underlay his earlier criminal behaviour:

> Have I mentioned My Search For God? Every lifer sooner or later
> sets out on that quest ... I am glad to say I managed to hold out
> for what I consider was a creditably long time. I had never really
> thought about religion and all that; this world had always been
> enough of a mystery for me without my needing to invent implau-
> sible hereafters ... True, I had, and have still, off and on, a hazy
> sort of half belief in some general force, a supreme malignancy in
> operation behind the apparent chaos and contingency of the
> world. There are times, indeed, when I even entertain the notion
> of a personal deity, a God out of the old books, He that laughs, the
> *deus ridens* ... In time, of course, I lapsed from my faith in this
> prankster God, preferring to believe in the Great Nothing instead,
> which when you think about it is itself a kind of force. (pp. 192–3)

The capitalization of Freddie's 'Search For God' is intended to have a dramatic effect by way of acknowledgement that such a search is potentially
stereotypical in desire as well as hackneyed in phrase. However, Banville
then has Freddie come as near to outright sincere prostration as any of
his narrators ever gets. Though the impact is a little diluted by the fact
that Freddie is now somewhat removed in space and time, this related
moment is one of the more moving passages of his three narratives:

> However, the moment came one impossible night in prison when
> I felt so far from everything, so lost in fear and anguish, that I
> found myself reaching out, like an abandoned baby reaching out
> its arms beseechingly from the cold cot, for someone or some-
> thing to comfort me, to save me from these horrors. There was no
> one there, of course, or not for me, anyway. It was like coming to
> in the dark on the battlefield amid the cries and the flying cannon-
> smoke and feeling around for a limb that had been shot off. I had
> never known a blackness so vast and deep as that which my grop-
> ing soul encountered that night. Almost as bad as the emptiness,
> though, was the fact of the need itself, that bleeding stump I could
> not bring myself to touch. (pp. 193–4)

As we saw in Chapter 1, the view of art as spilt religion lies at the
base of Banville's convictions on the function of the imagination.
Equally, however, there are some traceable ways in which the question

of religiosity has led to the adoption of specific lines of thought in the work itself. It is a platitude that once the basic tenets and oppositions of religion (good/bad; heaven/hell; God/Satan) have been posited, they cannot be easily erased as a regulative mode of seeing the world. In the same way that the autonomous aesthetic is an equal and opposite reaction to a perceived oppression from the outside, such oppositions may often be at their most powerful when strenuously questioned. It would be tempting here to invite in a psychoanalyst, catechism in hand, for a suppression session with Banville in the hope of revelations on his lapsed Catholicism and its consequences for his preoccupation with the idea of nothingness and moral vacuum. However, while Banville's upbringing as an Irish Catholic, even if sidelined by him subsequently, has surely left its solid residues – sifted through in Birchwood and The Newton Letter in the early period, and in Eclipse, Shroud and The Sea more recently – his treatment of guilt and redemption is also informed by philosophical and literary thought beyond that of any particular doctrine.

In an Irish Times article in 1998 (as unexpected at the time as his 1996 article about hurling) on the Catholic holy day of Good Friday, Banville testified in passing to the lasting impression made on him by the Vulgate masses of his childhood. He was almost nostalgic: 'I can vividly recall the Good Friday rites of my childhood, the shrouded statues, the sombre vestments of the priests … above all, I remember the awe-inspiring solemnity of the Latin texts bidding the faithful to kneel before the spectacle of the slain god.' The combination of aesthetics and spirituality in these rites is seen in terms worthy of the effusions of any nineteenth-century French aesthete lapsed from Catholicism: 'In the voice of the purple-clad priests … we fancied we could hear the cries of anguish at the foot of the cross, the rolling of thunder across the sky above the hill of Calvary, the terrible sound of the veil of the temple being rent.'[17] Alongside this admission of the lasting impression made on him by Irish Catholicism, Banville simultaneously reprofessed, as it were, his lapsed Christianity, mainly by reference to Nietzsche and his book The Anti-Christ (1895). This was an unsurprising move given Nietzsche's role as a philosophical reference point for secular opposition to Christianity; nonetheless, the move was sufficiently stark in its implications to provoke the venting of religious ire in subsequent letters to the Irish Times.

While Banville's view that the lapse of religion is pandemic cannot really be credited in view of present world circumstances, his generalizations are indicative of the intensity of his own convictions. The religious–areligious dialectic of his work is closely tied to certain damning interpretations of the nature of man and man's recent history. We live, he claims, 'in a post-religious age and I think that, historically, the turning point came during the Second World War. At that time people thought to themselves "if this kind of thing can happen and we can bring ourselves to the very edge of destruction in the most savage ways then the notion of a personal God is absurd". Religion died at that point.'[18]

These assertions that religious belief is impossible or redundant in the face of mankind's monstrous behaviour have been relentless in Banville's middle and late periods. Reading some work by the Polish existentialist writer Witold Gombrowicz (1904–69) in the year before The Book of Evidence was published, he was impressed by Gombrowicz's interpretation of The Rebel (1951), the classic high-existentialist work on man's revolt against the idea of God by Sartre's compatriot, Albert Camus (1913–60). Banville quoted Gombrowicz: 'I kill because you kill. You and he and all of you torture, therefore I torture. I killed him because you would have killed me if I had not. Such is the grammar of our time … We do not commit evil because we have destroyed God in ourselves, but because God and even Satan are unimportant if a deed is sanctioned by another man.' Banville's agreement came in the form of a 'Just so'.[19] His elaborations on this quick assent have been dramatic: 'I do really believe that we are absolute killers. We will destroy anything, including ourselves … we are the most dangerous thing that ever appeared on the face of the earth, if not the most dangerous thing in the universe. If we could destroy other worlds we would do it.'[20] One of the passages in his fiction that Banville has admitted to be self-expressive is a reflection of this view of human nature. Sailing for Ireland from Holyhead in The Book of Evidence, 'not entirely sober' and feeling like 'some lost, suffering wayfarer', Freddie ruminates on the strangeness of the world in his 'I have never really got used to being on this earth' passage. His own answer to his question about whether the ones who were actually meant for planet earth instead of humans are out there somewhere as baffled and homesick as we are concludes with a crucial emphasis: 'How could they survive, these gentle earthlings, in a world that was made to contain *us*?' (pp.26–7).

It is in Freddie's exculpatory interests to move from I to this *us*, to give the impression that his misdemeanours are merely part of a larger frame of monstrousness perpetrated by a whole species. But it would be a mistake to view his entire confession in the light of his prevarications. On one level Freddie is a highly individual creation, and on another a specific type derived from a range of precursory characters. On a further level, however, he is intended as a kind of representative figure, an Everyman *in extremis*. He is guilty because Banville believes this is essentially the human condition. This is perhaps the most challenging task undertaken by Banville in his entire career: the simultaneous probing of Freddie's disbelief in any transcendental moral order and of his seemingly contradictory belief that the burden of guilt must be confronted in the wake of specific transgression. And this probing is carried out mindful of what Banville calls the 'most terrifying discovery' in life: 'that we are free'.[21] Despite the hauteur of its uniform tone, the Trilogy is a deeply felt charting of that discovery.

MURDERERS AND FANCY PROSE STYLES: SETTING THE TONE IN
THE BOOK OF EVIDENCE

In the essay 'Thou Shalt Not Kill', Banville has provided some detail on his specific intent in devising Freddie Montgomery and the Trilogy. He reproduces the first few notes for *The Book of Evidence*, from April 1986. The three major jottings read:

> Browning's 'tender murderer'?

> 'There are no moral phenomena at all, only a moral interpretation of phenomena' – Nietzsche, *Beyond Good and Evil*.

> *Is it wrong to kill people?* [underlined twice]

A knowledge of both the literary type of the 'tender' murderer and of the import of the related second and third notes is vital to any understanding of what Banville intends in his characterization of Freddie. To Banville's own mind, the 'real origin' of the book, the 'real gleam in the progenitor's eye', was just that 'simple-seeming question: *Is it wrong to kill people?'*[22] This is Banville's strongest and most rigorously worked moral theme to date. He relentlessly re-emphasized it in and after the time the Trilogy was written, and identified the role Freddie takes on as a test-case for humanity generally: '"Is it wrong to kill people?" Assume there is no religion, there are no morals, there is no police force … is it actually wrong to kill other people? We have devised all these wonderful ethical systems, yet we still slaughter.'[23]

The parallels between Banville's Freddie and a real-life Irish murderer named Malcolm Macarthur are at this stage well known.[24] Of greater concern to Banville than Freddie's counterpart in real life were his numerous literary forebears. 'I was worried', Banville remembered afterwards, 'that The Book of Evidence would have echoes of other things … I did worry that I would be hackneyed … I mean, it is a hackneyed old story, but there is Freddie's voice and Freddie's style. If it has originality, that's where it lies.'[25] While Banville does sustain his usual careful balancing-act of combining intertextual imitations with a striking originality of character and treatment, a quick listing of the works and literary figures that inform Freddie's 'hackneyed old story' affirms his status as an 'emblematic figure':

> I did not attempt to create what book reviewers would call an 'original' character – there are, as we all know, no original characters. This one had a particularly luxuriant family tree, with many an odd bird squawking among its branches. Dostoyevsky's Underground Man is perched there, of course, sometimes in his own words (he figures darkly in that notebook of mine …). The narrator of Sartre's La Nausée flexes a blue-black wing, and Camus' Meursault is heard every so often to sound a weary note. Nabokov's Humbert Humbert flashes like a firebird. Oh, there is a whole aviary here: Goethe's Werther. Buchner's Wozzeck. Kleist's Judge Adam. Wilde's Dorian Gray. Musil's brutish killer Moosbrugger … and many, many more … Count Dracula is another of his forebears.[26]

These admitted presences can be placed in order, or at least itemized, in terms of their degree of importance for the thematics of murder. The equally intense idealization of a woman in Goethe's *The Sorrows of Young Werther* (1774) and idolization of painting in Oscar Wilde's *The Picture of*

Dorian Gray (1890–91) are closely interrelated cerebral acts in the context of Freddie's three narratives, and are important for Banville's interlocked treatment of painting and women. Judge Adam is from *The Broken Jug* (1811), the first of the three plays by Heinrich von Kleist that Banville has adapted. While Adam is a character who flouts the proprieties of morality and the procedures of law, he is more roguish than villainous and might thus be assumed to be mainly a shadow behind the more serious moral dimension of the Trilogy – he provides instead, perhaps, the resignedly comic view Freddie sometimes takes of his predicament.

The short play *Woyzeck* (1836–7), by the German dramatist Georg Büchner (1813–37), is maybe a more vital dramatic influence on Freddie's formation. Based on a true case of a crime of passion committed by the eponymous Woyzeck, this play concerns, at its thematic base, the question of whether or not man possesses free will in his actions, of whether inner compulsion can be controlled. The resultant quandary for the concept of accountability has obvious parallels with Freddie's situation in the Trilogy. Woyzeck as a character, however, is also only a shadowy presence behind Freddie, whose constructed personality is far more complex than in Büchner's bare outline for his original.

Moosbrugger is the sadistic sex killer in the multi-volume modernist novel *The Man Without Qualities* (1930–43) by the Austrian writer Robert Musil (1880–1942). Banville had expressed qualified admiration for this sprawling work in his early period, ten years before the appearance of Freddie. He pinpointed the character of Moosbrugger as one of its more admirable facets and quoted a line he later echoed in his 'Thou Shalt Not Kill' article: 'If mankind could dream collectively, it would dream Moosbrugger.'[27] Yet again, the close interaction, sometimes immediate and sometimes delayed, between Banville's own reading and the types of fiction he creates, is illustrated here. Walking in the crowded streets fresh from his murder, Freddie betrays an awareness of his new status: 'I saw myself, bobbing head and shoulders above them, disguised, solitary, nursing my huge secret. I was their unrecognised and their unacknowledged dream – I was their Moosbrugger' (*Book of Evidence*, p.163).

The more important influences indicated by Banville are those writers usually considered to be in the existentialist stream of fiction (Sartre, but particularly, in this case, Dostoyevsky and Camus), the Gothic tradition

(Dracula is accompanied in the Trilogy by a host of other similar presences), and Vladimir Nabokov, with whose *Lolita* Banville's novel would bear close comparison. These writers, works and characters are, on the level that Banville borrows from them, all in an identifiable tradition of criminal writing that goes back at least to romanticism. Banville self-consciously places Freddie in the lineage of a particular character type. This is more than a matter of the usual intertextual play that Banville likes to engage in and is inseparable from the fashion in which he works out the implications of his question 'Is it wrong to kill people?'

A distinct aesthetics of murder emerged in the literary and philosophical scene of romanticism in the late eighteenth and early nineteenth centuries. The general romantic fascination with grand mythical and literary transgressive figures (Prometheus, Satan, Cain, Faustus) became combined with the notional liberation of the aesthetic from other orders of knowledge by many eighteenth-century philosophers. This resulted in precise speculations on the suitability for art of the subject of outright immorality. A classic speculation of the type in English is 'On Murder Considered as One of the Fine Arts' (1827) by Thomas De Quincey (1785–1859) where, in a discussion of both actual and literary murders, it is ironically proposed that 'Enough has been given to morality; now comes the turn of Taste and the Fine Arts ... We dry up our tears, and have the satisfaction perhaps to discover, that a transaction, which, morally considered, was shocking ... when tried by principles of Taste, turns out to be a very meritorious performance.' De Quincey was particularly convinced of the satiric possibilities within the conviction that morality had no place in aesthetic concerns: 'Virtue has had her day; and henceforward, *Vertu* and Connoisseurship have leave to provide for themselves.'[28]

This somewhat facetious, but logical, result of theories of aesthetic disinterestedness proposed in the eighteenth century signalled the development of hedonistic aestheticism during the nineteenth century whereby the transgressor or murderer became a post-romantic kind of hero. Connoisseurship in murder became associated with those writers who insisted that literature, far from having duties to morality, should be a fine art practised only for art's sake. Gross transgression became the aesthete's choice accompaniment to the assertion that there is no such thing as a moral or immoral book and that literature should in fact strive to cultivate an interest in outright immorality.

As the nineteenth century progressed, impetus was added to the continued interest in immoral subjects by the emergence of new philosophical speculation on the nature of man's mind. One of the inaugural moments of existentialism proper was Kierkegaard's work and his general sense of the human personality as an essentially asocial 'incognito'. Subsequently, decadent and modernist literature began to focus even more intensely on the dissolution of the mind, on schizophrenia, madness and all varieties of extreme and antisocial behaviour. Continued interest in extreme subjects quickly became aligned with a determination towards a new psychological realism. The French poet Charles Baudelaire (1821–67), whose ideas on the relationship between childhood and imagination Banville has regularly mentioned inside and outside the work of his late period, was one of the major champions of this brand of writing. In his essay 'Of Virtuous Plays and Novels' (1851) he made the following demand while upending the common perception of what is morally appropriate thematically for the writer: 'Vice is alluring; then show it as alluring; but it brings in its train peculiar moral maladies and suffering; then describe them. Study all the sores, like a doctor in the course of his hospital duties, and the good-sense school, the school dedicated exclusively to morality, will find nothing to bite on.'[29]

As the mouthpiece of the Trilogy, Freddie is therefore an old kind of emblematic figure and conforms to this general profile of the romanticized transgressor. Though Freddie is one of the more complex contemporary instances of his kind, he engages directly in some self-serving romanticizing. Significantly, much of this happens in *Ghosts*, where he is supposedly reformulating his ideas. Just after referring to 'poor Oscar' he writes in what appears to be a deliberate echo of a specific passage in Wilde's long essay 'The Critic as Artist' (1890), that society 'needs its criminals, just as it needs its sportsmen and its butchers, for that vital admixture of strength, cunning and freedom from squeamishness' (pp.32–3). Freddie's typicality, at least in his own mind, is signalled from the very start of the Trilogy:

> I am kept locked up here like some exotic animal, last survivor of a species they had thought extinct. They should let in people to view me, the girl-eater, svelte and dangerous, padding to and fro in my cage, my terrible green glance flickering past the bars, give them something to dream about, tucked up cosy in their beds of a

night ... I confess I had hopelessly romantic expectations of how things would be in here. Somehow I pictured myself a sort of celebrity, kept apart from the other prisoners in a special wing, where I would receive parties of grave, important people and hold forth to them about the great issues of the day, impressing the men and charming the ladies. What insight! they would cry ... And there am I, striking an elegant pose, my ascetic profile lifted to the light in the barred window, fingering a scented handkerchief and faintly smirking, Jean-Jacques the cultured killer. (Book of Evidence, pp.3, 5)

Though ostensibly self-aggrandizing in his cherished wretchedness, Freddie views himself so consistently through the romantic lens that he is deflated from individual to mere type. He feels, he says, 'like the gloomy hero in a Russian novel', thus aligning himself with Dostoyevsky (pp.90–1). He speaks of himself throughout the Trilogy in terms of arch-predecessors. He is a 'poor, parched Nosferatu', thus calling on the dark romanticism of vampire literature generally (Ghosts, p.170). In Athena, he is 'Melmoth the bereft', a 'faltering Mr Hyde', a 'forlorn Baron Frankenstein' (pp.122, 179, 223), betraying by these references to three major gothic figures his romantic-tinted vision of himself. He is all familiar literary monsters rolled into one and is, in effect, well entitled to confer on himself, as he does, the status of a walking cliché.

Freddie is at his most obviously petulant when his romantic expectations of his stature are disappointed. It galls him that if he pleads guilty as he wishes, then his evidence will not be heard: 'It's not fair. Even a dog such as I must have his day. I have always seen myself in the witness box, gazing straight ahead, quite calm ... And then that authoritative voice, telling my side of things, in my own words. Now I am to be denied my moment of drama ... No, it's not right' (Book of Evidence, p.182). This desire conforms to the type of the idealized romantic murderer, who in the one sensibility contains the capacity for extraordinary refinements of taste and for vile acts that are nonetheless barbaric for being the pretext for a beauteous agony of conscience.

This juxtaposition is strikingly drawn by Banville. Though his lament cannot be taken at face value, Freddie believes he has 'a lamentable weakness for the low life. There is something in me that cleaves to the ramshackle and the shady, a crack somewhere in my make-up that likes to fill itself up with dirt. I tell myself this vulgar predilection is to be found in all true connoisseurs of culture but I am not convinced' (*Athena*, p.59). 'Madmen', he muses, 'do not frighten me or even make me uneasy. Indeed, I find that their ravings soothe me. I think it is because everything, from the explosion of a nova to the fall of dust in a deserted room, is to them of vast and equal significance, and therefore meaningless.' He follows grotesques in the street and wants, in a sidelong reference to the philosophy of the German pessimist Arthur Schopenhauer (1788–1860), to declare to them: '*my fellow sufferer, dear friend, compagnon de misères!*' (*Book of Evidence*, pp.94, 165).

The cultured criminal and killer Freddie Montgomery is closest to is Humbert Humbert, the narrator of Nabokov's *Lolita*, who does indeed, as Banville says, 'flash like a firebird' in *The Book of Evidence*. We saw the extent of Nabokov's influence on Banville in Chapter 2, and he has described *Lolita* as 'a singular achievement and one of the finest works of modern literary art'.[30] He particularly delights in the moral ambiguity of this Nabokov novel and its ironic delivery of outrageous transgression through a rarely equalled intensity of poetic prose: 'We know we are in the presence of evil, yet the surroundings are ravishingly (apt adjective) lovely'.[31] In their respective narratives, both Freddie and Humbert are incarcerated, and though both strenuously deny this, their confessions are both cases for the defence. It is thus natural that Humbert should insist at the beginning that 'you can always count on a murderer for a fancy prose style' since the lyricism of the prison cell, as with Freddie, is designed, whatever the claims to the contrary, with exculpatory intent.[32]

Some divergences between the two novels should be indicated nevertheless. Though his prose is as erudite and almost as baroque as Humbert Humbert's, Freddie is not quite so attitudinizing as his predecessor, and his dissembling more patently gives way to self-castigation. Only intermittently acknowledging the import of his crimes, Humbert is impressively ecstatic in his repeated vice and vanity, while Freddie is tormented by his unrepeated deed from the moment he commits it. Most importantly, Humbert is the consummately devious architect of things, while Freddie feels his life is without volition and direction.

The real parallels between *The Book of Evidence* and *Lolita* lie in the moral code at the centre of both, a code that is both more patent and more vital in *Lolita* than its high-aesthetic self-referentiality might suggest. Like *Lolita*, Banville's triumph in *The Book of Evidence* is to include, alongside a fairly standardized cultured killer, some highly original internal critiques of the tradition to which that killer belongs.

Determined confession, especially when it is filtered through an austere intellect like Freddie's, is accompanied by a kind of masochistic nostalgia for a regulatory system. One of the more easily ignored aspects of Freddie's story is his constantly reiterated craving for capture. He relishes, on three separate occasions, the prospect of confessing. 'Capture!' he gasps: 'I nursed the word in my heart. It comforted me. It was the promise of rest' (*Book of Evidence*, p.129). This is not just a passing fancy. His belief that committing his crime has made him free, authentic, is quickly displaced by the conviction that now only capture and punishment will allow him the exact same qualities:

> Did I want to be found out, did I hope to see my name splashed in monster type across every front page? I think I did. I think I longed deep down to be made to stand in front of a jury and reveal all my squalid little secrets. Yes, to be found out, to be suddenly pounced upon, beaten, stripped, and set before the howling multitude, that was my deepest, most ardent desire … To be rumbled. To feel that heavy hand fall upon your shoulder, and hear the booming voice of authority telling you the game is up at last. In short, to be unmasked … At any moment they might catch me, they might be watching me even now … First there would be panic, then pain. And when everything was gone, every shred of dignity and pretence, what freedom there would be, what lightness! No, what am I saying, not lightness, but its opposite: weight, gravity, the sense at last of being firmly grounded. Then finally I would be me, no longer that poor impersonation of myself I had been doing all my life. I would be real. I would be, of all things, human. (pp.161–2)

Only incarceration will complete Freddie's project, and when capture does come he is almost ecstatic: 'No more running, no more hiding and waiting, no more decisions. I snuggled down between my captors, enjoying the hot chafe of metal on my wrists' (p.193).

This is all part of the 'long course of lessons' Freddie decides is laid out for him (p.170). There are notifications throughout that he will accept responsibility, that he has, underneath his now crumbling exterior, some capacity for non-ironic feeling. He is annoyed when his solicitor originally encourages him to plead not guilty (p.209). At the very close of Part I, just after the murder, his admission could hardly be more self-condemning: 'I thought: I am not human' (p.119). He occasionally ruminates on the finer points of religious ordinance: 'inevitable, mind you, does not mean excusable, in my vocabulary. No indeed, a strong mixture of Catholic and Calvinist blood courses in my veins' (p.98). He is particularly encouraged by his tears in the immediate aftermath of his killing: they 'seemed not just a fore-token of remorse, but the sign of some more common, simpler urge, an affect for which there was no name, but which might be my last link, the only one that would hold, with the world of ordinary things' (p.115). He is determined to be above all else honest:

> Remorse implies the expectation of forgiveness, and I knew that what I had done was unforgivable. I could have feigned regret and sorrow, guilt, all that, but to what end? Even if I had felt such things, truly, in the deepest depths of my heart, would it have altered anything? The deed was done, and would not be cancelled by cries of anguish and repentance ... I was, I told myself, responsible, with all the weight that word implied. (p.151)

He even gives this recognition high cathartic significance with a quotation from Shakespeare's Macbeth that has the status of an italicized one-line paragraph: 'I am afraid to think what I have done' (p.126).

Banville formulates a distinction: 'As Freddie comes to realize, his crime was murder, but his sin was a radical failure of the imagination.'[33] Freddie has moved from the sheer ethics of authenticity, the insistence that one must be oneself above all else, towards the realization that to grant others their own authenticity is an equal imperative. As the Trilogy itself progresses, he moves away from his tendency to align his own crime with the general state of guilt of the human race and to accept individual responsibility.

Belief in Freddie's new moral code is a matter of whether his narrative is to be trusted or not. His deviousness as a character may be the exact equivalent of Humbert Humbert's, a 'vain and cruel wretch who manages to appear "touching"', as Nabokov described his own creation.[34]

Banville, when commenting on one of his favourite books on Nabokov, Michael Wood's The Magician's Doubts (1995), isolated a passage he felt made an 'important' distinction concerning Lolita. The ethical, argues Wood, 'is the realm of the unspeakable for Nabokov, but it is none the less (or for that very reason) everywhere implicit in his work ... Moral questions, like epistemological ones, are put to work in his fiction. Nabokov doesn't write about them; he writes them.'[35] This distinction is indicative of Banville's own preferred dynamism in books that have implicit moral motivations: rather than pontificate or provide the moral code by which a story should be read, the function of moral narrative is simply to illustrate the case in hand, to provide a book of evidence rather than judgement. As Banville points out, Freddie's narrative is no effort to prove innocence, but rather 'a kind of appalled act of witness'.[36]

Freddie does, however, engage in more straightforward moral rumination than does Humbert Humbert. Nabokov's scoffing description of his novel, via his parodic introduction, as a tragic tale progressing towards a moral apotheosis, could be applied to The Book of Evidence with much less irony. The complexities of Freddie's confession amount in the end not so much to a writing about as a writing of the involved issues of sin and redemption. It is one of the major achievements of The Book of Evidence that while its narrator is feverishly determined to tell us everything, Banville manages to show us the moral implications of this telling.

The writer who deals with the figure of the outsider or criminal can find that he is in a way writing about himself. (It is surely not coincidental that the murdered girl in The Book of Evidence, Josie Bell, has the same initials as her creator.) The aesthete-criminal is a suitable figure for the projection of the subjectivism of the artist and is a convincing way of examining the morality of this subjectivism. The Trilogy is, like the Tetralogy, Banville's way of writing, tangentially, about the artistic mindset and process. He has pointed out, for instance, that another novel of murder similar in many ways to The Book of Evidence, Patrick Süskind's Perfume (1985), is an 'allegory of the artistic life'.[37] In such cases the subject of criminality is a projection of the highly refined and potentially irresponsible and insensate aesthetic sensibility.

Though Freddie's moral apotheosis in The Book of Evidence is couched in prevarication, he does in the end see through his own solipsism and spends his entire three narratives trying to explain and make recompense for the way in which his private obsession with freedom and autonomy led him to commit the act of murder. His exasperation at the end of *Athena* thus involves as much a yearning for moral sense and order as an admission of intellectual failure: 'This is what is known, I believe, as the problem of evil. I doubt I shall ever solve it to my satisfaction'(p.229).

NOTES

1. John Banville, 'Ourselves and Other Animals', *Irish Times* (29 May 1999).

2. Helen Meaney, 'Master of Paradox', *Irish Times* (24 March 1993).

3. Arminta Wallace, 'A World Without People', *Irish Times* (21 September 2000).

4. Clíodhna Ní Anluain (ed.), 'John Banville', in *Reading the Future: Irish Writers in Conversation with Mike Murphy* (Dublin: Lilliput Press, 2000), p.35.

5. Michael Ross, 'Chaos Theory', *Sunday Times*, 'Culture Ireland' (19 November 2000).

6 Richard Bernstein, 'Once More Admired than Bought, A Writer Finally Basks in Success', *New York Times Book Review* (15 May 1990), p.13.

7. John Banville, 'Thou Shalt Not Kill', in *Arguing at the Crossroads: Essays on a Changing Ireland*, ed. Paul Brennan and Catherine de Saint Phalle (Dublin: New Island Books, 1997), p.134.

8. Eileen Battersby, 'Comedy in a Time of Famine', *Irish Times* (24 May 1994).

9. Anonymous, 'Oblique Dreamer', *Observer* (17 September 2000).

10. For the complete text of 'Long Lankin', see R.V. Williams and A.L. Lloyd (eds), *The Penguin Book of English Folk Songs* (London: Penguin, 1976), pp.60–1.

11. Ms. 10252.12.1. 'Sea Sequence'. A finished story.

12. Ms. 10252.2.1. Drafts of *Blood* [*Nightspawn*].

13. John Banville, 'Parables of Evil', *Hibernia* (21 October 1977), p.28.

14. John Banville, letter and selected poem, in *Lifelines: Letters from Famous People about their Favourite Poem*, ed. Niall MacMonagle, foreword. Seamus Heaney (Dublin: Town House, 1992), pp.31–2. The translation Banville uses is by Michael Hamburger.

15. Jean-Paul Sartre, *Nausea*, trans. Robert Baldick (London: Penguin, 1988), p.15.

16. Banville, 'Thou Shalt Not Kill', pp.136–7.

17. John Banville, 'Bad Friday', *Irish Times* (8 April 1998).

18. Joe Jackson, 'Hitler, Stalin, Bob Dylan, Roddy Doyle ... and Me', *Hot Press*, 18, 19 (5 October 1994), p.16.

19. John Banville, 'The Work as the Self', *Irish Times* (8 October 1988).

20. Jackson, 'Hitler, Stalin, Bob Dylan, Roddy Doyle ... and Me', p.16.

21. Banville, 'Thou Shalt Not Kill', p.140.

22. Ibid., pp.133–4.

23. Melvyn Bragg, 'John Banville', *The South Bank Show* (LWT/Ulster Television, 1993).

24. For an account of the relevant case, see Cathal O'Shannon, 'Murder in the Park', in *Thou Shalt Not Kill: True-Life Stories of Irish Murders*, by Kevin O'Connor *et al.* (Dublin: Gill

& Macmillan, 1995), pp.21–40.

25. Bernstein, 'Once More Admired than Bought', p.13.

26. Banville, 'Thou Shalt Not Kill', pp.135, 138.

27. John Banville, 'Odd Man Out', Hibernia (8 March 1979), p.17.

28. Thomas De Quincey, 'On Murder Considered as One of the Fine Arts', Selected English Essays, comp. W. Peacock, notes C.B. Wheeler (London: Oxford University Press, 1918), p.309.

29. Charles Baudelaire, Selected Writings on Art and Literature, trans. and intro. P.E. Charvet (London: Penguin, 1996), p.112.

30. John Banville, 'Vladimir Nabokov', Hibernia (5 August 1977), p.27.

31. John Banville, 'Nabokov's First Lolita', Sunday Independent (15 March 1987).

32. Vladimir Nabokov, Lolita, intro. Martin Amis (London: Everyman, 1992), p.9.

33. Banville, 'Thou Shalt Not Kill, p.138.

34. Vladimir Nabokov, Strong Opinions (New York: Vintage, 1990), p.94.

35. John Banville, 'Nabokov's Dark Treasures', New York Review of Books (5 October 1995), pp.4-6.

36. Banville, 'Thou Shalt Not Kill', p.138.

37. John Banville, 'A Scent of Power in the Age of Enlightenment', Sunday Tribune (16 November 1986).

CHAPTER SIX

Face Painting: The Arts of Self-Reflection in the Trilogy and the Late Period

PICTURE BOOKS: SEEING HOW BANVILLE'S IMAGINATION WORKS

From its beginnings it seems that literature has doubted itself, sometimes self-effacingly, sometimes paranoiacally. One way or the other, this doubt has usually been expressed by writers inside and outside their literary work in conjunction, or in contrast, with other arts, particularly painting and music. We have seen in Chapter 4 the ways in which musical parallels operate in Banville's compositional ideas. From the related analogue of science, we move on here to his second major analogue, one that has both compositional and thematic implications: painting and the pictorial generally. Banville's alignments of science and literature − at least his preferred kind of literature − were designed to show their mutual recourse to imaginative processes. His comparisons of literature with the pictorial arts, present in the work from the beginning and intensifying in the middle and late periods, have tended to be more complex and ambivalent.

On the one hand, Banville often appears literally and figuratively to idolize painting as the acme of the arts and thus to demote any claims for literature made in its shadow. On the other, and aside from the fact that he has frequently admitted that he started off wanting to be a painter, his choice of the medium of the word as ideally figured in the lyrical novel has involved a regular affirmation of the supreme and unique achievements of heightened language. A resolution of this ambivalence depends, really, on which side the reader might most notice at any given time.

The appropriate categorical term to use for various visual emphases in Banville is *ekphrasis* − that is, his intense description of things, his pictorialism, and certain related occult ideas he has about the power of writing.[1] Studies of the background to ekphrasis and other aspects of what have always been called the 'sister arts' are voluminous, and a dizzying array of aesthetic and philosophical concepts is involved. Regardless of which of the many aspects of the intersection of prose and painting in Banville one might want to focus on, and regardless of whether one might want to emphasize the positive or negative side of the intersection, it is clear that there is a series of established traditions in dealing artistically and critically with the sister arts. Banville's often conscious alignment with these traditions is perhaps the strongest of the array of relationships he has cultivated with precursors and customary literary analogues and themes.

A broad critical hazard in Banville studies must be avoided here. Banville is often suspected, if not exactly accused, of unoriginality in his work. He closely employs and adapts ideas and character types from his chosen models. Readers of his work who generally expect to find perceptibly new material in novels, rather than ingeniously new combinations of traditional material, can therefore sometimes be frustrated. To resign to such frustration, however, would be to miss the point that Banville has always consciously sought to place himself in certain traditions of thought and style. He is highly aware that literature, along with being in some way about, and placed in, the world, is also about, placed within, literature as a simultaneous world of the imagination, a kind of eternal paradisal Library. Banville's debts to this ideal Library are no mere matter of lazy allusions or self-aggrandizement by way of the invocation of recognized masters and masterpieces. When he aligns himself with particular traditions he makes those traditions work hard to his own genuine purposes, and this hard work is perhaps nowhere so evident in the œuvre as in his incorporation of the sister arts tradition.

There is a broad historical and continuing context for the use of pictorial paradigms in fiction, and any Banville researcher looking for a specialized area of investigation in the œuvre would find much excitement in placing him against this background. What is striking in Banville's case is the combination in single works of the range of distinct pictorial concerns displayed individually by other writers: a preoccupation with portraits and the eroticism of the female figure; a fascination with beauty and the potential irresponsibility of the artist; an investigation of the idea of the artist as anatomist; an occasional focus on sculpture; an assimilation of certain artists' biographies reminiscent of his use of his scientists' lives in the Tetralogy; a resounding treatment of the idea of art as forgery or fraudulence.

These are only a few examples. Various forms of pictorialism have inspired a wide variety of writers, not least novelists, and allowed them to embody particular themes, especially when an implicit or explicit discussion of the matter of representation itself is part of the project. In his formational period, Banville often seemed to deploy pictorialism to merely decorative ends. But in retrospect we can see that this was the foundation for extensive interpretative usages that emerged more fully in the early period, that reached a particular intensity in the Trilogy of the middle period, and that he continues to refine in the late period.

Banville's idiosyncratic use of the pictorialism tradition is centred on literary representation in a particularly self-doubting manner. Three matters relating to this self-reflective doubt will be explored here: sex and the erotic; painting and self-portraiture; the relationship between writing and autobiography. These all relate not simply to Banville's own formidably deft sense of humour as inscribed in the books, but also to his distinct conception of writing and all art as an important kind of cerebral playfulness.

Aside from there being no prohibition on critics having their own illustrative fun when engaging with a writer's work, Banville has regularly and rightfully complained that the different kinds of comedy in his work often seem passed over in the criticism. Banville's fictional ways with women, particularly his constant hint that feminine idealization is one of the key problems of the intellectual man, were for too long ignored. But this situation is now rapidly being reversed. Along the way there is a potential for gender-modulated criticism to lapse into solemnity, not least when Banville's erotic topics are discussed in tandem with his pictorial concentrations.

Yes, the tradition of literary pictorialism appears endemically to involve stark male/female oppositions. It seems that pictorialism has almost always involved a lustful male gaze that loudly seeks to appropriate in narrative a simultaneously alluring and threatening beautiful female presence or image that insists, by way of providing a productive tension, on remaining silent. Pictorialism is particularly central to a psychological approach to creativity which sees man's artistic endeavours as a kind of mythic claim of a biological function, a virtual substitute for the actual birthing faculties of woman. And enactments of female death, usually with violent overtones, have often appeared a requirement in this aestheticized negotiation between the sexes.

But no, it should not be forgotten that with literary pictorialism we are dealing with a highly mannered traditional set of themes and procedures. The concept of the male gaze (predatory, lustful, idealizing) is just that: a concept, a literary and artistic figure or trope. To believe that it has a direct correspondence with the actual would be only to betray a wilful condemnatory intent. Literary pictorialism, at least as Banville adapts it, is more ambiguous and complex than allowed for by many of the more simplistic or moralizing investigations of its male/female oppositions.

Related to the concept of the aggressive male gaze in the tradition of pictorialism – and this is especially so in Banville – is the notionally balancing concept of the 'innocent eye' whereby a casting off of language (male and predatory, lustful and idealizing) is attempted in favour of unmediated visual experience (female, apparently, and innocent, poised and realist). E.H. Gombrich, the art historian alluded to by Banville in the third painting set-piece of *Athena* (p.76), provided strong arguments against the 'myth of the innocent eye'.[2] We can readily extend this corrective to the innocent eye's counterpart of the male gaze. With these elements of the pictorial tradition, we are already in a highly artificial zone. And this is doubly so when the writer involved is Banville, whose aim has increasingly been to heighten the sense of artificiality in his fictions.

This sense of artificiality is also important to keep in mind when it comes to a major aspect here of self-reflective doubt in Banville's work: the figure of the author, and the pointing up of a potential lack of depth of meaning in his art (and, by implication, in all art). A chief component of the radical doubt about the claims of language and literature Banville has always expressed through his work is his increasing ridicule of the solemn author or artist, or simply the obsessively speaking monologist, who presumes in his megalomania that his endeavours at explaining both himself and the world have some claim to originality, authenticity or truth.

To repeat: the decision on whether Banville upholds the claims of narrative to have aristocratically autonomous force or, instead, scuppers these claims in some kind of allegedly postmodern democratic gesture, is a matter of those aspects of his narratives one might accentuate in any given context. Banville retains on one level an absolute faith in narrative art as a way of imposing aesthetic, if not necessarily rational, meaning or order on the world. But there are also important moments in his novels when there appears to be nothing so essentially funny as the figure of the author who has thrust himself onto the stage of art and the world to talk about himself and stake his claims.

The endings of Banville's novels underline an ambivalence here. Occasionally they close on a note of confidence about narrative – *Athena* may be the only certain example. Most frequently they close on an ambiguous note, as with the first edition of *Long Lankin*, *Copernicus*, *Kepler*, *Mefisto*, *The Book of Evidence*, *Ghosts*, *The Untouchable*, *Shroud* and *The Sea*. Sometimes a clear note of combined linguistic and existential exaspera- tion is sounded, as at the ends of *Nightspawn*, *Birchwood*, *The Newton Letter* and *Eclipse*. The point is that in keeping with Banville's overarching philosophy and theme of the bafflement of intellectual man, his principals and nar- rators typically waver between confidence and self-doubt in their own narratives. The pictorial tradition is assimilated by Banville to particularly acute effect in portraying this bafflement, both in the sense of conjuring up representative pictures of the mournfully comical author and of using the illusory dimension of painting to underline his own suspicions about the potential artificiality and inauthenticity of literature.

Banville uniformly uses the pictorial tradition to set up complex self- reflective analogues for creativity generally. In the early period it was the more arcane processes of science; in the middle and late phases it is the notionally more direct arts of the eye. As Banville said of *The Book of Evidence* and *Ghosts* – and we can extend this to *Athena* and, with some nuances, to *Eclipse*, *Shroud* and *The Sea* – he was intent on 'an investigation of the way in which the imagination works'.[3] The metaphors of the stage and the actor might arguably be a third analogical movement in Banville, but here we will accommodate this to his pictorial obsessions and examine their role in his intensified examination, in his late period, of the imagination's function in what might, without punning, be termed the drama of the self, the theatrical ways in which the self imag- ines itself into uncertain being.

SUBLIME SEX: THE TRILOGY IN CONTEXT

Let's not entirely tame it with the more genteel synonym erotic: there is a decidedly sexual tinge to certain elements of Banville's use of pictorialism. Some of these elements are motivated by a kind of negative definition that both psychoanalytical and denominational readers might enjoy. Banville recalls being told by a priest when young that there was a 'sin of looking', and he sees painting in particular as 'an almost erotic gaze fixed on the world'.[4] This sin of looking is clearly an idea that has stuck because it is directly referred to in the late period in *The Sea* (p.120). As Banville treats it, the eroticism involved in the sense of sight, at least as it features in literature and art, is a particular kind of fetishized love. The erotic gaze is classically figured in the Trilogy of the middle period where Banville works in detail with an idiosyncratic version of the classical story of Pygmalion, the sculptor who carves a statue of a woman so lifelike that it actually does come to life. In the Pygmalion-like Trilogy, various aspects of the pictorial tradition are particularly well combined, especially the problem of realism, the aura of the feminine, and the idea that literature is a virtually 'real' dimension.

Athena is heavily influenced by a curious novel that has at its centre the scenario of the imagination seeking its own pleasures. *Athena* could, Banville admits, be considered a homage to the pornographic *Story of O* (1954) by the French author Anne Desclos (1907–98) writing under the pseudonym of Pauline Réage. Banville considers this work a masterpiece. When devising *Athena*, he was trying to look at 'that strange hinterland between pleasure and pain, between control and submission', and *Story of O* 'does catch something essential about the relationship between men and women':

> You read *Story of O* when you're an adolescent, as a 'dirty book' then read it again and realise how subtle it is. When you read it in adolescence you think this woman is having all these terrible things done to her. Then you realise, afterwards, she is the one in control throughout. She's the one with the power. I wanted to do something like that.[5]

Though *Athena* is not so extensively sexual as Réage's novel, the correspondence in terms of theme is close. Banville's inverted heroine, A., is also the focus of erotic and masochistic attention, and he had even thought at first of directly calling her O. The Trilogy in general is characterized by the dual sense of idealized Woman as figured in Réage's character of O. On the one hand Woman appears as malleable male fantasy; on the other she appears as a manipulator of men.

The nature of the feminine was a preoccupation of Banville's when he was writing the Trilogy. In his public voicing of this, he tended to use something of an extreme vocabulary, and he has left himself somewhat open to accusations of attitudinizing for some comments he made on the nature of Woman. Men, apparently, 'have a deep, deep fear of all women. They fear the power women carry. The power to cause them pain, the power to rob them of their equilibrium, which, of course, has to do with the mother, but also has to do with the ways in which men are taught to treasure women.' And then he dropped this clanger: 'I've always felt that women came from Mars! We were put here, then the spaceships came down and the women sprang out of pods and men said "my God! Look at this" and stood there with their mouths open – which is how we've been ever since! Forget this stuff about spare ribs, women are pods from Mars!' But then more familiar Banville territory comes into view: 'But they are just so absolutely ravishingly beautiful. They are everything we're not. They have this kind of tentativeness and seem to understand how things work, whereas we spend a lifetime trying to find out the same things.'[6]

Umbrage may be taken at these associated ideas of Woman as extraterrestrial and as heavenly beauty. Yet this sense of Woman is not a matter of throwaway hyperbole. Words very similar to those used by Banville here on women appeared a year later in *Athena*:

> [W]hen it comes to what is called love and all that the word entails I am a dolt. Always was, always will be. I do not understand women, I mean I understand them even less than the rest of my sex seems to do. There are times when I think this failure of comprehension is the prime underlying fact of my life, a blank region of unknowing which in others is a lighted, well-signposted place. (p.46)

One of the more consistent ironies of the œuvre has to do with this matter of the confusions of love and sex. Banville's stylistic concern with the visual coexists with an extended thematic preoccupation with the female as icon. In *Nightspawn*, through Banville's first reference to a specific painter, this is already predicted. In a metaphor that is later reiterated in his own narrative, and also in Birchwood, Ben White admits that he cannot find the words to describe his beloved Helena, and he resorts to this: 'I think of certain summer days when the air itself seems to sing, and I think of the perfection of silence caught by the best music; I think of Botticelli's maiden of abundant spring' (p.116). The reference is to the Renaissance painter Sandro Botticelli (1445–1510), one of whose specialities was the depiction of mythical female figures. This imagistic connection between women and art continues through Godkin's cherished photograph in Birchwood, for which, in his search for time misplaced, he has great hopes. His entire picaresque quest for a meaningful past is motivated by this picture, and this is the description:

> Printed in yellowish brown tints, with a white crease aslant it like a bloodless vein, it was of a young girl dressed in white, standing in a garden, one hand resting lightly on the back of a wrought-iron seat ... Half of the scene was in sunlight, half in shade, and the girl with her eyes closed leaned from the dark into the light smiling blithely, dreamily, as though she were listening to some mysterious music. (p.5)

Banville's iconic concerns are always linked to such female depictions, and Godkin's Rose is also likened to 'one of Botticelli's maidens' (p.6). After his tutor aunt reads him a story, approximately entitled by his memory The Something Twins, the photograph begins to metamorphose and take on life for Godkin: 'On a little low table by the bookshelves there was a small framed photograph of a young girl in white standing among leaves in a garden, leaning out of the tree's deep shade into a mist of sunlight. In one hand she held a flower. A rose. Look!' (pp.42–3). Godkin is in essence fetishizing his picture into life.

This fetishization, which will later infuse the Trilogy, is also patent in The Newton Letter. When the historian has begun to idealize his old girlfriend Ottilie, he tries to conjure up an image that will illustrate an indefinable sense of absence and things lost. So he resorts to a description of a photograph in which the sense of the ethereal is typical: 'In it she is sitting on a fallen tree, in winter sunlight. Her gaze is steady, unsmiling, her hands rest on her knees ... There is something here, in this pose, this gaze at once candid and tender, that when I was with her I missed; it is I think the sense of her essential otherness, made poignant and precious' (p.78).

Such an idealized girl, and her accentuated 'otherness', also appears in *Kepler* in the figure of the scientist's stepdaughter, Regina. Again, the very silent, ocular and oracular presence of this girl intimates for Kepler a sense of essential beauty and harmony: 'There was in her an air of completeness, of being, for herself, a precise sufficiency ... She was like a marvellous and enigmatic work of art', and he is 'content to stand and contemplate with a dreamy smile, careless of the artist's intentions'. The girl's idealization is complete when her accepting silence is relished: 'To try to tell her what he felt would be as superfluous as talking to a picture' (pp.13, 100).

In his first narrative of the Trilogy, Freddie Montgomery's sensual delight in his wife is also mediated through the fetishized iconic. 'I wanted to caress her', he says, 'as I would want to caress a piece of sculpture, hefting the curves in the hollow of my hand, running a thumb down the long smooth lines, feeling the coolness, the velvet texture of the stone' (*Book of Evidence*, p.8). His desire to scrutinize only Daphne's physical surface is illustrated in a scene that reuses the figure of Banville's earliest idealized girl in the uncollected story 'The Party', from 1966.[7] This story would bear considerable comparison with the sections of Joyce's short story 'The Dead' from *Dubliners* (1914) where the protagonist, Gabriel, is at one point captivated by his wife on the stairs and wonders about painting her. In 'The Party', the narrator feels desire for a laconic ghostly girl he sees gazing out of a window at a party:

> For some reason the window, which was high and wide, and set in a sort of little alcove, looked nice to me. The moonlight was coming in through it, and splashing on the floor and falling silvery on the dancers as they moved slowly about like some kind of ghosts. Thin lace curtains hung before the alcove, moving with tiny little rippling movements in the little wind which came in through the open window. I don't know. I can't explain it. It just looked, well, nice. Then I noticed that there was a girl standing behind the curtains, looking out the window.

He has the feeling of being on the brink of something, but, owing to sleepiness and the lights going up at the party, he forgets the girl. Then the lights go out again:

> And the window was beautiful, really lovely. I suppose it's silly to

say that something like a window was beautiful, but there in that hot, smoky room, with the smell of bodies all around me, that window seemed to be the only thing that was clean, something that no one or nothing could dirty. Silly I suppose.

Then I began to notice the girl again, the one behind the curtains. She was still standing there. Like me, she hadn't moved either. She was so still, like a statue.

There follows an unremarkable awkward exchange, but this is followed by the two gazing out at the garden 'dark and deep in shadow, the masses of the trees black and silent', and the narrator suddenly feels an overwhelming desire to tell her something, to confess his loneliness. The girl remains silent and he eventually retreats from the party, holding the thought of this mysterious stranger as a kind of talisman of enigmatic sadness and strangeness. In *The Book of Evidence*, Freddie reconstitutes the objectification of that girl in his image of Daphne, and he regrets having woken her from her reverie at that window 'when [he] could have hung back in the shadows and painted her, down to the tiniest, tenderest detail' (p.72).

The broad significance of the non-individualized, artistically idealized nature of Banville's girls is indicated when Freddie at one point wonders in *Ghosts* if he might be a 'sly old Faustus' trying to turn Flora into '*das Ewig-Weibliche*' (p.70). This is a reference to an idea about 'the eternal Womanly' contained in Goethe's *Faust* (1808–1832) which has proved enduringly influential on Banville. The female figure, or at least its metamorphosis in the agonized male intellect as Banville represents it, always possesses the enviable completeness of Kepler's Regina. Godkin, with the help of his ethereal pictured girl, decides that all the sorry scraps of his life point to the 'awesome and abiding fact ... that somewhere I had a sister, my twin, a lost child ... Half of me, somewhere ... A part of me stolen, yes, that was a thrilling notion. I was incomplete, and would remain so until I found her' (*Birchwood*, p.78–9). While the various versions of a character named Felix are the more obvious, mischievously diabolic twins to Banville's narrators, this vision of the 'eternal Womanly' comprises an adjoining, and equally phantasmic, sense of the split self. If Felix is the demon within, then Banville's madonnas appear to be the saving angels without, at least initially. Indeed, Godkin's ministering angel is explicitly called on to help him deny his particular Felix, his 'real' twin brother Michael. 'There is no girl. There never was', he admits at the end: 'I believed in a sister in order not to believe in him, my cold mad brother' (Birchwood, p.168).

This idea of Woman as salvation has endured through all Banville's periods, though the former tone of colder admiration has perhaps become tinged with avidity. Cleave in Eclipse, for instance, is almost cloying in his idealizations, and he comments on the women 'who have been drawn into the orbit of my life over the years. They have cared for me, they have sustained me; however precipitate my behaviour may be at times, they are always there to break my fall' (pp.8–9).

The ironic moment comes with regard to 'the eternal Womanly' when Banville carefully indicates the gap between Woman and women. Just as the perceptions of Banville's male protagonists are always a little off-centre, always misreading things somewhat, the perfection of his angelic women is frequently suspect. An almost travestied dichotomy sometimes results. We can see this in all his periods. Compared to the 'iridescent ideal' of Godkin's photographic imago, his 'peasant girlchild with her grubby nails and sausage curls seems a tawdry thing' (Birchwood, p.63). When the girl Alicia is brought to him, Copernicus is impressed by her 'strange closed silence'; she seems to be 'turned inward somehow, away from the world, as if she were the carrier of a secret that made her inner self wholly sufficient'; but this could be merely symptomatic of her venereal disease (Copernicus, p.113). When Gabriel Swan in Mefisto returns from one of his reveries, he laments: '[Sophie] had so throbbed in my imagination that now, when I confronted the real she, it was as if I had just parted from her more dazzling double.' Sophie, one of Banville's most ethereally drawn figures, communicates 'in an airy, insubstantial language consisting not of words but moving forms'; but this is hardly avoidable since she is in any case a deaf-mute (pp.68, 55). And Freddie recalls that he started his downward free-fall with his conviction that the woman of his painting is 'unignorably there, more real than the majority of her sisters out here in what we call real life' (Ghosts, p.84).

Encounters with real girls are as extensively de-sublimated in Banville as his pictured girls are sublimated, and sexual scenes are almost invariably grotesque. When sex is not grotesque, it is transformed into either a fantasy troilism (Newton Letter, p.48) or an equally etherealized 'real' troilism (Book of Evidence, pp.67ff.). The bathos of this purposeful separation of the real from the ideal is accentuated in The Newton Letter and

Mefisto when it is respectively recognized that Charlotte's and Adele's airy grace is attributable to the fact that they both are doped out (*Newton Letter*, p.75; *Mefisto*, pp.156ff.).

With the Trilogy, Banville brought to the pictorial a new sexual intensity and fetishization. There is a particularized facet of literary pictorialism which tends to overdetermine a sense of female otherness. Banville's idealized Woman is the contemporary fetishized and idolized version of the beautiful women lyrically described in the idylls of classical Greek poetry, the original examples of pictorial obsession. All the expected adjuncts of male fantasy are figured in such pictorial work. Elements of pornography, voyeurism, masturbation and fetishism will frequently appear. The detail of this male desire for the pleasurable female image inscribed in the pictorial tradition can be schematized in a list of oppositions where painting and the pictorial generally are seen as silent, physical, externalized, feminine and beautiful, and poetry and language are seen as eloquent, cerebral, internalized, masculine and obsessed with sublime experience.

In the Trilogy, violence and fetishism are involved in the male desire for the pictorial feminine icon. The most readily recognized moment in this regard is Freddie's recollection in *The Book of Evidence* of the first time he sees the portrait that leads him towards murder. Though unidentified in the novel, this scene is based on an actual painting that Banville has identified as *Portrait of a Lady in Dark Blue*, a work, variously attributed, which hangs in the Museum of Fine Arts in Budapest. In general, the Dutch painter Vermeer (1632–75) is credited, and the title of the painting, as in the Budapest museum catalogue, is sometimes given as *Portrait of a Woman*. While Freddie will later kill for this virtual woman, on his first encounter he experiences what he thinks of as love. He berates those who would incriminate him for knowing nothing of his feeling for her: 'You do not know the fortitude and pathos of her presence. You have not come upon her suddenly in a golden room on a summer eve, as I have. You have not held her in your arms.' Importantly, Freddie remembers feeling under equal erotic scrutiny from the painted woman:

> I stood there, staring, for what seemed a long time, and gradually a kind of embarrassment took hold of me, a hot, shamefaced awareness of myself, as if somehow I, this soiled sack of flesh, were

the one who was being scrutinised, with careful, cold attention. It was not just the woman's painted stare that watched me. Everything in the picture, that brooch, those gloves, the flocculent darkness at her back, every spot on the canvas was an eye fixed on me unblinkingly. (Book of Evidence, p.79)

The state of absorption to be achieved in Banville's pictorial idealizations has already somewhat broken down here. Rather than gazing away, this woman stares at the observer. As the autonomous world of the painting thus breaks its code of silence, the segregation of art from life dissolves, producing the confusion of life and art that leads to Freddie's crime.

In Athena this extends to a virtual human copulation with the female art icon, as represented by the outrightly sexualized A. Freddie wishes to ravish his icon, to possess her silence. There are two scenes of troilism and voyeurism in a brothel (pp.164–5, 178); scenes where A. delights in performing for Freddie's voyeuristic attention (pp.155ff.); scenes where A. demands to be sadistically beaten (pp.171, 174–5). Freddie spends the entire story fetishizing his girl, carefully dressing her each day of his story whichever way he desires. At the end when he reports that she has left his life, he tries to 'make her appear' and proceeds to masturbate (p.220). Athena itself takes the form of a long love letter to an absent lover. According to Freddie, who repeatedly admits his self-obsession and solipsism, this fervent sexual remembrance is his variety of love.

Without necessarily wanting to defer to the high romantic notion of orgasm as the 'little death', the connections between lust and the imaginative yearning to confer metaphorical life in Banville's work, especially in the Trilogy, would be worth considerable attention. One further example from the late period will underline the connections for the moment. This concerns Cleave's description in Eclipse of the 'cache of dirty pictures' he discovers on top of the wardrobe in his old house: 'Antique smut it is, hand-tinted photographs of paintings from the last century, postcard-sized but rich in detail, all creams and crimsons and rose-petal pinks.' And then there is the typical moment of expectancy:

There are occasions, rare and precious, when, having brought myself to the last hiccupy scamper, with the pictures fanned out before me and my eyes agoggle, I will experience a moment of desolating rapture that has nothing to do with what is happening in my lap but seems a distillation of all the tenderness and intensity that life can promise. (pp.52–3)

The kind of fetishization of the female icon we see in the Trilogy has far-reaching illustrative implications within the novels and also for Banville's entire aesthetic. This is hinted at when the painted girl somehow demands things of Freddie: 'There is something in the way the woman regards me, the querulous, mute insistence of her eyes ... I squirm in the grasp of her gaze. She requires of me some great effort, some tremendous feat of scrutiny and attention ... It is as if she were asking me to let her live' (Book of Evidence, p.105). As Freddie proceeds to invent a four-page life for the woman, the sense of obligation involves an appropriation of occult powers for the active observing imagination.

The male birth metaphor applied to the imagination is vital here, and the occult idea behind the metaphor is indicated when Freddie compares the virtual world of art to a mirrored world: 'I think of the stillness that lives in the depths of mirrors. It is not our world that is reflected there. It is another place entirely, another universe ... Anything is possible there; even the dead may come back to life' (Ghosts, p.55). The analogy between this other universe and Banville's view of narrative is patent: narrative is the kind of mirror in which the life-and-death laws of the world it allegedly reflects do not hold sway. Simply, anything can happen within the fictional world; it is the occult's natural home, and men may give birth there.

Freddie's dead girl will be vicariously replaced in Athena as he conjures up a mortal life for a figure from his paintings: 'Each painting that I lifted up and set under my enlarging glass was a portent of what was coming. And what was coming, though I did not know it yet, was you ... Perhaps when I peered into those pictures what I was looking for was always and only the prospect of you ... You were the pictures and they were you' (p.81, 83). During the fifth catalogue piece, the girl and her life begin to interrupt Freddie's discussion; she notionally emerges from the paintings into the story outside. Impersonal third-person critique now becomes addressed to 'You' as A. takes on life (pp.129–31). The sixth catalogue piece gives way even earlier to this address to 'You': 'She [Diana of the painting] looks a little like you ... But then, they all look like you; I paint you over them.' At the end of this section, the critique fades perceptibly into the outside story as the final sentence cuts off and is taken up by the main narrative. The effect is that of the merging of two worlds (pp.167–71). By the seventh and final catalogue piece, the critique finds it difficult to even begin because the life of 'You' interrupts at the very beginning (pp.203–4).

The intent behind Freddie's imagined magic is to possess his idealized girl, to make her both sensual and sensory. Once he feels that his A. has been born, he describes his mental picture of her as having a crease running athwart it 'like a bloodless vein' (p.232). This is the same bloodless vein running through Godkin's photograph in Birchwood, and the idea is the same: that life has been half-created, flesh and blood taken out of the pictorial icon. It is out of the primary quality of the pictorial icon that Freddie creates his girl. 'You appear out of silence', he says of A. 'That is how I think of it, as if the silence in the room had somehow materialised you and given you form.' Freddie sees the silence of his paintings as paradoxically athrob with 'mute eloquence. Athrob, yes, for this voluminous inaudible din with which they filled the place ... did not bring calm but on the contrary provoked in me a kind of suspenseful agitation, a tremulous, poised expectancy that was all the more fraught because there seemed nothing to expect' (pp.84, 79).

The imaginative energy of the pictorial in Banville is designed to cope with the potentially painful sublime, a paradoxical pain most famously described as an 'aesthetic idea' by the German philosopher Immanuel Kant (1724–1804). The sublime is 'that representation of the imagination which induces much thought, yet without the possibility of any definite thought whatever, i.e. *concept*, being adequate to it, and which language, consequently, can never get quite on level terms with or render completely intelligible'.[8] The occult power of creativity in the pictorial allows the imagination to confront head-on the evasiveness of the sublime. In consciously working with the problem of the sublime, Banville is yet again indebted to Rilke, and he has pointed to a particular parallel in the Trilogy with an aesthetic idea expressed in Rilke's poem about a unicorn in Sonnets to Orpheus (1923). This poem is a crucial illustration of the idea of the sublime as Banville works with it. It is the fourth poem of the second part of the Sonnets, and concerns the conjuring-up of a unicorn by some maidens. Its first verse reads:

Oh this is the animal that never was.
They hadn't seen one; but just the same, they loved
its graceful movements, and the way it stood
looking at them calmly, with clear eyes.[9]

'It is a beautiful poem', says Banville: 'In the end, because of the maidens' concentration on him, the Unicorn begins to be. This is the way of *Athena*. It was quite difficult to do, because A. has to be physically palpable – but not present.' Freddie has to 'imagine a creature into existence' in the same way Rilke describes his maidens' imaginative feat, though in the end A. is 'even less present than the unicorn in the poem, for all the precise description'.[10]

Athena can be taken as success of a kind, however. The practical acknowledgement in the way Banville works with the pictorial through his morally suspect narrators is that the aesthetic dimension cannot in reality make an ideal object 'present' as such. It can only make it virtually 'palpable', and therefore it is distinct from the real. This ambivalent realization that occult hopes for the imagination will ultimately be thwarted is the moral centre of Banville's use of art and the pictorial as analogues for creativity. His variety of aesthetic self-reflexivity is ultimately inseparable from a probing self-reflection about the moral credibility and worthiness of art as a potentially self-contained dimension.

The extent to which Banville is holistically self-reflexive in this theme of the ambivalent desires of the sublime imagination suggests that the theme may be the most organically dominant one of his œuvre. And far from assenting to the stark contrasting of the craving male gazer with the sublimely evasive female that seems a prerequisite of the pictorial tradition, Banville's women and men are ultimately not to be separated in this respect. They are firmly united in his grand theme of the Imagination. In the late period, for instance, the detailed use in *The Sea* of the French painter Pierre Bonnard (1867–1947), who compulsively painted his adored wife, is designed to painfully emphasize Morden's complex but nonetheless deep love for his own lost companion.

One particularly hidden parallel in the late period will serve to illustrate the extent of this unification. Banville's most enigmatic and completely depicted woman from any of his periods is Cass Cleave, the damaged daughter of the narrator of *Eclipse* and the potential instigator of downfall for the narrator of *Shroud*, a novel that gives extensive third-person coverage to a female character. Although her name is Catherine, Vander refers to her as 'my Cassandra' (*Shroud*, p.223), and this is literally and metaphorically a Trojan Horse reference. In Greek legend, Cassandra was the beautiful daughter of King Priam who tried to warn the Trojans against the infamous horse. She was, however, also familiarly known as Alexandra, and thus, by this reference, Cass actually has the same root name as her father, Alexander Cleave of *Eclipse*, and, anagrammatically, the same name as the narrator's assumed identity, Axel Vander, in *Shroud*. It might be further remarked that Axel Vander is one-eyed. This may be a partial reference to the 'Cyclopses of culture', the 'frightful energies' that Friedrich Nietzsche, the ghost that haunts that novel, argued were the innovators for humanity. More importantly for our context here, Vander's second feminine eye is symbolized by Cass in her legendary role as a seer or prophetess who came to represent the romantic yearning to communicate. Cass is, just as with Freddie Montgomery's women in the Trilogy, a picture of what's inside the head, a projection of an idea. 'Did she think, or was she thought?' is the essential question Cass asks herself in *Shroud* (p.141).

There would therefore be little point in taking to a reading of Banville any conventional accusation that he refuses, thematically at least, to have his men separate their gaze from the independent female 'other'. Desire and the object of desire operate as a union in Banville, but this must be thought of not in terms of any discussions about real or accurate characterizations of women but as a symbolic enactment of the concept of the sublime.

SELF-PORTRAITS OF THE AUTHOR AS A FIGURE OF FUN:
PAINTING IN THE TRILOGY

With the Trilogy, Banville's ekphrastic sense reached a level of intensity far beyond the considerable pictorialism of the early period. Up to Freddie's portrait in *The Book of Evidence*, there is mention of eight individual painters in the work. In the Trilogy there are references to three sculptors, one photographic artist and forty individual painters. Freddie, a renowned scientist who gives up on science in his first narrative, becomes the amanuensis of a famous art historian in *Ghosts*, and by *Athena* he is a fully fledged art critic and expert on provenance. A plethora of painters, paintings and genre moods combine to create scenes, and the extended painting descriptions in the Trilogy are in some aspects fastidiously modelled on real paintings. These deserve some attention, especially with regard to an artist who, in *Ghosts*, became Banville's first extensively self-reflective pictorial model.

At the heart of *Ghosts* is the fictional *Le Monde d'or* (pp.94–5), and the mood of the narrative emerges from a compendium of Golden Age paintings. The real painting in the isolated catalogue description at the theoretical centre of the novel is more important. Though Banville does not mention a title, the painting behind the short section three of *Ghosts* (pp.225–31) is entitled *Gilles* by the French rococo artist, Jean-Antoine Watteau (1684–1721). Watteau's painted world has had considerable influence on European writers who have wanted to achieve a sense of charming artificiality or airiness in their work. *Gilles* acts as an intrusive backdrop earlier in *Ghosts*, where a reproduction hangs on the wall of Flora's room and enters her dreams (pp.46–9, 64). The figure of Gilles was the French adaptation of Pierrot, the general patsy and scapegoat of the *Commedia dell'arte*, and in Watteau's representation he is particularly isolated and vulnerable. The general air and posture of this Pierrot is for Banville a model of the self-conscious writer's predicament of isolation, and his reading of an extended symbolic narrative into *Gilles* leaves little room for the notion of the innocent eye.

The physical description Banville provides in his fictional catalogue piece corresponds in some minute details with the original which hangs in the Louvre in Paris, from the fine observation of Gilles' setting slightly to the left of centre, and the extended nuancing of the colours of the painted sky, down to the sixteen buttons on his twill coat. Some additional features are transferred on to the canvas by Banville, however. As Freddie declares through his expert recourse to X-ray analysis, in a reference to the alterations carried out on a painting evinced in earlier versions that can be discovered behind the surface of the finalized canvas: 'Pentimenti will out.' Banville carries out a literary pentimento on Watteau – most importantly, he paints in a club for Gilles, in memory of Freddie's murderous hammer.

Gilles is the prime version of the self-reflective figure of the clown who has appeared in Banville from the outset, sometimes in different guises. He has always used the image of the author as jester, from the harlequin-like Julian of *Nightspawn*, through the troupe of theatrical folk moving across the demesne in the uncollected story 'Mr Mallin's Quest' and their eventual proper figuration as the circus people of *Birchwood*, from the acrobats of 'De Rerum Natura', into the more devilish joking doubles of the Tetralogy. With the figure of Gilles, however, the image takes on a more intense, more mournful and more obvious self-reflexivity (conveniently enhanced by the fact that *Gilles* is often assumed to be a self-portrait by Watteau).

This applies specifically to a kind of reverse version of pictorial hope whereby Banville communicates the fear that the virtual realm of literary art can picture nothing successfully. The comprehensiveness of this fear is established by Banville's use of less specified Watteau paintings for the mood of *Ghosts*. There are two possibilities for the reference point of repeated allusions in the novel to Cythera, the mythic isle of happy dreaming, both of which are 'Cythera' paintings by Watteau. The scenes of these Cythera paintings become mixed with the description of *Gilles* in the course of the novel. Banville has acknowledged the importance of the Watteau background, particularly as informed by the book *Watteau: 1684–1721* (1984) by Grasselli and Rosenberg, and he has also precisely identified the purpose of using this painter in particular:

> I wanted to give a sort of superficiality to the book. I wanted to give a sense of theatricality, and one of the things that fascinate me about Watteau and that was useful for me in this book was that Watteau never painted from life, he painted actors portraying life. I wanted this sense of, literally, *imitation* of life.[11]

This sense of the theatrical double distance of art from reality, further informed by details such as allusions to photographs of sculptures by the French photographer Eugène Atget (1857–1927), contributes to the extensive self-consciousness of the Trilogy. Vaublin, the fictitious painter Freddie is studying with Professor Kreutznaer in *Ghosts*, is closely modelled on Watteau. Like Watteau, Vaublin is a painter of *pèlerinages* and *fêtes galantes*, and is later given the exact same life dates as Watteau (*Ghosts*, p.30; *Athena*, p.230). Descriptions of Vaublin's work in *Ghosts* are self-reflective comments on Banville's own work, particularly the novel in progress. His fictitious paintings are full of 'quietude and remoteness'; they 'hardly need to be glazed, their brilliant surfaces are themselves like a sheet of glass, smooth, chill and impenetrable'; he is 'the master of darkness, as others are of light'; he is the painter of absences and endings and in his work 'something is deliberately not being said ... it is this very reticence that lends his pictures their peculiar power' (p.35). And Vaublin's masterpiece, *Le Monde d'or*, may itself be taken as a painted analogue of the novel in which it appears (pp.94–5).

Such analogical commentary, not self-deprecatory by any means, dominates in *Athena*. Each of the seven catalogue pieces here contains authorial self-depictions. Indeed, if Banville's playing is taken to the extreme, the seven pieces might be seen to correspond to each of the seven novels Banville had written up to *Athena*; and *Athena* itself, like the one painting that is not given its own critical piece, might be seen as the final, eighth work. The fictitious paintings are all dated and sized, and dates are also provided for the painters. Banville gives, as painter of each fictitious piece, anagrams, or approximate anagrams, of his own name, and, to get the fun underway, Godkin's circus alias of *Birchwood*, Johann Livelb, resurfaces as the painter of the first piece.

All is meant as a good wheeze no doubt, but above all Banville's self-reflective tics, this use of anagrams is the most jaded. Further, all his self-ironic cards are shown through these mock catalogue pieces to the extent that the game at hand leaves little room for the ambiguity he likes to have in a novel. Johann Livelb 'adapts his vision to the dictates of available form' and maintains 'a kind of ersatz classical repose, an enervated stillness at the heart of seeming frenzy'. Of the painting in question, 'there have been suggestions that this is a self-portrait but no evidence has been adduced to support the theory' (pp.17–19). Evidence of self-portraiture is perhaps too obvious as the subsequent critical pieces develop. L. van Hobelijin's canvas 'gives more the impression of a still life than the scene of passionate activity it is intended to be' (pp.41–3). Giovanni Belli paints in 'highly worked, polished textures' and engages in 'the obsessive pursuit of stillness, poise' (pp.75–7). Job van Hellin's work has a 'coolness of approach – a coldness', a 'remoteness and classical stillness' (pp.103–5). L.E. van Ohlbijn's work has an 'almost vertiginous sense of elevation and dreamlike buoyancy' and is remarkable for its 'softness of textures and the diaphanous quality of the paint surface' (pp.129–31). J. van Hollbein's effect is one of 'stillness and silence' (pp.167–9). Jan Vibell's art is 'subtle and ambiguous' (pp.203–4).

Occasionally in these pieces, Banville does include more pointedly self-effacing comments. Belli's 'constant effort of transcendence' produces a 'mannered, overwrought style', and his work is 'too self-conscious, too deliberate in its striving for pure beauty' (p.76). And Hollbein is described as 'no scholar, despite the many classical references which appear in his work' (p.167). Here, too, Banville again takes up the practice, begun in *The Newton Letter*, of including references to academics to accentuate the parodic scholarly effect. Popov, the footnoted fictional historian of the novella, reappears to comment on Livelb. Actual academics are also invoked, and real-life experts in painting are quoted to self-reflexively describe Livelb's highly rhetorical style and Belli's quest for ideal forms.

Though arguably extreme, such self-reflexivity is something of a natural characteristic of pictorial literature, which is overwhelmingly concerned with the power of imagination and therefore the power of artists to conjure up the impression of a real sensory world. The Trilogy is even more centripetal, more self-obsessed and self-analogical than the Tetralogy. Fascination with another art form turns literature in on itself and doubly removes it from any proposed reality outside of the aesthetic medium. Pictorial literature such as Banville's might thus be described as the imagination mirroring its own desire because this is perhaps more eminently achievable than the mirroring of the world.

COMING TO THE (SUR)FACE: *ECLIPSE, SHROUD, THE SEA*

As is the case with so many of the seeming symbolic incidentals in his early work, Banville afterwards employs the simultaneously comic and threatening possibilities of his harlequins and attendant *Commedia* figures with an intensity that makes their earlier figurations seem like foreseen preparation of the ground. The same applies to the metaphor of the mirror, references to which have momentarily characterized all the work, even before the depth of Banville's fascination with it is properly revealed in the late period. With stock clowns and mirrors in Banville, we are in a world and mood of high theatricality, and this theatricality is key to an understanding of the close interrelations between *Eclipse* and *Shroud*. These are not exactly partner novels in the manner of the Tetralogy or the Trilogy, but, as well as the fact that the character of Cass, Banville's most enigmatic female figure, is central to both, together they are impressive illustrations of the way clowning interacts with the over-arching theme of representation in Banville's pictorial self-reflections.

An increasingly dominant philosophic presence in Banville's work is crucial here. In Banville's middle and especially his late periods, Friedrich Nietzsche has taken a place in his intellectual affections that rivals that of those earlier exemplars we have already mentioned: Rilke, Stevens, Kafka, Steiner, Hofmannsthal and James. For Banville, this German philosopher is 'one of the greatest and most profound thinkers of the modern age. Without him, it would be hard to imagine the philosophical and literary map of the twentieth century, from Heidegger to Paul de Man, from Freud to Lacan, from Thomas Mann to Milan Kundera.' Nietzsche's philosophy, he says, 'fits the world ... Nietzsche was the first to say there can be no system'.[12] Insofar as we might wish to categorize Banville under any single philosophical heading, we could say that he is a Nietzschean.

This can be seen implicitly in all the novels, and more explicitly in the middle and especially the late period. For instance, perhaps even before Banville became so convinced a devotee, Nietzsche's preferred ironic attitude to history as propagated in his famous essay on historiography, 'On the Uses and Disadvantages of History for Life' (1874), could easily be found in the autonomous approach to national history in Birchwood. Freddie Montgomery's devised predicament in The Book of Evidence is an enactment of the moral implications of Nietzsche's philosophy of system-smashing and the resultant experience of nihilism and existential free-fall. Given the appearance of Nietzsche in the formational notes for The Book of Evidence, it is safe to argue that his philosophy forms more than a mere backdrop to the novel. 'Nietzsche is there in the pages', Banville admits, sometimes 'quoted directly, without acknowledgement'.[13]

The Nietzschean idea of life as primarily a matter of provisionality and invention, an idea closely aligned with Banville's convictions on the central role of the imagination in all of life, has implications for the theme of free will in the Trilogy that would be worth pursuing beyond what we have time for at the present. It might, for momentary example, initially seem fanciful to think of Freddie Montgomery's murder weapon of the hammer in the light of Nietzsche's description of his own thought as 'philosophizing with a hammer' and his subtitling of one of his key works, Twilight of the Idols (1888), with the phrase 'or How to

Philosophise with a Hammer'. But we are clearly invited by Banville to think symbolically about these hammers when he has his version of Gilles in *Ghosts* carry a club, and when references to clubs and hammers are scattered throughout *Shroud*.

A large part of Banville's continued attraction to Nietzsche is the philosopher's focus on *style* in thinking, on heightening the artistic forms of his poetic writing, book after book, to suit the density, the momentousness, of what he wanted to say. Nietzsche's emphasis on music as the prime art and on the idea that life only has full meaning when it is aestheticized also proves naturally amenable to Banville's own ideas on the function of the lyrical novel.

One instance of Freddie Montgomery's deviousness, despite his apparent acceptance of responsibility, is the frequency with which he returns to the idea that he has never been in control of his life, and this will serve to make other Nietzsche connections for us here. Insisting that his 'journey' had 'not been a thing of signposts and decisive marching, but drift only, a kind of slow subsidence', he argues that it is wrong to assume 'that actions are determined by volition, deliberate thought, a careful weighing-up of facts, all that puppet-show twitching which passes for consciousness. I was living like that because I was living like that, there is no other answer' (*Book of Evidence*, pp.37–8).The direct comparison of puppets to consciousness here, only one instance of many in Banville, is vital.

Theatrical puppets or dolls are closely related in the European tradition to *Commedia* figures, and have provided a number of writers, all organically related in Banville's personal canon, with symbols or metaphors for discussions of the problems of consciousness. More particularly, the use of doll figures and related ideas has provided for examinations of the problem of the artistic *representation* of consciousness. Heinrich von Kleist, the original German author of Banville's three stage adaptations and the dramatist regularly mentioned directly and indirectly by the actor Cleave in *Eclipse*, is the key writer here, though Rilke also devised some of the major relevant theories, and dolls are particularly noticeable in Banville's beloved *Duino Elegies*. Kleist's short essay 'On the Marionette Theatre' (1810) is an important instalment in dramatic theory, and Banville invoked it in his work long before its more perceptible usage in the late period – the first part of *Mefisto*, for instance, entitled 'Marionettes', includes scenes with broken puppets and theatrical costumes, and in his narrative Swan repeatedly refers to himself as a 'Pinocchio' who is trying to be real (pp.45, 63, 118, 176).

The vital parallel between Kleist's theory of puppets and Banville's examination of consciousness and its literary representation concerns a particular notion of innocence. The matters of the innocent eye and the non-innocence of the morally compromised principals of Banville's middle and late period are involved here. More crucial for present purposes is the metaphysical loss of innocence which afflicts Banville's highly self-conscious intellectual men. Freddie Montgomery of the Trilogy, Alexander Cleave of *Eclipse*, Max Morden of *The Sea*, and, most especially, Axel Vander of *Shroud*, suffer an extreme version of the excessive self-awareness that Banville's principals have always felt as a threat. Ever-receding self-reflection on their part – which operates for Banville as an analogue of the general problem of the artist – brings with it a sense of doubtful self-identity, suspect authenticity, and an agonized yearning for a sublimely idealized, preconscious, and therefore innocent, self.

'On the Marionette Theatre' focuses on 'how consciousness can disturb natural grace'. Kleist's puppets would have the advantage over living dancers of never being 'guilty of affectation':

> For affectation is seen, as you know, when the soul, or moving force, appears at some point other than the centre of gravity of the movement. Because the operator controls with his wire or thread only this centre, the attached limbs are just what they should be ... lifeless, pure pendulums, governed only by the law of gravity. This is an excellent quality ... Grace appears most purely in that human form which either has no consciousness or an infinite consciousness. That is, in the puppet or in the god.[14]

Amid their mixed motives and supercilious tones, this absence of graceful innocence is keenly felt by Banville's men in their moments of heightened self-reflection. They feel that they are potentially fakes, fraudulent in motivation as well as in being. This, they feel, is largely because of their 'insupportable excess of self' (*Eclipse*, p.88), their 'over-consciousness of self' (*Shroud*, p.41).

A natural adjunct to Banville's usage of Kleist's theory on puppets are the theories on acting proposed by the French intellectual Denis Diderot

(1713–84), whose theories on statues and acting are invoked a number of times in the Trilogy and who shows up again behind Cleave's ruminations on acting in *Eclipse*. Cleave has 'corpsed' on stage and the problem is that he is unable any longer to sustain by sheer feat the actor's pose either on or off the stage. His personal and professional acting were only a provisional displacement of his deeply felt absence of innocence of sensibility. This is what Diderot had to say on the necessary coldness and detachment, the 'sublime piece of clowning', of the successful actor in both the personal and professional senses:

> [The] actor has spent a long time listening to himself; and he's listening to himself at the very moment when he moves you, and all his talent consists not in feeling, as you suppose, but in giving such a scrupulous rendering of the outward signs of the feeling that you're taken in. His cries of pain are marked out in his ear. His gestures of despair are memorized and have been prepared in a mirror.[15]

In close inverse correspondence with Kleist, whose essay tells the story of how the natural poise of one talented and graceful young man was destroyed by his performances in front of a mirror, the paradox of the actor for Diderot is exactly the paradox Banville addresses. Cleave's natural grace and equilibrium is destroyed by self-reflective or self-mirroring practice. Yet, adult grace is also perhaps possible for him only when there has been a recognition that once his childhood (to the site of which he flees as a pretext for the action of the novel) has been left behind there is no returning to its innocent naturalness. So a heightened artistic play, an acting at grace sustained by the self-conscious intelligence, is the only existential option, the only way of achieving a workable unity of being.

Related references to masks and mirrors and acting figure heavily in Banville's late period. In working with these he regularly defers to the particularly ironic solution to the problem of depth of consciousness in Nietzsche (who provided his own versions of Kleist on puppets and Diderot on acting):

> I believe that art is about surfaces, and of course painting is the quintessential art of surfaces. But as Nietzsche says, 'It's on the surface where there's real depth', and I love the way in which paintings can

give a sense of enormous depth, I don't just mean in terms of perspective, but depth beyond the flat surface of the canvas reaching into the world. Depth both forward and backwards, reaching outward from the picture plane and backwards into it as well. And I like to think that that's what the novel is at its best.[16]

Any reasonably close reading of Banville, especially the work of the middle and late periods, will reveal his close 'picturing' attention to the surface of the world, the plain, but minutely described sensory experience of it. But this paradoxical insistence that true depth lies on the surface also extends more complexly into Banville's interrelated themes of self-reflection, self-doubt, play and innocence.

In his late period, Banville has reviewed more books on Nietzsche than on any other single author. Of the work of this period, it is *Shroud* that offers us a full-blown Nietzsche narrative. *Shroud* is set in Turin where, in the late 1880s, Nietzsche famously went mad after an extraordinarily productive period during which he wrote many of his greatest works, most particularly the related *Twilight of the Idols* and *The Anti-Christ* (1894). Banville is keen on the irony that these works came to fruition in the city of the greatest of Christian relics, the Turin Shroud, and he has a *Commedia* version of Zoroaster, the ancient Iranian prophet who provided Nietzsche with his eponymous prophet for *Thus Spoke Zarathustra* (1883–85), stalk the narrator Axel Vander in the way most of Banville's principals are shadowed by clownish doubles. Banville has always assessed Nietzsche beyond the simplicities of the standard accusation that he provided, in part at least, the philosophical basis for the rise of Nazism. Yet the setting of Vander's remembered youth in the period leading up to the Holocaust makes for precise historical inferences, accompanied by a characteristic theatrical vocabulary:

> Oh, yes. Here it is, my deepest, dirtiest secret. In my heart, I too wanted to see the stage cleared, the boards swept clean, the audience cowed and aghast. It was all for love of the idea, you see, the one, dark, radiant idea. Aestheticise, aestheticise! Such was our cry. Had not our favourite philosopher decreed that human existence is only to be justified as an aesthetic phenomenon? ... We would have, I would have, sacrificed anything to that transfiguring fire. I whisper it: *and I still would.* (p.223)

The aestheticization of all life promoted by Nietzsche is a matter of accepting the necessity of dramatically invented surfaces or appearances. Ideas about masks and playfulness, regulated by the mood of the *Commedia*, can regularly be seen behind the various versions of aestheticization in the philosopher's work. Here is a digest of one of the stronger versions:

> As an aesthetic phenomenon existence is still *bearable* for us ... At times we need a rest from ourselves by looking upon, by looking *down* upon, ourselves and, from an artistic distance, laughing *over* ourselves or weeping *over* ourselves ... Precisely because we are at bottom grave and serious human beings ... nothing does us as much good as a *fool's cap*.[17]

Because of the enduring hazard that Banville's adoptions of, and allusions to, other works and writers might be seen as mere cleverness or self-elevating trickery, the fact that *Shroud* is a detailed fictional treatment of these aspects of Nietzschean philosophy is worth heavily emphasizing. From another source, here is Nietzsche again:

> We are the first era that is truly learned so far as 'costumes' are concerned – I mean moralities, articles of faith, esthetic tastes, and religions. We are better prepared than any time has ever been for the Great Carnival, the most spirited Mardi-Gras laughter, the most reckless fun, for the transcendental summit of the utmost idiocy, for a truly Aristophanean mockery of the universe.

And the alignment of man with puppet-show is total: 'Perhaps we can be the parodists of world history, the punchinellos of God.'[18]

One final Nietzsche illustration will draw together this strand with the sexualization of art and of the sublime imagination by Banville that is figured, in the case of *Shroud*, in the peculiar sexual relationship between Vander and Cass. Vander – who tells us 'I approach the female body on the knees of my soul' – has more in mind than simple sexual conquest (p.325). He is 'dazzled by the otherness' of Cass and asks, with a mood and imagery that recollect Rilke's unicorn poem: 'Who was she, what was she, this unknowable creature, sitting there so plausibly in that deep box of mirrored space?' The sexual vocabulary continues in the implicit comparison of Cass's 'impenetrable mysteriousness' to the unattainable sublime:

Yet it was that very she ... that I suddenly desired, with an intensity that made my heart constrict. I am not speaking of the flesh, I do not mean that kind of desire. What I lusted after and longed to bury myself in up to the hilt was the fact of her being her own being, of her being, for me, unreachably beyond. Do you see? (p.335)

This, and similar passages on the sexualized sublime in Shroud and in Banville's work generally of the middle and late periods, are all analogues for creativity, for one particular explanation of the origin of the work of art.

The most resounding and intense version of the explanation is contained in the Nietzsche notebooks from which Banville takes the epigraph to Shroud. An extraordinary self-contained section there, not least because of its emphasis on the visual, could stand as an encapsulation of everything we've been thinking about here:

On the genesis of art. – That making perfect, seeing as perfect, which characterizes the cerebral system bursting with sexual energy ... – every perfection, all the beauty of things, revives through contiguity this aphrodisiac bliss. (Physiologically: the creative instinct of the artist and the distribution of semen in his blood –) The demand for art and beauty is an indirect demand for the ecstasies of sexuality communicated to the brain. The world become perfect, through 'love' –[19]

In a more obvious way, through the Turin Shroud Vander identifies himself directly with Christ and with Nietzsche, who often referred to himself in his incipient madness as 'the Crucified'. Generally, this identification is deftly accumulative, evoked through Vander's mention, for instance, of catching his reflection in the marble floor of his bathroom and thinking of 'that bronzen portrait of the dead Christ by what's-his-name, first the feet and then the shins, the knees, and dangling genitals, and belly and big chest, and topping it all the aura of wild hair and the featureless face looking down' (pp.38–9). The reference is to the painting Dead Christ by the Italian Renaissance artist Andrea Mantegna (1431–1506). Banville is perhaps ultimately too determined that his readers not miss the point when he has Vander describe himself lying on his back 'under a humid sheet with my hands folded on my chest like the dead Christ in his shroud' (p.362).

The inherent problem regarding authentication of the Turin Shroud, comically contained in the eventual failure of Vander and Cass actually to see it on display, is a major symbolic aspect of Banville's play here with matters of self-reflection and artistic representation. As constructed in the novel, we must think of the face of Christ on the Shroud in the light of other references to faces, especially to the idea that the face is literally and metaphorically the surface identification of the self.

A key structure of references involves the deconstructionist literary theorist Paul de Man (1919–83), whose 'life and various works' are acknowledged by Banville at the end. Paul de Man is of natural interest to Banville beyond the immediate matter of suspect morality (in the late 1980s, the period during which *Shroud* is set, it was revealed that de Man had written collaborationist journalism during his youth in Nazi-occupied Belgium). Heavily influenced by Nietzsche, de Man developed his literary theories in and around the problem of reference and meaning in literary language, a problem which has always preoccupied Banville. Many of de Man's essay titles are alluded to in Vander's account of his own concocted academic career. Besides the important fact that de Man wrote one of the major studies of Kleist's puppet theory, the essay Vander considers his 'first major piece of work', entitled 'Shelley Defaced', is a reference to de Man's 'Shelley Disfigured'.

Banville's changing of 'disfigured' to 'defaced' points up the particular concern with faces. The major reference comes when the title of the essay from which Vander has chosen to read in Turin, 'Effacement and Real Presence', turns out to be a combined borrowing from a title of one of George Steiner's books, *Real Presences*, and from de Man's essay 'Autobiography as De-Facement'. One of de Man's major perpetual subjects was the concept of the self, and one of his principal studies in this regard is entitled 'Self (Pygmalion)', an essay which relates directly to many aspects of the yearning pictorial imagination we are covering here. In this curious essay on autobiography, de Man wonders if even the most literally self-centred literary genre or mode can ever hope to represent in language something like the essential self of the writer.[20]

The answer is no. In de Man's view of self-centred writing (in the case of *Shroud* and most of Banville's writing we can extend this to include fiction in the first-person autobiographical mode), the natural assumption we generally make – that an autobiographically designed narrative records or reports a life – is simply but astonishingly reversed. Contrary to our assumption, de Man suggested, the devised project of autobiography, the particular stylistic and structural demands of this genre of writing, produces and determines the very idea that an individual life is recordable. Central to the way de Man works with this paradox of self-representation is *prosopopeia* (from the Greek: *face-making*), the rhetorical trope of personification whereby an inanimate or alien object, potentially including a dead or absent person, is addressed as if present and alive and with human qualities. In accordance with de Man, and in exact correspondence with Banville's own views on the purpose of language that we covered in Chapter 4, we should understand the whole of language itself as prosopopoeia, as a system that humanizes phenomena so that we feel they belong to us and are under our control.

As a system of alleviating for us the strangeness and distance of things, language, in de Man's metaphor, gives the world a familiar face. In this context, the interesting aspect of de Man's theory of autobiography as it applies to *Shroud* is the argument that this form of writing, despite its apparent purpose, does not capture or communicate reliable self-knowledge. Autobiographically motivated narrative is designed to identify the unique life associated with a particular face. But since autobiography is a construct of language, and since language is a systematically artificial giving of a face to things, then it must be recognized that the self that autobiographical narrative purports to capture for the writer and to communicate to the reader is by definition itself elusive and strange and open-ended. The argument offered by de Man is that there is an eternal difference and distance between the silent surface of the world and the meaningful face man tries to impose on that surface through words. The point is not so much that an autobiographical narrative may not be saying what we think it's saying, but that, because it is an artificial system regulated by predetermining generic rules, it may be saying nothing at all, nothing with any revelatory significance, and therefore it might as well stay silent. Silent picture meets silent to-be-pictured in the suspect shroud that is writing.

As illustrated in all Banville's work in his middle and late periods, and at a particularly high pitch in *Eclipse* and *Shroud*, the narrating self, even when autobiographically concentrated, can get as lost in words as any object. The systems of language – in our case here, the lyrical novel –

which seek to represent the alleged depth of the self and the surface of the world have on some level to admit that they are artificial, that they are aesthetic expressions of a beautifully basic desire for possession. A *nostalgia* for the self, and therefore a nostalgia for art's claims to authenticity on behalf of the artist, are perhaps the only things that can be properly recorded in autobiographically designed or toned narrative. Cleave puts it clearly:

> I passed the years of my youth practising for the stage. I would prowl the back roads of the town, always alone, playing out solitary dramas of struggle and triumph in which I spoke all the parts, even of the vanquished and the slain. I would be anyone but myself. Thus it continued year on year, the intense, unending rehearsal. But what was it I was rehearsing for? When I searched inside myself I found nothing finished, only a permanent potential, a waiting to go on. At the site of what was supposed to be my self was only a vacancy, an ecstatic hollow. And things rushed into this vacuum where the self should be. (*Eclipse*, p.33)

That 'permanent potential' of Cleave's is the sublime; those 'things' rushing in, along with his women, are the provisional self-portraits of the artist.

Perhaps a major reason for the success of *The Sea* is that Banville leaves behind these more tortuous versions of psychiatric uncertainty and the absences of the self and focuses instead more clearly on what is deep down within the self and on what comes from these depths to the surface. Sheer *depth* of consciousness is now the subject, and the whole thing seems more direct, more fleshly, less filtered through the cerebral range of cross-references and involutions we can find in *Shroud*. With *The Sea* Banville's fiction seems to have emerged – in the familiar but resounding formulation – as more *human*.

Even adoring readers might carp at the immediate mention of 'the gods' in the very first sentence of *The Sea*, thereby believing they are simply being returned to yet another figuration of the allusive classicism for which Banville is at this stage famous. But any resistance beyond that first sentence is futile. By his own intent, Banville's prose in his late period reads more and more like absolute music. Once the long second sentence rolls in with its description of the 'strange tide' of the titular sea, the reader is sunk, seduced even by sound alone. In any case, the gods here turn out to be of a different order. They are, with the attendant classical echoes, the Graces, a family of twin children, Chloe and mute Myles, who, with their parents Carlo and Constance, are remembered into being by the monologue of Max Morden who spent a life-changing summer in their idealized presence at a southern Irish seaside town when he and the twins were aged somewhere around 10 or 11.

Morden brings to mind his namesake, the proprietor of the suspect paintings in *Athena*, and he brings to his story certain established elements that Banville had not used extensively since *The Untouchable*. Morden is a dilettantish 'second-rater', a gentleman art critic (courtesy of the inherited wealth of his wife, Anna) who is trying to finish a seemingly interminable project on Pierre Bonnard.

As with Bonnard's work, the story that Morden tells is intimately domestic and is obliquely figured in parallel information provided on Bonnard's love for his wife, his favourite subject for his nude studies. Morden is writing exactly a year after he and Anna first visited the aptly named consultant, Mr Todd, the Dr Death who diagnoses Anna's cancer. Anna has now died, and Max has run away from the year-long experience of her death to youthful memories and to The Cedars, the house where his befriended Graces summered, now a lodging house occupied by the mysterious spinster, Miss Vavasour, and by Colonel Blunden, one of Banville's best ever clownish creations. It is perhaps Banville's overarching achievement here to retain his uncompromising commitment to a technically perfected art while writing a meditation on childhood and age that is, especially in its closing scenes where Morden takes a tumble and a bad turn, plainly moving. While this new narrator comes with the comedy Banville always brilliantly attaches to his self-obsessives, Morden is perhaps his most kindly treated principal since the eponymous *Kepler*, not least in his depicted relationship with his 'bluestocking' daughter, Claire.

Poking at his memories, insomniac and regularly anaesthetized by his hip flask, Morden sits pushing his paragraphs around, unable any longer to grasp quite what it is writing is supposed to do. He is metaphorically writing against the tide, feeling that he might almost be able to turn back time if he can concentrate sufficiently on the art of recollection. Almost tear-stained feeling suffuses his memories of Anna, even though she is the vehicle for clinical descriptions of the horrors of decaying flesh. The moment when he curses her for leaving him alone and the passages where he describes the photographs she took, when dying, of other hospital patients contain some of Banville's most viciously arresting prose to date. It is one of the greatest moments of the entire œuvre that when Morden, because he is so perfectly exhibited, so deftly shown to us rather than told to us literally in his own words, bursts out with 'You cunt, you fucking cunt, how could you go and leave me like this, floundering in my own foulness, with no one to save me from myself. How could you' (p.196), it seems within the story like nothing but the purest declaration of love.

As a direct counterpoint to the experience of ageing and death, Morden's ceremonial remembrance celebrates the ethereal Chloe, who, as the eponymous and metaphoric figuration of grace, is remembered by Morden as 'the true origin in me of self-consciousness' (p.168). So when Chloe mysteriously drowns, in a metaphor that would bear considerable comparison with the characteristic reference in traditional psychoanalysis to the 'sea' of the unconscious, she has descended to the depths of Morden's memory, the faculty that in all Banville's work is simultaneously the site of all artistic evocation and self-reflecting trouble. The members of the Grace family are all an echo of the perception of the unconscious grace that Kleist insists in his essay is the key facility of puppets when compared to overly self-aware, and therefore awkward, humans. This is a grace Morden might have had unawares when he was a youth, but he has spent his adult life trying to achieve it, or reclaim it, by intellectual means. He is especially directly concerned with the self-reflective nature of his narrative:

> When I consider my face in the glass like this I think, naturally, of those last studies Bonnard made of himself in the bathroom mirror at Le Bosquet towards the end of the war after his wife had died ... but in fact what my reflection most reminds me of, I have just realised it, is that Van Gogh self-portrait, not the famous one with bandage and tobacco pipe and bad hat, but that one from an earlier series, done in Paris in 1887, in which he is bare-headed in a high collar and Provence-blue necktie with all ears intact, looking as if he has just emerged from some sort of punitive dousing ... (pp.130–1)

The 'punitive dousing' Morden is undergoing is his self-reflecting immersion in memory and the yearning for a grace that is now permanently elusive for him, a sublime concept that can never be attained.

If the imagination in Banville is unsure of sublime attainments, its transcendent capabilities, it is confident that it is free to transform things on the surface. Once again in *The Sea*, Banville is deploying a kind of aesthetic autobiography. The estrangements and rearrangements of conventional perceptions – or, more precisely, descriptions of perceptions – performed by Morden's kind of stylizations carry implied imperatives: you must smell more, you must hear more, you must touch more, you must, above all, see more. Whether or not we like to have the starkest of final realities mythologized for us, whether or not it is the siren's song that will finally drown us, we can hear in Banville's sensorily replete prose in *The Sea* an evidential fascination with life lived in face of the peculiar but certain knowledge that the element from whence we came will reclaim us. In the dying Anna's words: 'Strange ... To be here, like that, and then not ... To have been here' (pp.211–12).

Contrary to all resentful blindness in the post-Man Booker critical fall-out, *The Sea* is easily the key work thus far in this regard because it concerns the only two ages of man that matter in the intellectual adult male's sense of time as Banville has always portrayed it: youth, and the end. Banville's provision of evidential views of the world is classically motivated by a desire to transcend temporality; in this, his aesthetic of autonomy has a metaphysical intensity. When asked what he would like future readers to find in the work, he replied: 'A sense of passion, a sense of – I'll risk using a word taken from religion – a sense of witness, that there was somebody at some point who saw these things ... I'd like that. Not in any sense of being a social chronicler, but in the small, seemingly inconsequential things that my books notice.'[21] Max Morden's hope for the memorialization of the world and himself and his loved ones in the art that emerges out of the sea of his past and his unconscious is thus a hope that carries with it the hesitant vocabularies of transubstantiation:

> I am not speaking here of a posthumous transfiguration. I do not entertain the possibility of an afterlife, or any deity capable of offering it. Given the world that he created, it would be an impiety against God to believe in him. No, what I am looking forward to

is a moment of earthly expression ... I shall be delivered, like a noble closing speech. I shall be, in a word, *said*. Has this not always been my aim, is this not, indeed, the secret aim of all of us, to be no longer flesh but transformed utterly into the gossamer of unsuffering spirit? (p.185)

Properly heard through the ear as well as through the intelligence, that is a sacral sounding of Banville's entire calling as a novelist. And it is a salutary and challenging call to us to echo these things in our reading.

NOTES

1. John Kenny, 'Well Said Well Seen: The Pictorial Paradigm in John Banville's Fiction', *Irish University Review*, 36, 1 (Spring/Summer 2006), pp.52–67.

2. E.H. Gombrich, *Art and Illusion: A Study in the Psychology of Pictorial Representation* (Princeton, NJ: Princeton University Press, 1969).

3. Susannah Hunnewell, 'Art and the Stillness of Things', *New York Times Book Review* (28 November 1993), p.33.

4. Kate Kellaway, 'Behind the Curtains', *Observer* (4 April 1993).

5. Joe Jackson, 'John Banville', *Hot Press*, 24, 21 (8 November 2000), p.85.

6. Joe Jackson, 'Hitler, Stalin, Bob Dylan, Roddy Doyle ... and Me', *Hot Press*, 18, 19 (5 October 1994), p.16.

7. All references are to 'The Party', *Kilkenny Magazine*, 14 (Spring/Summer 1966), pp.79–82.

8. Immanuel Kant, *The Critique of Judgement*, trans. James Creed Meredith (Oxford: Clarendon Press, 1952), pp.175–6.

9. Rainer Maria Rilke, *The Selected Poetry of Rainer Maria Rilke*, ed. and trans. Stephen Mitchell, intro. Robert Hass (London: Picador, 1987), p.241.

10. Hedwig Schwall, 'An Interview with John Banville', *European English Messenger*, 6, 1 (1997), p.14.

11. Melvyn Bragg, 'John Banville', *South Bank Show* (LWT/Ulster Television, 1993).

12. John Banville, 'The Last Days of Nietzsche', *New York Review of Books*, 45, 13 (13 August 1998), p.25; Schwall, 'An Interview with John Banville', p.15.

13. John Banville, 'Thou Shalt Not Kill', in *Arguing at the Crossroads: Essays on a Changing Ireland*, ed. Paul Brennan and Catherine de Saint Phalle (Dublin: New Island Books, 1997), p.133.

14. Heinrich von Kleist, 'On the Marionette Theatre', in *Essays on Dolls* (Heinrich von Kleist, Charles Baudelaire, Rainer Maria Rilke), trans. Idris Parry and Paul Keegan, intro. Idris Parry (London: Penguin Syrens, 1995), pp.8,5–6, 12.

15. Denis Diderot, *Selected Writings on Art and Literature*, trans., intro. and notes Geoffrey Bremner (London: Penguin, 1994), pp.107–8.

16. Bron Sibree, 'Flashbacks on a Charmed Detour', *The Canberra Times* (8 July 2006).

17. Friedrich Nietzsche, *The Gay Science*, trans. and commentary Walter Kaufmann (New York: Vintage, 1974), pp.163–4.

18. Friedrich Nietzsche, *Beyond Good and Evil*, trans. and intro. Marianne Cowan (Chicago, IL: Gateway, 1967), p.147.

19. Friedrich Nietzsche, *The Will to Power*, ed. and commentary Walter Kaufmann, trans. Walter Kaufmann and R.J. Hollingdale (London: Weidenfeld & Nicolson, 1968), p.424.

20. My discussion here draws on de Man's essays 'Self (Pygmalion)' from *Allegories of Reading: Figural Language in Rousseau, Nietzsche, Rilke and Proust* (New Haven, CT: Yale University Press, 1979), pp.160–87, and 'Autobiography as De-Facement', from *The Rhetoric of Romanticism* (New York: Columbia University Press, 1984), pp.67–81.

21. Clíodhna Ní Anluain (ed.), 'John Banville', in *Reading the Future: Irish Writers in Conversation with Mike Murphy* (Dublin: Lilliput Press, 2000), p.40.

Select Bibliography

WORKS BY JOHN BANVILLE

Fiction

Long Lankin (London: Secker & Warburg, 1970).
Nightspawn (London: Secker & Warburg, 1971).
Birchwood (London: Secker & Warburg, 1973).
Doctor Copernicus (London: Secker & Warburg, 1976).
Kepler (London: Secker & Warburg, 1981).
The Newton Letter: An Interlude (London: Secker & Warburg, 1982).
Long Lankin, rev. edn (Oldcastle, Co. Meath: Gallery Press, 1984).
Mefisto (London: Secker & Warburg, 1986).
The Book of Evidence (London: Secker & Warburg, 1989).
Ghosts (London: Secker & Warburg, 1993).
Athena (London: Secker & Warburg, 1995).
The Untouchable (London: Picador, 1997).
Eclipse (London: Picador, 2000).
Shroud (London: Picador, 2002).
The Sea (London: Picador, 2005).
Christine Falls (London: Picador, 2006). [Published under the pseudonym Benjamin Black.]
The Silver Swan (London: Picador, 2007). [Published under the pseudonym Benjamin Black.]

Uncollected Fiction/Non-Fiction/Plays/Films

'The Party', *Kilkenny Magazine*, 14 (spring/summer 1966), pp.79–82.
'Mr Mallin's Quest', *Transatlantic Review*, 37–8 (autumn/winter 1970–71), pp.29–34.

'Rondo', *Transatlantic Review*, 60 (1977), pp.180–3.

Reflections, an adaptation of *The Newton Letter*, dir. Kevin Billington (Court House Films for Channel 4 Productions, in association with Bord Scannán na hÉireann/RTÉ, 1983).

The Broken Jug: After Heinrich von Kleist (Oldcastle, Co. Meath: Gallery Press, 1994).

Seachange, dir. Thaddeus O'Sullivan (RTÉ television, 1994).

The Ark, illustrated by Conor Fallon, with the assistance of John Kelly (Oldcastle, Co. Meath: Gallery Press, 1996).

The Last September, by Elizabeth Bowen, dir. Deborah Warner (Scala Thunder Productions, 1999).

God's Gift: A version of Amphitryon by Heinrich von Kleist (Oldcastle, Co. Meath: Gallery Press, 2000).

Prague Pictures: Portraits of a City (London: Bloomsbury, 2003).

A World too Wide, prod. Cathryn Brennan (RTÉ radio, 8 February 2005).

Love in the Wars: A version of Penthesilia by Heinrich von Kleist (Oldcastle, Co. Meath: Gallery Press, 2005).

'First Light', *The Faber Book of Best New Irish Short Stories, 2006–7*, ed. David Marcus (London: Faber & Faber, 2007), pp.1–14.

Conversation in the Mountains: a play for radio (Oldcastle, Co. Meath: Gallery Press, 2008).

Manuscripts

Note: Banville's manuscripts are held by Trinity College Dublin (MS. 10252). The items listed here are those mentioned in the text.

MS. 10252.2.1–3. Drafts of *Blood* [*Nightspawn*].

MS. 10252.3.15. Notes for the filming of *Inheritance* [*Birchwood*].

MS. 10252.4.6. Notebook for *Doctor Copernicus*, with drafts of *The Song of the Earth*, an abandoned novel.

MS. 10252.12.1. 'Sea Sequence'. A finished story.

Other Writings by John Banville

'Inutile Genius', *Hibernia* (25 May 1973), p.23.

'Essays into Sanity', *Hibernia* (2 November 1973), p.16.

'An American Monster', *Hibernia* (14 December 1973), p.22.

'Opinions Better Kept Private', *Hibernia* (7 June 1974), p.29.

'Cracker-Barrel Philosopher', Hibernia (2 May 1975), p.19.

'Bread or Madeleines', Hibernia (30 May 1975), p.20.

'A Sense of Proportion', Hibernia (30 January 1976), p.26.

'Beginnings', Hibernia (7 January 1977), p.32.

'Heavenly Alchemy', Hibernia (4 February 1977), p.28.

'Adieu Tristesse', Hibernia (1 April 1977), p.26.

'Vladimir Nabokov', Hibernia (5 August 1977), p.27.

'Act of Faith', Hibernia (2 September 1977), p. 20.

'Fowles at the Crossroads', Hibernia (14 October 1977), p.27.

'Parables of Evil', Hibernia (21 October 1977), p.28.

'It is Only a Novel', Hibernia (11 November 1977), p.23.

'Monument to H.J.', Hibernia (27 January 1978), p.24.

'Odd Man Out', Hibernia (8 March 1979), p.17.

'A Talk', Irish University Review, 11, 1 (spring 1981), pp.13–17.

'The Dead Father', Irish University Review, 12, 1 (spring 1982), pp.64–8.

'Place Names: The Place', in Ireland and the Arts (special issue of The Literary Review), ed. Tim Pat Coogan (Dublin: Namara Press, 1983), pp.62–5.

'Silent in Several Languages', Sunday Tribune (16 October 1983).

'Masterfully Manic', Sunday Tribune (20 November 1983).

'Out of the Abyss', Irish University Review, 14, 1 (spring 1984), p.102.

'Physics and Fiction: Order from Chaos', New York Times Book Review (21 April 1985), pp.1, 41–2.

'A Scent of Power in the Age of Enlightenment', Sunday Tribune (16 November 1986).

'Nabokov's First Lolita', Sunday Independent (15 March 1987).

'The Work as the Self', Irish Times (8 October 1988).

'What do We Mean by Meaning?', Irish Times (1 July 1989).

'Samuel Beckett Dies in Paris, Aged 83', Irish Times (25–27 December 1989).

'Survivors of Joyce', in James Joyce: The Artist and the Labyrinth, ed. Augustine Martin (London: Ryan Publishing, 1990), pp.73–81.

'The Legend of the Man who Fell to Earth', Irish Times (2 June 1990).

'Portrait of the Critic as a Young Man', New York Review of Books, 37, 16 (25 October 1990), pp.48–50.

Paperback review of The Great Gatsby, Irish Times (8 May 1991).

'Winners', New York Review of Books, 38, 19 (21 November 1991), pp.27–9.

Article on favourite books of 1991, Irish Times (30 November 1991).

'Put Up What Flag You Like, It's Too Late', Observer (1 December 1991).

Letter and selected poem, in Lifelines: Letters from Famous People about their Favourite Poem, ed. Niall MacMonagle, foreword Seamus Heaney (Dublin: Town House, 1992), pp.31–2.

'Master of the Universe', Irish Times (1 February 1992).

'At the Manor', Irish Times (23 May 1992).

'Making Little Monsters Walk', in The Agony and the Ego: The Art and Strategy of Fiction Writing Explored, ed. Clare Boylan (London: Penguin, 1993), pp.105–12.

'The Master and the Madness of Art', Irish Times (9 January 1993).

'A Great Tradition', Sunday Times (21 March 1993).

'Northern Lights and the Mystery of Mr James', Irish Times (22 May 1993).

'Living in the Shadows', New York Review of Books, 40, 13 (15 July 1993), pp.23–4.

'Micks on the Make Find True Selves in Exile', Observer (3 October 1993).

'Travelling Light in Foreign Parts', Irish Times (9 October 1993).

'Nabokov's Dark Treasures', New York Review of Books, 42, 15 (5 October 1995), pp.4–6.

'The Ireland of de Valera and O'Faoláin', Irish Review, 17–18 (winter 1995), pp.142–52.

'Introduction', in The Deeps of the Sea and Other Fiction, by George Steiner (London: Faber & Faber, 1996), pp.vii–xi.

'Passing Beautiful in Yellowbelly Heaven', Irish Times (31 August 1996).

'Thou Shalt Not Kill', in Arguing at the Crossroads: Essays on a Changing Ireland, ed. Paul Brennan and Catherine de Saint Phalle (Dublin: New Island Books, 1997), pp.132–42.

'The Real Presence of a Passionate Mind', Irish Times (5 July 1997).

'Bad Friday', Irish Times (8 April 1998).

'Beauty, Charm and Strangeness: Science as Metaphor', Science Magazine, 281, 5373 (3 July 1998), pp.40–1.

'The Last Days of Nietzsche', New York Review of Books, 45, 13 (13 August 1998), pp.22–5.

'Ourselves and Other Animals', Irish Times (29 May 1999).

'Pushed from the Centre of Creation', Irish Times (31 December 1999).

'Are We Who We Say We Are?', Irish Times (4 March 2000).

'How to Read a Novel? Lovingly', Irish Times (26 August 2000).

'Champion of the "Real Presence"', *Irish Times* (12 May 2001).

'Summon the Gods', *Irish Times* (4 August 2001).

'Introduction', in *Troubles*, by J.G. Farrell (New York: New York Review of Books, 2002).

'Introduction', in *The Lord Chandos Letter and Other Writings*, by Hugo von Hofmannsthal, selected and trans. Joel Rotenberg (New York: New York Review of Books, 2005), pp.vii–xii.

'A Day in the Life', *New York Review of Books*, 52, 9 (26 May 2005), pp.42–4.

'Personally Speaking I Blame Agatha for Turning Me to Crime', *Sunday Telegraph* (11 February 2007).

INTERVIEWS WITH JOHN BANVILLE

Adair, Tom, 'Meet the Other Half', *Scotsman* (21 October 2006).

Anonymous, 'Oblique Dreamer', *Observer* (17 September 2000).

Battersby, Eileen, 'Comedy in a Time of Famine', *Irish Times* (24 May 1994).

Bernstein, Richard, 'Once More Admired than Bought, A Writer Finally Basks in Success', *New York Times Book Review* (15 May 1990), p.13.

Bragg, Melvyn, 'John Banville', *The South Bank Show* (LWT/Ulster Television, 1993).

Carty, Ciaran, 'Out of Chaos Comes Order', *Sunday Tribune* (14 September 1986).

Fay, Liam, 'The Touchable', *Hot Press*, 21, 13 (9 July 1997), pp.44–6.

———— 'Wexford's Winner', *Sunday Times* (Ireland edn), (16 October 2005).

Garvey, Michael (prod. and dir.), *Undercover Portrait: John Banville* (Orpheus Productions for RTÉ television, 2000).

Greacen, Lavinia, 'A Serious Writer', *Irish Times* (24 March 1981).

Hanly, David, 'Interview with John Banville', *Bookside: Writer in Profile* (RTÉ television, 1992).

Hederman, M.P. and R. Kearney (eds), 'Novelists on the Novel: Ronan Sheehan Talks to John Banville and Francis Stuart' (1979), in *The Crane Bag Book of Irish Studies* (1977–1981) (Dublin: Blackwater Press, 1982).

Hogan, Ron, 'The Beatrice Interview: John Banville', 1 June 1997, <www.beatrice.com/interviews/banville>.

Hunnewell, Susannah, 'Art and the Stillness of Things', *New York Times Book Review* (28 November 1993), p.33.

Imhof, Rüdiger, 'My Readers, that Small Band, Deserve a Rest', *Irish University Review*, 11, 1 (spring 1981), pp.5–12.

———— 'Q. and A. with John Banville', *Irish Literary Supplement*, 6, 1 (1987), p.13.

Jackson, Joe, 'Hitler, Stalin, Bob Dylan, Roddy Doyle … and Me', *Hot Press*, 18, 19 (5 October 1994), pp.14–16.

———— 'John Banville', *Hot Press*, 24, 21 (8 November 2000), pp.58–61, 85.

Kellaway, Kate, 'Behind the Curtains', *Observer* (4 April 1993).

McCarthy, Charlie (dir.), *Being John Banville* (Ice Box Films for RTÉ television, 2007).

McGee, Harry, 'Freddie's Back as Banville Grapples with Alien Planet', *Sunday Press* (28 March 1993).

Meaney, Helen, 'Master of Paradox', *Irish Times* (24 March 1993).

Murphy, Mike, 'John Banville', *The Arts Show* (RTÉ radio) (8 February 1995).

Ní Anluain, Clíodhna (ed.), 'John Banville', in *Reading the Future: Irish Writers in Conversation with Mike Murphy* (Dublin: Lilliput Press, 2000).

O'Mahony, Andy, 'John Banville', *Off the Shelf* (RTÉ radio, 24 April 1997).

O'Toole, Fintan, 'Stepping into the Limelight – and the Chaos', *Irish Times* (21 October 1989).

Padel, Ruth, 'The Patient English', *Independent on Sunday* (27 April 1997).

Ross, Michael, 'Chaos Theory', *Sunday Times*, 'Culture Ireland' (19 November 2000).

Schwall, Hedwig, 'An Interview with John Banville', *European English Messenger*, 6, 1 (1997), pp.13–19.

Sibree, Bron, 'Flashbacks on a Charmed Detour', *Canberra Times* (8 July 2006).

Wallace, Arminta, 'A World Without People', *Irish Times* (21 September 2000).

WORKS ON JOHN BANVILLE

Berensmeyer, Ingo, *John Banville: Fictions of Order – Authority, Authorship, Authenticity* (Heidelberg: Universitätsverlag [C. Winter], 2000).

Connolly, John, 'Joining the Criminal Fraternity', *Irish Times* (30 September 2006).

D'Hoker, Elke, *Visions of Alterity: Representation in the Works of John Banville* (Amsterdam: Rodopi, 2004).

Hand, Derek, *John Banville: Exploring Fictions* (Dublin: Liffey Press, 2002).

———— (ed.), Special Issue: John Banville, *Irish University Review*, 36, 1 (spring/summer 2006).

Imhof, Rüdiger, *John Banville: A Critical Introduction*, 2nd edn (Dublin: Wolfhound, 1997 [1989]).

———— (ed.), Special Issue: John Banville, *Irish University Review*, 11, 1 (spring 1981).

Izarra, Laura P. Zuntini de, *Mirrors and Holographic Labyrinths: The Process of a 'New' Aesthetic Synthesis in the Novels of John Banville* (San Francisco: International Scholars Publications, 1999).

Kenny, John, 'Connoisseur of Silences: John Banville and the Belief in Autonomy' (National University of Ireland, Galway, 2002, TH 4746).

———— '"Appallingly Funny": John Banville's *The Broken Jug*', in *Beyond Borders: IASIL Essays on Modern Irish Writing*, ed. Neil Sammells (Bath: Sulis Press, 2004), pp.83–103.

———— 'Well Said Well Seen: The Pictorial Paradigm in John Banville's Fiction', *Irish University Review*, 36, 1 (spring/summer 2006), pp.52–67.

McMinn, Joseph, *John Banville: A Critical Study* (Dublin: Gill & Macmillan, 1991).

———— *The Supreme Fictions of John Banville* (Manchester: Manchester University Press, 1999).

McNamee, Brendan, *The Quest for God in the Novels of John Banville 1973–2005: A Postmodern Spirituality* (New York: Edwin Mellen, 2006).

Steiner, George, 'To be Perfectly Blunt', *Observer* (4 May 1997).

Tonkin, Boyd, 'The Wrong Choice in a List Packed with Delights', *Independent* (11 October 2005).

OTHER WORKS

Adorno, Theodor, *Aesthetic Theory*, ed. Gretel Adorno and Rolf Tiedemann, trans. C. Lenhardt (London: Routledge & Kegan Paul, 1984).

———— *Notes to Literature*, ed. Rolf Tiedmann, trans. Shierry Weber Nicholsen, 2 vols (New York: Columbia University Press, 1991, 1992).

Bakhtin, Mikhail, *The Dialogic Imagination: Four Essays*, ed. Michael Holquist, trans. Caryl Emerson and Michael Holmquist (Austin, TX: University of Texas Press, 1981).

———— Speech Genres and Other Late Essays, ed. Caryl Emerson and Michael Holquist, trans. Vern W. McGee (Austin, TX: University of Texas Press, 1986).

Baudelaire, Charles, Selected Writings on Art and Literature, trans. and intro. P.E. Charvet (London: Penguin, 1996).

Beckett, Samuel, Proust / Three Dialogues with Georges Duthuit (London: Calder & Boyars, 1970).

Broch, Hermann, The Death of Virgil, trans. Jean Starr Untermeyer (New York: Vintage, 1995).

De Man, Paul, Allegories of Reading: Figural Language in Rousseau, Nietzsche, Rilke and Proust (New Haven, CT: Yale University Press, 1979).

———— The Rhetoric of Romanticism (New York: Columbia University Press, 1984).

De Quincey, Thomas, 'On Murder Considered as One of the Fine Arts', in Selected English Essays, compiled by W. Peacock, notes C.B. Wheeler (Oxford: Oxford University Press, 1918), pp.303–53.

Diderot, Denis, Selected Writings on Art and Literature, trans., intro. and notes Geoffrey Bremner (London: Penguin, 1994).

Eliot, T.S., Collected Poems 1909–1962 (London: Faber & Faber, 1974).

Flaubert, Gustave, Selected Letters, trans. and intro. Geoffrey Wall (London: Penguin, 1997).

Gombrich, E.H., Art and Illusion: A Study in the Psychology of Pictorial Representation (Princeton, NJ: Princeton University Press, 1969).

Grasselli, Margaret Morgan and Pierre Rosenberg, Watteau: 1684–1721 (Washington, DC: National Gallery of Art, 1984).

Heidegger, Martin, Poetry, Language, Thought, trans. Albert Hofstadter (New York: Harper & Row, 1971).

Hofmannsthal, Hugo von, Selected Prose, trans. Mary Hottinger et al., intro. Hermann Broch (New York: Pantheon, 1952).

Huyssen, Andreas, After the Great Divide: Modernism, Mass Culture and Postmodernism (London: Macmillan, 1988).

James, Henry, The Critical Muse: Selected Literary Criticism, ed. and intro. Roger Gard (London: Penguin, 1987).

———— Henry James: A Life in Letters, ed. Philip Horne (New York: Viking, 1999).

Jameson, Fredric, *The Ideologies of Theory: Essays 1971–1986*, 2 vols (Minneapolis, MN: University of Minnesota Press, 1988).

———— *Postmodernism, or The Cultural Logic of Late Capitalism* (London: Verso, 1991).

Jordan, Neil, 'Imagining Otherwise', in *Across the Frontiers: Ireland in the 1990s*, ed. Richard Kearney (Dublin: Wolfhound, 1988), pp.196–9.

Kant, Immanuel, *The Critique of Judgement*, trans. James Creed Meredith (Oxford: Clarendon Press, 1952).

Kleist, Heinrich von, 'On the Marionette Theatre', in *Essays on Dolls (Heinrich von Kleist, Charles Baudelaire, Rainer Maria Rilke)*, trans. Idris Parry and Paul Keegan, intro. Idris Parry (London: Penguin Syrens, 1995), pp.1–12.

Longley, Edna, *The Living Stream: Literature and Revisionism in Ireland* (Newcastle upon Tyne: Bloodaxe, 1994).

Lyotard, Jean-François, *The Postmodern Condition: A Report on Knowledge*, trans. Geoff Bennington and Brian Massumi, foreword Fredric Jameson (Manchester: Manchester University Press, 1984).

Martin, Augustine, 'Inherited Dissent: The Dilemma of the Irish Writer', *Studies*, 54 (spring 1965), pp.1–20.

Nabokov, Vladimir, *Lolita* (London: Everyman, 1992).

———— *Strong Opinions* (New York: Vintage, 1990).

Nietzsche, Friedrich, *Beyond Good and Evil*, trans. and intro. Marianne Cowan (Chicago, IL: Gateway, 1967).

———— *The Will to Power*, ed. and commentary Walter Kaufmann, trans. Walter Kaufmann and R.J. Hollingdale (London: Weidenfeld & Nicolson, 1968).

———— *The Gay Science*, trans. and commentary Walter Kaufmann (New York: Vintage, 1974).

O'Shannon, Cathal, 'Murder in the Park', in *Thou Shalt Not Kill: True-Life Stories of Irish Murders*, by Kevin O'Connor *et al.* (Dublin: Gill & Macmillan, 1995), pp.21–40.

Rilke, Rainer Maria, *Where Silence Reigns: Selected Prose*, trans. G. Craig Houston, foreword Denise Levertov (New York: New Directions, 1978).

———— *The Selected Poetry of Rainer Maria Rilke*, ed. and trans. Stephen Mitchell, intro. Robert Hass (London: Picador, 1987).

Sartre, Jean-Paul, *What is Literature?* trans. Bernard Frechtman (London: Methuen, 1967).

———— *Nausea*, trans. Robert Baldick (London: Penguin, 1988).

Steiner, George, *Language and Silence: Essays 1958–1966* (Harmondsworth: Peregrine, 1979).

———— *Real Presences: Is There Anything in What We Say?* (London: Faber & Faber, 1989).

Symons, Arthur, *The Symbolist Movement in Literature*, intro. Richard Ellmann (New York: E.P. Dutton, 1958).

Tóibín, Colm, 'Martyrs and Metaphors', in *Letters from the New Island*, ed. Dermot Bolger (Dublin: Raven Arts Press, 1991), pp.44–55.

Williams, Raymond, *Resources of Hope: Culture, Democracy, Socialism*, ed. Robin Gable, intro. Robin Blackburn (London: Verso, 1989).

Williams, R.V. and A.L. Lloyd (eds), *The Penguin Book of English Folk Songs* (London: Penguin, 1976).

Wittgenstein, Ludwig, *Tractatus Logico-Philosophicus*, trans. D.F. Pears and B.F. McGuinness, intro. Bertrand Russell (London: Routledge & Kegan Paul, 1997).

Index